Praise for previous editions of

Tennessee

Off the Beaten Path™

"...very inclusive and interesting..."
—*The Pike County* (PA) *Courier*

"*Tennessee: Off the Beaten Path* ...gives a glimpse into some not-so-widely-known areas in Tennessee that may quench your thirst for a little adventure and exploration.... O'Brien lists dozens of diversions for the traveler who'd like to see more of the Volunteer State.... [O'Brien has an] uncanny ability to find ...out-of-the-way places.... O'Brien opens a window into many ...communities.... [A]s its name promises, the heart of O'Brien's book beats the fastest when it's off the well-traveled road."
—*Johnson City* (TN) *Press*

Help Us Keep This Guide Up to Date

Every effort has been made by the author and editors to make this guide as accurate and useful as possible. However, many things can change after a guide is published—establishments close, phone numbers change, hiking trails are rerouted, facilities come under new management, etc.

We would love to hear from you concerning your experiences with this guide and how you feel it could be made better and be kept up to date. While we may not be able to respond to all comments and suggestions, we'll take them to heart and we'll also make certain to share them with the author. Please send your comments and suggestions to the following address:

The Globe Pequot Press
Reader Response/Editorial Department
P.O. Box 833
Old Saybrook, CT 06475

Or you may e-mail us at:
editorial@globe-pequot.com

Thanks for your input, and happy travels!

OFF THE BEATEN PATH™ SERIES

Tennessee

FOURTH EDITION

Off the Beaten Path™

by
Tim O'Brien

Old Saybrook, Connecticut

To my late, but great parents, Jim and Ann,
for instilling in me the wanderlust
that has always given me the desire to travel
the world's least-traveled byways.

Copyright © 1990, 1993, 1996, 1999 by Tim O'Brien

Off the Beaten Path is a trademark of The Globe Pequot Press.

Illustrations by Carole Drong
Cover and text design by Laura Augustine
Maps created by Equator Graphics © The Globe Pequot Press
Cover photo by Images © PhotoDisc, Inc.

Library of Congress Cataloging-in-Publication Data

O'Brien, Tim.
   Tennessee : off the beaten path / Tim O'Brien. —4th ed.
   p. cm. —(Off the beaten path series)
  Includes indexes.
  ISBN 0-7627-0279-6
  1. Tennessee—Guidebooks. I Title. III. Series.
  F434.3.O27 1999
  917.6804´53—dc21   98-41944
                     CIP

Manufactured in the United States of America
Fourth Edition/First Printing

The Lookout Mountain Incline Railway, Chattanooga

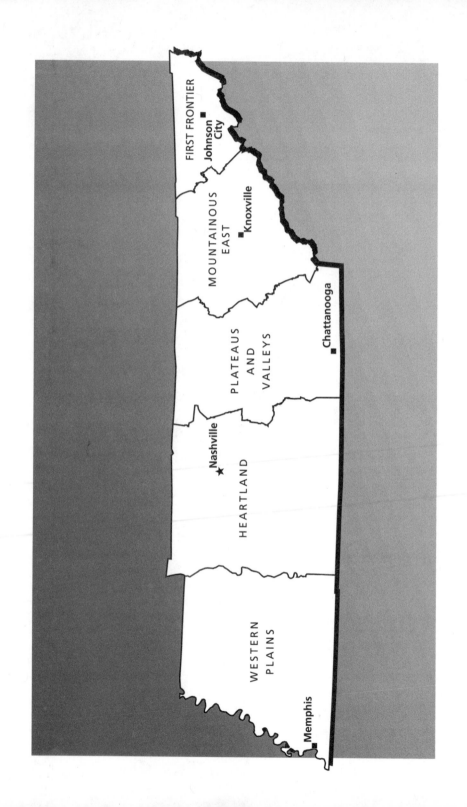

FIRST FRONTIER
■ Johnson City

MOUNTAINOUS EAST
■ Knoxville

Chattanooga
■

PLATEAUS AND VALLEYS

HEARTLAND
★ Nashville

WESTERN PLAINS

■ Memphis

Contents

Foreword

You don't have to look far to find something to love in Tennessee—whether you're a country music fan, a mountain climber, or a history buff.

I should know. I grew up here, and as Tennessee's senior United States Senator, I get a chance to see every corner of the state in my travels. It never gets old.

Whether you're visiting the Great Smoky Mountains National Park, Historic Shiloh, or the Grand Ole Opry, I know you'll enjoy your Tennessee experience, too.

Senator Fred Thompson

Acknowledgments

It's amazing how many people know so much, and it sure was nice that they all wanted to share that knowledge with a stranger.

As I drove the blue-line highways of the state of Tennessee searching for off-the-beaten-path sorts of things, I stopped and talked to many people, and to the best of my recollection each one I approached was able to help me in some fashion. It was from these people that I discovered many of the items in this book, and I thank them for their Southern hospitality.

I also wish to thank the folks at the tourism departments and at the various chambers of commerce where I stopped by, most always unannounced, requesting further information. These people are true professionals who know their areas. They provided me with a wealth of information by furnishing a plethora of insightful local color. Special thanks go out to individuals who went beyond the call of duty to help. Valerie Parker, of the Memphis Convention & Visitors Bureau, for trekking us through her neck of the woods and pointing out the sites, and to Johnna Rogers, of the Obion County Chamber of Commerce, for giving up a weekend to make sure we saw and experienced everything her part of the state has to offer.

Barbara Parker of the Tennessee Department of Tourist Development was a big help once again, as was Landon Howard of the Chattanooga Area Convention & Visitors Bureau. Jim Perry's assistance in the northwest portion of the state was most helpful and led to my discovery of the many treasures up there.

Molly and Carrie, my two daughters, were also a great help in this edition. They traveled most of the state with me and pointed out a great many things I probably would have missed. Their help in traveling and in fact checking was everything a proud father could ask for.

Introduction

The state of Tennessee is a fun and funky state to explore. From the mountainous areas in the east to the delta plains of the Mississippi River in the west, the variety of natural wonders and attractions the state has to offer is awesome.

It would take volumes to detail all of Tennessee's highlights. In Tennessee: *Off the Beaten Path*™, we've narrowed down your choice considerably by taking you off the interstates and onto the side roads, where the character of the state shines through.

The state is an easy one to get around in. Major highways and interstates are abundant, and even though you won't be spending much time on those behemoths, it's nice to know they're there if you have to make a quick escape back to civilization.

The Tennessee Scenic Parkway System covers 2,300 miles of primarily two-lane roads that connect the state's parks, major lakes, historical sites, recreational attractions, and this book's lesser-known attractions. The parkways are marked with a sign sporting a mockingbird, the state bird. They are mounted directly above the state highway designation numbers along the roads at key intersections.

If you follow the suggestions in this book, you'll find yourself driving up steep mountain roads, across rolling plains, over a few century-old bridges, and down many a gravel road. You'll also find yourself floating on a lake 300 feet below the earth's surface, playing miniature golf on the side of a mountain, cruising along on a lake created by the strongest earthquake on record, and eating the world's sweetest-tasting, vilest-smelling vegetable.

As in any area with a great deal of tourist traffic, Tennessee has its share of tourist traps along the well-worn trails. Sometimes our trip down the less-traveled paths of the state will intersect with those trails in order to highlight an event, an attraction, or a person worth visiting. We have found that sometimes it's worth fighting a crowd to see something that we'll probably never get a chance to see again. You'll find many of those once-in-a-lifetime opportunities in Tennessee.

Music is a big attraction in the state. From the birthplace of the blues in Memphis to the birthplace of the Grand Ole Opry in Nashville to the songs of the Appalachian Mountain folk, music of all kinds has played an important part in the heritage of Tennessee. Our tour of the state will touch on much of that heritage and the people who have contributed to it. We'll visit the commercial monuments that honor Elvis Presley,

Carl Perkins, Tina Turner, Dolly Parton, Loretta Lynn, Conway Twitty, and many others.

Southern hospitality is more than a myth in Tennessee, and our people may well be the state's friendliest attraction. There is one thing you'll never have to worry about as you travel through the state: You'll never truly be lost. Knock on any door or stop by any store, and chances are you'll get the directions you need, plus a whole lot more. Just when you think you've met the world's most colorful person, you'll meet one just a bit more fun. That's the way it is in Tennessee.

The state is full of crossroad communities with colorful and descriptive names. Usually, the community has little more to offer than a gas station–general store combination, but here's where you'll usually find the most intriguing characters of the area.

In the summer, these folks will be sitting on the porch of that store solving the world's problems. In the winter, you'll find them sitting around the potbellied stove. There are more than a hundred such communities around the state with colorful names, including Fly, New Flys Village, Defeated Creek, Ugly Creek, Pretty Creek, Dull, Soddy-Daisy, Bell Buckle, Gilt Edge, Finger, Frogjump, Nutbush, Bucksnort, Only, Who'd A Thought It, and Skullbone.

This book has been broken down into five major areas:

The First Frontier. More than 200 years ago, this part of the state was America's new frontier. Explorers, including Daniel Boone, blazed paths across the Appalachian Mountains, establishing some of the first settlements outside the original thirteen colonies.

Much of the area is heavily forested, with the extreme east and southeast parts quite mountainous. Davy Crockett was born here, and the state of Franklin, which never quite made it to statehood, was formed here several years before Tennessee became a state.

The Mountainous East. As the name implies, this area is probably the most rugged of all Tennessee terrain. The 500,000-acre Great Smoky Mountain National Park and its foothill communities provide beauty incomparable to what you'll find elsewhere in the Southeast United States.

Throughout the area several museums have dedicated their collections and grounds to the preservation of mountain life, and many communities have preserved that lifestyle by their very existence.

Plateaus and Valleys. Forested and rugged, the Cumberland Plateau rises like a gigantic wall that spans the width of the state, forming the western boundary of the Tennessee Valley.

Although relatively flat, the area has many spectacular streams that have carved out deep gorges in the sandstone, making it one of the best areas in the state for white-water enthusiasts. In fact, the 1996 Olympic Games white-water events took place here.

The Heartland. Also known as Middle Tennessee, the area is a region of gently rolling hills, sloping green meadows, and miles of river and lake frontage.

At the heart of the area lies Nashville, "Music City USA," the home of the Grand Ole Opry. Musical attractions are popular in this area, as are Tennessee Walking Horse farms, sour mash whiskey distilleries, and the homes of two U.S. presidents.

The Western Plains. An area of fertile bottomlands and dense hardwood forests, the Western Plains is bordered on the east by the Tennessee River and on the west by the Mississippi.

A few of the state's most colorful folk heroes—frontiersman Davy Crockett, train engineer Casey Jones, and Walking Tall sheriff Buford Pusser—have strong roots here, as do Roots author Alex Haley and the King of Rock 'n' Roll, Elvis Presley.

The 520-mile-long state is divided into four telephone area codes, 423, 901, 931, and 615, and about half of it lies in the eastern time zone and half in the central zone.

Although care has been taken to ensure accuracy in all listings in this book, visitors would be advised to call ahead before traveling any great distance. Life throughout Tennessee is slow paced and mellow, so if a day appears to be going a bit slow, it isn't uncommon for a proprietor to close early and go fishing. Phone numbers and admission prices have been included in listings where appropriate.

Most of the attractions are open on a year-round basis, but some cut operations a bit during the winter months.

Before venturing forth, you may want to contact the state tourism bureau and load up on brochures and maps of the areas you plan on visiting. In the material you receive from the state, there will be a list of local tourism bureaus that will be able to provide even more specific information.

Write to Tennessee Tourist Development, P.O. Box 23170, Nashville, TN 37202, or call (615) 741–2158; www.state.tn.us/tourdev/

Tennessee Facts

State Symbols

Bird: Mockingbird

Insect, two of them: the firefly and the ladybug

Gem: Tennessee river pearls

Tree: Tulip Poplar

Rock: Limestone

Wildflower: The passion flower

Flower: Iris

Songs, five of them: "My Homeland"; "Tennessee"; "When it's Iris Time in Tennessee"; "My Tennessee"; "Tennessee Waltz"; and "Rocky Top"

Animal: Raccoon

Amphibian: Tennessee cave salamander

Reptile: Box turtle

Butterfly: Zebra Swallowtail

Tourism Web Sites

State of Tennessee Tourism
www.state.tn.us/tourdev/

State of Tennessee
www.tenn.net/

Nashville
www.nashville.net/

Memphis
www.memphistravel.com/

Pigeon Forge
www.pigeon-forge.tn.us/

Smoky Mountains
www.smoky-mtns.com/

Chattanooga
bertha.chattanooga.net/chamber/index.html

INTRODUCTION

Rhea County
rheacounty.com/

Oak Ridge
www.oakridgeonline.com

Gatlinburg
www.Gatlinburg.com

Bed and Breakfast Inns

Bed and breakfast inns can be found throughout the state. Many are listed in this book. Here are a few contacts to call for information on more locations:

Natchez Trace Bed & Breakfast Reservation Service
Information on lodging along the Natchez Trace Parkway
(800) 377–2770

Bed & Breakfasts—About Tennessee
Reservation and information service for more
than 100 small inns and private homes
(615) 331–5244

Tennessee Bed & Breakfast Innkeepers Association
Call for listing of the state's top inns
(800) 820–8144
www.bbonline.com/tbbia

The prices and rates listed in this guidebook were confirmed at press time. We recommend, however, that you call establishments before traveling to obtain current information.

The First Frontier

Corner of the Frontier

Bristol is about as far north as one can go in the state and stay in Tennessee. In fact, about half the city is in Virginia. The state line runs down the middle of State Street in the heart of the downtown shopping district. But other than the small state markers embedded in the street between the double yellow lines, there's little evidence that the city has two mayors, two city councils, and two telephone area codes.

A big, old-fashioned neon sign forms an archway across State Street, near Randall Street, and proclaims "Bristol is a good place to live." Arrows point to the Tennessee and Virginia sides.

Although Nashville, about 300 miles to the west, gets credit for being the center of country music, it was here in Bristol that the Carter Family and Jimmie Rodgers recorded the first country-and-western music that was distributed nationwide. That recording took place on August 2, 1927, and put the area on the musical map. A monument honoring those musical pioneers stands at Edgemont Avenue and State Street. Farther down State Street, a large mural on the side of a building presents a visual memorial to that event.

To celebrate that musical heritage and to salute the culture, arts, crafts, and history of this unique area of the state, the annual ten-day Autumn Chase Festival is held in Bristol in late August or early September. With more than 120 events during the family festival, this is a fun celebration, with everything from a chili cook-off to a hot-air balloon rally. There are also sundown concerts, a flower show, children's activities, and all sorts of family activities.

Tennessee Ernie Ford was born Ernest Jennings Ford on February 13, 1919, in Bristol, and before he became the booming voice behind many hit country songs, including "Sixteen Tons," "The Shot Gun Boogie," and "Mule Train," he was a radio staff announcer and a bombardier during the war. He was elected to the Country Music Hall of Fame in 1990 and died in October 1991.

Today, the house where Ernie Ford was born has opened as a lasting

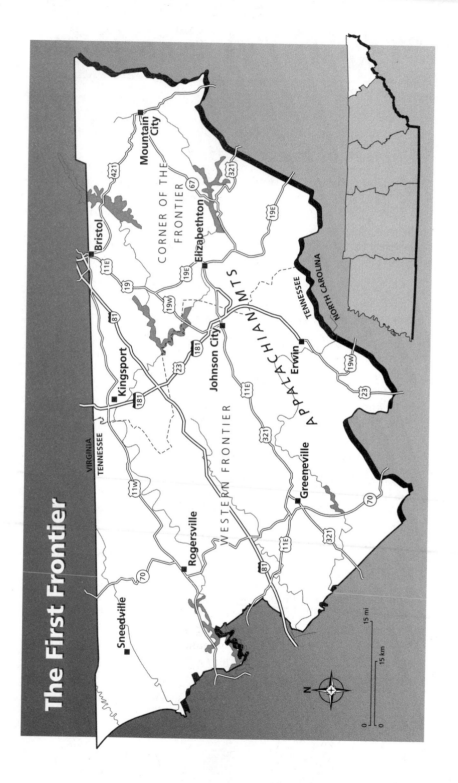

The First Frontier

CORNER OF THE FRONTIER

Mountain City

Bristol

Elizabethton

Kingsport

Johnson City

Erwin

Rogersville

Sneedville

Greeneville

WESTERN FRONTIER

APPALACHIAN MTS

VIRGINIA
TENNESSEE

TENNESSEE
NORTH CAROLINA

15 mi

15 km

N

THE FIRST FRONTIER

TIM'S TOP TEN PICKS
THE FIRST FRONTIER

Tennessee Ernie Ford Home

Ridgewood Restaurant

Shady Valley Trading
Company

Kissing Bridge

Unicoi County Heritage
Museum

Archie Campbell Days

Wilderness Road

Trade Days

Hale Springs Inn

Appalachian Fair

memorial to the city's favorite son. Located on Anderson Street, the home is garnished with memorabilia of his long musical and television career. The home isn't open on a regular basis, but call (423) 989–4850 for a schedule.

In nearby Kingsport early travelers through the area exchanged their Virginia currency for Tennessee money at a stagecoach stop known as the **Exchange Place.** Today the small farmlike village and crafts center is open Thursday through Sunday during the warmer months. If you visit on a Thursday, you're likely to see a group of ladies working on a quilt. The Fall Folk Arts Festival and an open-house celebration take place during the last weekend of September. The village is located just off Highway 11W at 4812 Orebank Road. Admission is free. (423) 288–6071.

Lots of fun and action takes place in the downtown area of Kingsport. On the weekend after Labor Day, a large arts and crafts festival is presented, attracting people from all over the region. During the winter what is billed as the largest "first night" celebration in the state takes place every December 31 throughout the downtown area. A true nonalcoholic family activity, **First Night Kingsport** is a popular New Year's Eve event that is supported by 125 businesses, 23 churches, 700 volunteers, and 17 media groups in the area. There's plenty to do as well; look at this sampling: twenty-four indoor performance sites plus several outdoor entertainment areas featuring local and regional entertainers; ten food vendors inside a warm hospitality tent, storytelling, carnival rides, and a fireworks show at the train station. This is the kind of great low-key celebration that you won't find in too many communities in Tennessee or for that matter, in the United States.

Unlikely as it seems, a major U.S. boatyard was in operation along the Holston River here in Kingsport in 1802. William King's boatyard had a reputation for quality that stretched as far as New Orleans. On the hill across the stagecoach road from the yards was the always-busy **Netherland Inn,** an inn and tavern where the likes of the state's three presidents, Andrew Jackson, Andrew Johnson, and James K. Polk, whiled away hours with their friends. The inn has been restored and is open to the public as a museum. Several other buildings on the property, including a shop and wagon shelter, have also been restored. A log cabin that was moved here from Virginia and once served as Daniel Boone's home from 1773 to 1775 is now a children's museum; it is a must if there are any small travelers with you. Start your visit at the Log Cabin Visitors Center and Gift Shop, located behind the inn. The boatyards are now a city park that stretches for miles down the river. Open weekends only, May through October. Admission is charged. (423) 247–3111.

Within the city limits of Kingsport, tucked away between the Holston River Mountain and Bays Ridge, is the secluded and tranquil **Bays Mountain Park.** The 3,000-acre, city-owned facility has a wildlife park, a planetarium, a wildlife tour on the forty-four-acre lake, a natural-history museum, 22 miles of hiking trails, and the unique Harry Steadman Mountain Heritage Farmstead Museum.

The museum contains a collection of old tools and implements the founders of the area used in their daily lives. "It gives you a great feel of the hardships and the size of the tasks they were faced with," Valerie Wood of the park staff told me. "Everything was donated to us from local families." In the park there's an unusual gray wolf habitat and a brand new snake habitat.

The park is a great way to spend a quiet, laid-back afternoon away from the crowds usually associated with natural parks of this size. The park is located 3 miles off I–181 at Bays Mountain Road, and it is open daily during the summer; open weekends only in off-season. (423) 229–9447.

The city fathers of Blountville say that there are more original log houses along their city's main street than in any other town in the state. Whether that's true or not, there are a great many vintage buildings to see here. One of those, **The Deery Inn,** played an important part in the frontier era of this part of the state. Built during the late 1700s, the building is actually three buildings: a two-story hewn-log house, a three-story cut-stone house, and a two-story frame structure, all built adjacent to one another and joined together. It's now a private residence, but the architecture can still be appreciated from the sidewalk.

A walking-tour map of Blountville is available, and most of the buildings are decorated and open to the public around Christmas.

For the best barbecue meal in eastern Tennessee, go to Bluff City south of Blountville on Highway 37, and head out Old Highway 19E (not the new four-lane Highway 19E). There you'll find the **Ridgewood Restaurant.** Grace Proffitt and her restaurant are legendary in these parts. She has been dishing up barbecued pork and beef since 1948, and most barbecue experts from coast to coast agree that hers is some of the best in the country.

THE FIRST FRONTIER

ALSO WORTH SEEING IN THE FIRST FRONTIER

Appalachian Caverns, Blountville, (423) 323-2337

Hands-On! Regional Museum, Johnson City, (423) 434-HAND

Bristol Caverns, Bristol, (423) 878-2011

Dickson-Williams Mansion, Greeneville, (423) 639-0695

Tipton-Haynes Historic Site, Johnson City, (423) 926-3631

Farmhouse Gallery & Gardens, Unicoi, (800) 952-6043

Wetlands Water Park, Jonesborough, (423) 753-1553

Much of the cooking is done out front where patrons can watch. Although many other items take up space on the menu, it's the barbecue that brings people through the doors. She makes about sixteen gallons of her special sweet-and-sour sauce a day. "It's a secret recipe, and I keep it in my head," she claims. Her son Terry, who works the eatery with her, is the only other person who knows the exact blends.

Coleslaw is put on all barbecue sandwiches, and various other hot sauces accompany hers to the table. Great northern white beans are prepared in her sauce and served along with hand-cut French fries on the popular platters. No reservations are taken, and the weekends tend to get crowded. Open every day but Monday; (423) 538-7543.

Perhaps one of the most historically significant extant structures in the state is **Rocky Mount,** a two-story log cabin in **Piney Flats.** Built in 1770, Rocky Mount is the oldest original territorial capital in the United States and one of the oldest buildings in the state.

It was the capital of "The Territory of the United States south of the river Ohio" from 1790 until a new capitol was built in Knoxville. With two stories and nine rooms, pine paneling, and real glass windows, the structure was a mansion by frontier standards, and it quickly became a gathering place for people across the entire frontier.

Today the house is open to the public daily, as is the adjoining **Over-mountain Museum,** which shows the early life of the area. First-person interpretation provides visitors with a true sense of what was taking place in 1791. Guides talk with you as they would have in that year and stay in character for your entire visit. On Route 11E; (423) 538-7396.

Johnson County is surrounded by the hills of the Appalachian Mountains, and the businesses and attractions reflect that way of life quite nicely. Throughout the county you'll see small handwritten signs hanging from mailboxes advertising handmade quilts or birdhouses for sale. Farther down any road, you'll pass through a crossroads community with a small general store stocked with local Appalachian crafts.

Diane Howard calls the Shady Valley area genuine "God's country." "Come into the valley across one of the three mountains and you'll think you've died and gone to heaven," she told me. With an elevation of 3,000 feet, the 12-mile long valley is home to the community of Shady Valley, where the *Shady Valley Trading Company* is located.

An old general store building houses an assortment of handmade mountain items, crafts, gifts, and souvenirs, and an adjacent gallery and museum tells the story of the area through artifacts and artwork. Hungry? In the back room of the store a fifty-seat restaurant serves up breakfast, lunch, and dinner. There are different specials every night, with Saturday being steak night and Wednesday featuring spaghetti. If you're camping or exploring the area, the folks at the restaurant will pack you a picnic.

The store and restaurant are open year-round. The store is open daily 9:00 A.M. to 9:00 P.M., the restaurant is open every day until 7:00 or 9:00 P.M. Located at the intersection of Highway 421 and Highway 91; (423) 739–9393 (store), (423) 739–9395 (gallery).

When the glaciers came through this area, they brought a few cranberry seeds with them, and today cranberries grow wild in the marshy areas of the valley. A Cranberry Festival, which benefits the seventy-student elementary school, is held on the second weekend in October, during the peak of the fall colors in the area, according to Diane Howard, who is co-chairperson of the festival.

The school is turned into an exhibit hall, with each room featuring various subjects ranging from Indian relics to quilt making. Tours of the private cranberry bogs are given, and more than sixty local craftsmen set up business around the school. Music is continuous, and there's several hours of storytelling.

In *Mountain City,* about the only thing you won't find are crowds. Within a few-block area of the downtown section, you'll find numerous antiques and gift shops selling a whole variety of neat things.

A great place to start your East Tennessee mountain trek is at the Johnson County Welcome Center & Museum, located on Highway 421 in Mountain City. In addition to maps, brochures, and great stores by the attendants, there's a historical museum with a large selection of Native American and pioneer artifacts. (423) 727–5800.

South of Mountain City on Highway 421 is *Trade,* the oldest unincorporated community in the state. It's the spot where, in 1673, the first English-speaking white man set foot on Tennessee soil. Situated on an old buffalo trail, the community flourished as a resting place for those traveling the three major paths through the wilderness that crossed at this point.

By the 1790s, the area had a country store, a post office, a blacksmith shop, and a handful of cabins, and today it's about as low-key as it was then—no big signs and no souvenir shops. "Trade Days" is held each June, when the entire county comes out to celebrate the heritage of the area.

Wilderness Road, one of the three major paths that converged at Trade, continues through East Tennessee to Cumberland Gap, where it heads northward into Kentucky and on to the "Great American West." Today, the **Tennessee Wilderness Road** tour follows as closely as possible the original trail of the pioneers. The leisurely drive along the path takes you through a landscape of spectacular valleys dotted with church spires, old towns, and, if you take the time to explore on your own, plenty of unique experiences. Use the designated roads as your main route, but don't hesitate to follow a few side roads now and then to experience even more. There's a brochure that maps your way and highlights all the sites and attractions. For a copy, call the NorthEast Tennessee Tourism Association at (800) 468–6882.

Sycamore Shoals the first permanent settlement outside the thirteen colonies, was a muster point for the Overmountain Men on their way to the battle of King's Mountain. Today, it is a State Historic Area and offers a museum, along with a reconstructed Fort Watauga that interprets the role this area played in the early settlement of what is now Tennessee and in the expansion of America's western boundary. An outdoor drama, *The Wataugans,* is presented during mid-July.

There are plenty of hiking trails here among the park's forty-five acres and there are several boat launch ramps for the lake. Beautifully shaded and peaceful, this is truly an off-the-beaten-path mixture of history and recreation. Highway 321 in Elizabethton. (423) 543–5808.

One of the state's remaining original covered bridges crosses the Doe River in downtown Elizabethton and is the focal point for the city's riverside park. Built in 1882, **The Kissing Bridge** (as the locals call it) is the oldest such structure in the state.

The Covered Bridge Celebration takes place the first week of June. Activities include concerts, a crafts show, an antique car show, and kid's games and contests. (423) 547–3850.

For many years a tall Frazier fir tree on Elk Street near downtown Elizabethton was considered the tallest such tree in the world. Then the gloomy day came when officials found it was only the second tallest. But since the tallest is never decorated at Christmas, they now decorate the fir in Elizabethton, making it the tallest decorated Frazier fir tree in the world.

Flying missionaries to and from remote parts of the world is quite difficult and requires pilots trained in a seat-of-the-pants style of piloting. In Elizabethton, **Moody Missionary Aviation** trains pilots to do just that. A division of Chicago's Moody Bible Institute, the aviation school provides three years of technical training for a student who has already completed two years of missionary studies.

Once students graduate, they are "free agents" who can work for any missionary organization. "Our pilots are capable of flying in the worst of conditions with no instruments and, most often, no formal landing strip," said one flight instructor. "And since they are also trained missionaries, they understand the importance of their jobs."

The entire operation is open for public tours. (423) 543–3534.

About 20 miles southeast of Elizabethton on Highway 143 is **Roan Mountain State Park.** The park itself lies at the foot of Roan Mountain, one of the highest peaks (6,285 feet) in the eastern United States, but that's not what makes this park so special. On the side of that mountain is one of the largest rhododendron gardens in the country. More than 600 acres of color bloom each June, making the area a striking display of pinks and purples. The Rhododendron Festival, held in mid-June, features native arts and crafts, mountain music and dancing, local food festivals, and wildlife tours. The park is the best place in the area to view fall foliage. A campground and cabins offer overnighters grand vistas of the mountains.

Walking and hiking trails line the mountain with numerous scenic overlooks. The **Dave Miller Homestead,** a preserved farm, is located in a hollow atop Strawberry Mountain. The Miller family first settled in the area around 1870 and for generations lived in virtual seclusion. Today the farm is preserved intact and serves as a model of early Appalachian life. Jackie Grindstaff, great-granddaughter of Dave, is the caretaker and is eager to share her knowledge and humor with visitors. The park is open year-round; the homestead is open only during the warmer months. Admission is free. (423) 772–3303.

Farther down Highway 321 toward Johnson City is the **Sinking Creek**

Baptist Church. The log structure, built in 1803, is the oldest Baptist church in the state and is open to the public on weekends during the warmer months. It's located next to the new church. (423) 928–3222.

South of I–81, on Highway 36 headed toward Johnson City, is the little community of *Boone's Creek.* Daniel Boone loved this area and he came back often to hunt. On one of his trips, he brought along William Bean, who liked the area so much he decided to settle his family here in 1769, thus becoming the first permanent white settlers in Tennessee. He built his first cabin on the site of Boone's hunting camp next to Boone's Creek. A monument now marks that spot.

The *Boone's Creek Museum* now consists of three old classrooms within the Boone Middle School, located along Highway 36. Inside, the locals have put together a collection of artifacts from Daniel Boone, William Bean, and other pioneers of the area. The museum is not open on a regular basis, but if you call ahead someone will meet you there to walk you through. (423) 477–7925.

Across from the school is the waterfall that Boone hid under to escape the Indians, and less than a mile down the road is a historic marker showing where Boone carved his own monument into a beech tree, which read "D. Boon cilled a bar in 1760." The tree is now dead, but a short walk off the highway will take you to the spot, which is now fenced in.

The sites aren't marked well, but the locals all know where everything is, so don't be shy—stop and ask. They'll be more than happy to point out the way.

Western Frontier

The Unicoi County seat community of *Erwin* probably holds the distinction of being the only town ever to put an elephant on trial for murder, find it guilty, and carry out the death penalty.

"Murderous Mary," a circus elephant who trampled her owner to death, was hanged from a railroad derrick before 5,000 spectators in 1916. Newspaper clippings and photos of that event are but a few of the interesting items in the *Unicoi County Heritage Museum,* housed in a turn-of-the-century home on the grounds of the *National Fish Hatchery* on Highway 23.

The hatchery was established in 1894, and the ten-room superintendent's residence was constructed in 1903. By the early 1980s the house wasn't being used by the superintendent, so the federal government signed an agreement allowing the county to use it as a museum. In addition to the story of Murderous Mary, various displays highlight local pottery production, the history of local railroading, and on the second floor is a replica of the city's turn-of-the-century Main Street.

In "Grandmother's Attic" is a display of quilts, antique dolls, and children's toys, all displayed as they might be in your own grandma's attic.

Outside, the fish hatchery is still in operation and produces about eighteen million rainbow trout eggs each year. Tours are available at the hatchery as well as at the museum. Admission is charged. (423) 743–4712 for the hatchery, (423) 743–9449 for the museum.

Bring your lunch; the entire area is a beautiful parklike setting, complete with a picnic pavilion and rest rooms.

A fun event to catch in Erwin each fall is the Apple Festival. Held the last weekend in September, there is continuous music, dancing, handmade crafts, the famous Blue Ridge Pottery Club Show and Sale, and various local food vendors.

The sixteen counties that now make up the eastern tip of Tennessee were at one time united in an effort to become a state by themselves. The framework for the would-be *state of Franklin* was set when about 30,000 white settlers crossed the Appalachian Mountains and founded several settlements in this area, which was a part of North Carolina at the time.

Leaders met in Jonesborough and created a bill of rights for their new state and requested the lawmakers of North Carolina to allow its creation. They refused, but Franklin, under the leadership of John Sevier,

The Bad-Shot President

*O*nce, a long time ago, a small crowd of onlookers followed a fiery lawyer named Andrew Jackson from a courtroom in Jonesborough to a nearby meadow, where Jackson and his opponent, attorney Waightstill Avery, squared off, and a duel began.

Crack! A pistol shot rang out. Crack! Another shot.

Yet both men still stood, unharmed. Each dueler, it seems, had fired wildly into the air, and a deadly conclusion was avoided. Moments later, the two adversaries shook hands.

Jackson went on to become the seventh president of the United States.

continued the battle for several years, until 1788. Several skirmishes between Franklin and North Carolina militia took place in the area.

Although never recognized as an official state, Franklin operated like a sovereign government with an assembly, administered justice, and negotiated treaties with the Indians.

Eight years after the fight for the quasi state ended, Sevier became the first governor of the state of Tennessee, which incorporated the former boundaries of Franklin. Jonesborough, chartered in 1779, seventeen years before there was a Tennessee, holds the distinction of being the oldest incorporated area in the state. And thanks to an ambitious restoration effort, much of the city appears as it did more than a century ago. Jonesborough was the first Tennessee town placed on the National Register of Historic Places.

There are more than twenty-seven points of interest on the walking-tour map of the historic downtown area, including the historic *Chester Inn,* where a young Andrew Jackson stayed while working on his law degree in 1788. Now owned by the state of Tennessee, the inn houses the National Association for the Preservation and Perpetuation of Storytelling. (423) 753–2171.

Many of the old buildings along the main streets now house a wide array of specialty shops. One particular structure, the *Old Town Hall,* at 144 East Main Street, was restored in 1982 and now houses about fifty crafts-oriented shops.

Behind the courthouse, at 102 Woodrow Avenue, the *Parson's Table Restaurant* is located in the circa-1870 First Christian Church building and parsonage. Owned by "Chef" Jeff Myron, the Victorian dining hall offers classical music, linen tablecloths and napkins, and about twenty entrees for dinner every night except Monday. A Sunday buffet is served and there is a daily luncheon special. This is truly an oasis of elegant dining among the barbecue restaurants of eastern Tennessee. Complete dinners range from $15 to $27. No alcohol is sold, but bring your own wine and they'll keep it chilled for you. Reservations are suggested for all meals. (423) 753–8002.

The Hawley House Bed & Breakfast is located on Lot #1 and is the oldest house in the state's oldest town! Built in 1793, the house offers three bedrooms with private baths and a full breakfast. Prices range from $80 to $125 per couple. (423) 753–8869.

The *Jonesborough History Museum,* at 117 Boone Street, is located inside the visitors center and is a good place to start your visit to this historic area. Brochures, maps, and a short film will get you started in the right direction. Horse-drawn carriage tours of the area are available. The museum is open daily. (423) 753–5961.

There are two great festivals in town you won't want to miss. An old-fashioned, family-oriented July 4 celebration known as Historic Jonesborough Days features arts and crafts, southern cooking, and clogging. In early October, the *National Storytelling Festival* is a celebration of the country's top storytellers. (423) 753–5281.

If you're in this part of the state during the third week of August, be sure to visit the *Appalachian Fair,* which is held at the fairgrounds in Gray. This nine-day event is the largest fair in east Tennessee and features one of the best carnival companies in operation today, The Great James H. Drew Exposition. There are all kinds of live Appalachian crafts demonstrations, farm and home exhibits, and various agricultural exhibits and competitions. This is truly an old-time country fair complete with tractor pulls, demolition derbies, mud-drag racing, baby shows, baking contests, and top-name country music entertainment. (423) 477–3211.

Contrary to the myth started by Walt Disney, Davy Crockett was not born on a mountaintop in Tennessee; he was born along the banks of the Nolichuckey River, near the mouth of Limestone Creek. Today that birth spot, just outside of the small community of Limestone, is marked by the *Davy Crockett Birthplace State Historical Area.*

Born in 1786, David (he never signed his name Davy) went on to become the "King of the Wild Frontier." His name and legend can rightfully be claimed by many areas in the state. He was born here in the east, he ran a gristmill in middle Tennessee, and he was elected to Congress from western Tennessee.

But here is where it all began. A reproduction of his birthplace cabin has been constructed, with the cornerstone of his original cabin on display. Probably the most unusual aspect of this park is the monument erected in the late 1960s by a local civic organization. In honor of Crockett's stature as a national hero, each of the fifty states is represented in the wall of the monument. Stones native to each state are incorporated in the wall and engraved with the respective state's name.

The park, located off U.S. Highway 11E, has a campground, swimming pool, picnic facilities, and a visitors center. Open year-round; cabin open daily during the warmer months; (423) 257–2167.

Within walking distance of the park is the *Snapp Inn Bed and Breakfast* at 1990 Davy Crockett Park Road. Owned by Dan and Ruth Dorgan, the inn is a restored 1815 Federal brick home chock-full of antiques. Rates are $65 per couple and include a full breakfast. Nonsmoking patrons only; (423) 257–2482.

Fifteen minutes down Highway 321 is the county seat city of Greeneville, which happens to be the only Greeneville in the United States that uses that middle *e* in its name.

It was to this city that an eighteen-year-old boy moved in 1826 to establish a tailor business for himself. Several years later that boy, Andrew Johnson, became the country's seventeenth president. Today Johnson's Greeneville years are highlighted at the *Andrew Johnson National Historic Site,* in the downtown section. His small tailor shop has been preserved and is inside

Davy Crockett Birthplace, Limestone

the site's visitors center. Across the street is the brick home in which he lived during the early 1830s. On Main Street is the Homestead, his home from 1851 to 1875 while he was president. The cemetery where he and his family are buried is a few blocks away. All four attractions are open every day except Christmas Day. The visitors center is located at the corner of College and Depot Streets. The visitors center is free, but there is a $2.00 fee to tour the Homestead. (423) 638–3551.

Across Depot Street from the Johnson site is the *Ye Olde Tourist Trappe* crafts cooperative. Managed by Sue Hice, the shop features works from more than 150 local craftspeople and includes everything from quilts to wooden toys to wreaths to cookbooks of local delicacies. It's open daily. (423) 639–1567.

A walking-tour map of Greeneville is available that highlights thirty-six historic areas or structures of the community.

Greeneville's *Tusculum College,* founded in 1794, is the oldest college south of the Ohio River and west of the Allegheny Mountains. It was the twenty-eighth college founded in America, is the oldest college in the state, and is the oldest coed college associated with the Presbyterian Church.

Eight buildings on the campus were constructed between 1841 and 1928 and comprise the college's historic district. A walking tour of the campus is included in the city's walking-tour brochure.

The college's **Andrew Johnson Library and Museum** is the state's largest presidential library and houses a great many of the president's books, papers, and manuscripts, as well as those of his family. In addition, the library houses almost 200 original Civil War–era newspapers from throughout the country. (423) 638–1111.

Five miles southeast of town off Highway 70 on Allens Bridge Road, the **University of Tennessee** has an experimental farm that specializes in research on **burley tobacco.** The farm, according to Phil Hunter, its superintendent, concentrates on developing disease-resistant varieties and on labor-saving production practices. The fall is the best time to visit the farm. That's when the cutting, handling, and drying procedures are undertaken, but Hunter assures us that if you're not familiar with tobacco production, a trip to the agriculture station at any time would be quite fascinating. Tobacco is the leading cash crop of Tennessee, which is the third-largest tobacco producer in the country. (423) 638–6532.

The **Tennessee Mountaineer Restaurant,** on Highway 11W in Church Hill, specializes in Hillbilly Fried Chicken. "It's not the way we fix them that's so special," said the owners. "It's the chickens themselves. They have one leg shorter than the other so they can walk on the side of the mountains around here."

Whether you believe that or not, you can believe that only good food is served up in this family restaurant.

Make sure you leave room for dessert. The kitchen turns out peach cobbler, hot fudge cake, and chocolate pie. Open daily at 6:00 A.M.; (423) 357–5511.

In downtown **Rogersville,** the **Hale Springs Inn** is considered to be the oldest continuously operating inn in the state. Built in 1824 the inn has been totally restored and today offers a dining room and nine guest rooms, all but one with fireplaces. Much of the original 1824 structure is evident, including the staircases and the wooden floors throughout. Each room is furnished with antique furniture. All three Tennessee presidents, Johnson, Jackson, and Polk, stayed here, and all have guest rooms named after them. Room rates, which range from $40 to $70, include breakfast. (423) 272–5171.

Down the street from the inn is the circa-1890 **Depot Museum.** Located at 415 South Depot Street, at the railroad, the structure was renovated in 1989 and now holds a printing museum. (423) 272– 2186.

Most of the old structures in downtown Rogersville have been restored, and the entire district is listed on the National Register of Historic Places. A walking tour of the historic district includes the Hawkins County Courthouse. Built in 1836 the building is the oldest original courthouse still in use in the state.

Hale Springs Inn, Rogersville

Most of the Main Street retail businesses now sell antiques or crafts, but there are still a few old-time offices and clothing stores along the way.

There's a fascinating natural phenomenon a few miles outside of Rogersville on Ebbing & Flowing Spring Road that you won't want to miss. The *Ebbing & Flowing Spring* is one of only two known springs in the world to flow and stop at regular intervals. The way it was explained to me was that the underground hollow is filled slowly with water, and as it nears the surface of the ground, a suction is formed and the water begins to be siphoned out of the ground into the spring basin. The siphon continues to drain the hollow until it dries up, breaking the siphon and stopping the flow. It then fills up and starts all over again. This has happened for at least the past 200 years at two-hour-and-forty-seven-minute intervals. The water remains at a constant thirty-four degrees.

Legend claims that any couple drinking from the spring at the height of its flow will marry within the year. The flat rock nearby was a favorite courting spot and the site of many marriage proposals.

The Ebbing & Flowing Spring School was built in the early 1800s by families of its first students. Generations of the Amis family, the original land grant owners of the land, were taught here until the dismissal bell rang for the last time in 1956.

The Ebbing & Flowing Spring United Methodist Church met in the school when it was organized in 1820 until a permanent church was built between the school and the cemetery in 1898. It still stands today with its original timbers and interior and is used regularly by the congregation.

From the center of Rogersville, head east on old Highway 11W (not the bypass) for about a mile to Burem Road. Bear right at the Amis House historical marker, and go little more than 2 miles and turn left on Ebbing & Flowing Spring Road, a narrow country road. You'll go by ruins of a stone mill on your right. In less than a half a mile, you'll come to a stream crossing the road. Immediately to your left is the spring. The road on your right leads to the church and school. Call the Depot Museum for more information. (423) 272–2186.

Out on Highway 11E at Highway 66, is the little community of **Bulls Gap.** Named after local gun maker John Bull, who settled here in the mid-1790s, this natural gap in Bays Mountain later became a strategic location when the railroad through here was completed in 1858. During the Civil War both the North and South wanted to control the railroad through the mountains, and, as a result, Bulls Gap was the site of several skirmishes.

Even though the area has more than 200 years of history and architecture going for it, the event that put it on the map more than anything else was the birth of comedian Archie Campbell, who went on to become a member of the Grand Ole Opry in Nashville and to star on the long-running television show *Hee Haw.* He died in 1987.

Today a reconstruction of his birthplace is open in the town park, alongside the Caboose Museum and the Quillen Store building. A fun time to visit is during Labor Day weekend, when **Archie Campbell Days** takes place. In addition to the Campbell complex, there's an Old Town historic district walking tour. Campbell's birthplace is located 2 1/2 miles off exit 23 of I–81, at 139 South Main Street. (423) 235–5216.

Scott Collins works at the courthouse in Sneedville, and he's considered to be a member of the nation's smallest minority. He's a **Melungeon,** and there are not too many true Melungeons left.

For years there had been various theories of where the Melungeons came from, but Collins said no one was able to prove any of them true or false. Then, in mid-1992, an Atlanta researcher, himself part Melungeon, was able to trace the race back to A.D. 710 to southern Spain and Portugal. In a nutshell, Melungeons are descendants of the Phoenicians and the Carthaginians, the conquerors of both of those countries.

Through a series of events, they were forced to leave their homelands, and a group of several hundred was put ashore off the coast of South Carolina sometime between 1530 and 1614. Known then as Moriscos, members of the group made their way inland and eventually settled in the mountains of western North Carolina and eastern Tennessee. During their heyday the center of their life in this county was high atop Newman's Ridge.

Characteristically, Melungeons had smooth olive-colored skin, straight black hair, dark eyes, and high cheekbones. The women were shorter than average, and the men were tall and straight.

Because of mixed marriages during the 200 years or so the Melungeons called this area home, there are no "true" members of the race. "There are no distinctive traits evident in us today that make us look any different than anyone else," Collins said.

Up on Newman's Ridge today, you'll find a few old, grown-over buildings and a cemetery. There are no good roads to get there, and most of the year it takes a four-wheel-drive vehicle to do so.

Collins is kind of the unofficial historian of the race as well as the area, and his office wall is covered with photos dating back to before 1900. Researching his race is almost impossible, since the county courthouse burned down twice over the years, destroying all records. Call Collins at the courthouse when you're in town, and he'll be glad to invite you over to see the photos and to talk about the Melungeons. (423) 733–4524.

You have to be going to *Sneedville* to get there. No major highways lead there, and there are only three state highways in the entire county. In a way, the area is a part of the state that time has forgotten. There aren't too many pre-1900 structures in the county, and most of Sneedville proper reminds you of the 1950s.

In mid-1989 the county received its first national food franchise, a Hardees restaurant. All other businesses are local, family-owned establishments. Total county population is about 7,000.

Located off Highway 31, 7 miles south of Sneedville, is *Elrod Falls,* one of the great hidden treasures of this sparsely populated county. Flat Gap Creek cascades more than 100 feet to the lower pool, where swimming is permitted in the cool, deep water. Take the unnamed gravel road off Highway 31 at the sign for the falls and follow it approximately 1 mile to a small picnic area. Park there, and the walk is a very short, easy one to the falls.

PLACES TO STAY IN
THE FIRST FRONTIER

BLOUNTVILLE
Rocky Top Campground
496 Pearl Lane
Cable TV, pets allowed
(423) 323–2535

BRISTOL
Holiday Inn Medical Center
111 Holiday Drive
Restaurant, lounge,
exercise, pool
(423) 968–1101

ERWIN
Nolichucky Campground
1 Jones Branch Road
Showers, flush toilets,
fishing
(423) 743–8876

GREENEVILLE
General Morgan Inn
111 North Main Street
Restaurant, room service,
fireplaces
(423) 787–1000

JOHNSON CITY
Garden Plaza Hotel
211 Mockingbird Lane
Restaurant, lounge, pool
(423) 929–2000

JONESBOROUGH
Bugaboo Bed & Breakfast
211 Semore Drive
Full breakfast, hot tub,
scenic, fireplace
(423) 753–9345

Hawley House Bed &
Breakfast
114 East Woodrow Avenue
Built 1793, private baths,
full breakfast
(423) 753–8869

KINGSPORT
Fox Manor B&B
1612 Watauga Street
In old neighborhood,
private bath, full breakfast
(423) 378–3844

LIMESTONE
Davy Crockett Birthplace
State Park (Camping)
Off Highway 11E
Hiking trails, playground,
scenic riverside
(423) 257–2167

Snapp Inn Bed & Breakfast
1990 Davy Crockett
Park Road
Restored 1815 Federal
home with antiques
(423) 257–2482

MOUNTAIN CITY
The Butler House B&B
309 North Church Street
Private baths, secluded
quiet, great views
(423) 727–4119

ROGERSVILLE
Hale Springs Inn
110 West Main Street
Fireplace in most rooms,
antique furniture
(423) 272–5171

PLACES TO EAT IN
THE FIRST FRONTIER

BLUFF CITY
Ridgewood Restaurant
Old Highway 19E
Barbecued pork and beef
Opens at 11:30 A.M.
Tuesday–Sunday
(423) 538–7543

BRISTOL
Confetti's Cafe
3285 West State Street
Monday–Saturday, lunch
and dinner;
dinner only Saturday
(423) 764–7600

CHURCH HILL
Tennessee Mountaineer
Restaurant
On Highway 11W
Hillbilly Fried Chicken
Open daily at 6:00 A.M.
(423) 357–5511

GREENEVILLE
Deidra's
140 West Depot Street
Located in historic district
Lunch, Monday–Sunday;
Dinner, Tuesday–Saturday
(423) 636–8806

HAMPTON
Captain's Table
2340 Highway 321
Overlooking Lake Watauga,
open seasonally
Specialty is seafood,
also steaks and chicken
(423) 725–2201

JOHNSON CITY
The Firehouse Restaurant
627 West Walnut Street
In circa-1900 building, fire-
fighting memorabilia
Pit-cooked barbecue,
ribs, steaks
Lunch and dinner daily
(423) 929-7377

Galloway's Restaurant
807 North Roan Street
Dine on porch
or by fireplace
Pasta, sandwiches and
soup, all from scratch
Monday–Friday, lunch
and dinner;
dinner only Saturday
(423) 926-1166

JONESBOROUGH
Harmony Grocery
1121 Painter Road
In old country store
Cajun cuisine, BYOB
Dinner: Tuesday–Sunday;
Lunch: Sunday
(423) 348-6183

Main Street Cafe
& Catering
117 West Main Street
Located in old post office
Monday–Friday, lunch
and early dinner
Saturday, lunch only
(423) 753-2460

Parson's Table Restaurant
102 Woodrow Avenue
In circa-1870 First Christ-
ian Church building
and parsonage
Elegant dining, barbecue
Dinner Tuesday–Sunday,
Sunday buffet, lunch daily

The Mountainous East

Of Lincoln and Boone

The quaint little village of Cumberland Gap rests just a few miles from one of the most historic natural passageways of all time. Much of the westward movement of early America came through this V-shaped indentation in the Appalachian Mountain chain, a wall of rock that stretches from Maine to Georgia.

It was 1775 when Daniel Boone and his thirty axmen hacked out the Wilderness Road through the gap to open up the "western frontier" and the fertile farmlands on the other side. It was the first road platted by a white man in the state. That byway became a major thoroughfare and was a four-lane highway for decades.

Now the Cumberland Gap Tunnel, which opened October 18, 1996, takes that highway (25E) through the mountain instead of up and over the top. With the rerouting of that busy and noisy highway, the area on the mountain surrounding the original road is being restored to resemble, as closely as possible, the path used by the pioneers of the late 1700s.

At the top of the gap, a marker in the *Cumberland Gap National Historic Park* shows where the states of Kentucky, Virginia, and Tennessee meet. It is said that from the top, those three states, plus Georgia and North Carolina, can be seen on a clear day. A visitors center and museum are part of the park. (606) 248–2817.

To reach the park's visitors center, go through the tunnel to Middlesboro, Kentucky. Inside the center is an informative museum about the park, the gap, and the early life in the area. A good way to see the terrain of the mountains is to drive 4 miles up to The Pinnacle, where you'll park in Kentucky, walk into Virginia, and overlook the village of Cumberland Gap in Tennessee. You can look down on the actual gap where Daniel Boone

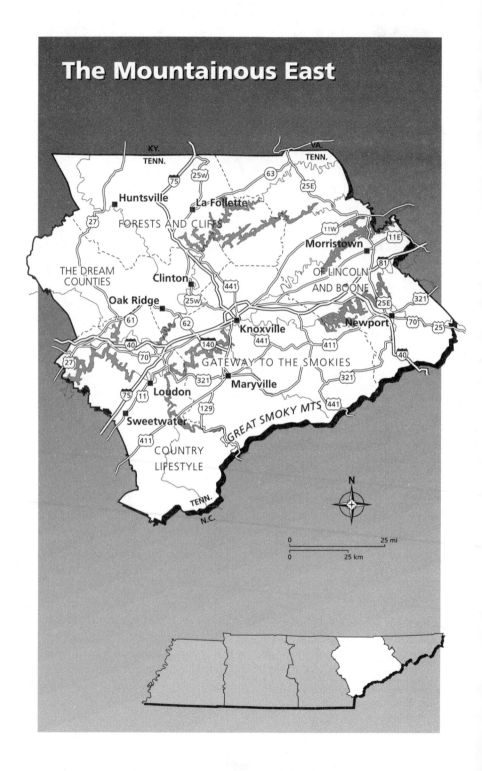

The Mountainous East

THE MOUNTAINOUS EAST

Tim's Top Ten Picks
THE MOUNTAINOUS EAST

World's Largest Stalagmite

Moonshine Capital
of the World

Davy Crockett's
Marriage License

Hillbilly Golf Course

Mel's Diner

Carbo's Police Museum

The Lost Sea

Museum of Appalachia

Rugby Utopian Community

Dollywood

came through and you'll see the old highway that follows the original Wilderness Trail.

While that trail is being restored, special guided walking programs led by the national park rangers take guests into Cudjo's Caverns and to the isolated village where Sherman Hensley lived until 1951. In 1904, he decided to get away from it all and moved, along with several relatives, to the mountaintop a few miles from Cumberland Gap. They all became self-sufficient during the period when the rest of America was learning to rely more on each other for basic needs.

Since 1965 the National Park Service has restored parts of the Hensley Settlement, including three houses, several barns, many of the fences, the schoolhouse, and the cemetery. Many of the fields are back in use, and the area is once again a working farm, run by the park service. The public is invited to visit. It's not an easy place to get to, but what an adventure it is! The most popular way of getting there is on foot via a 3¹/₂-mile path up the side of the mountain, or you can be shuttled there by park-operated vehicles. The settlement is free to visit. Call (606) 248–2817 for directions and a schedule of special events.

During the construction of the Cumberland Gap tunnel, Cudjo's Caverns, located deep in the mountain directly underneath the historic Wilderness Road, was closed but will open again when the original trail is opened to the public. The cavern is the home of the "Pillar of Hercules," the *World's Largest Stalagmite.* The formation is 65 feet high, 35 feet in circumference, and it is still growing. It's estimated to be eighty-five million years old.

The village of Cumberland Gap was founded by English settlers and today shows a strong English influence in its architecture. The downtown section has been virtually untouched by modernization for the last fifty years. The opening scene of a movie was filmed here in 1988, and according to one of the downtown businessmen, only one sign had to be removed to make the village look like a small town of the 1930s.

"Instead of getting bigger, this place is smaller now than it was in the 1960s," said Harvey Fuson, owner of *The Old Drugstore* in the village of Cumberland Gap. From his front door one can look up and see the entrance to Cudjo's Caverns, where he worked as a guide during high school. His shop was built as the town drugstore by his pharmacist father and uncle in 1950.

Located at 515 Colwyn Avenue, Fuson's store today is a combination of pharmacy museum, gift shop, and ice cream parlor. He makes the best peanut-butter milk shakes in this part of Tennessee! Open daily. (423) 869–0455. Other gift, variety, antiques and craft shops can be found up and down Colwyn Avenue.

On Wilderness Trail at the end of town is the historic Newlee Iron Works iron furnace, built in the early 1820s. It was used to make iron that was shipped off to Chattanooga and to blacksmiths throughout the region. At its peak, the furnace created more than thirty-five tons of pig iron a week. To the left of the furnace is a path that is part of the original Wilderness Trail that you can follow to get up to the historic gap itself.

A few miles south on Highway 25E is Harrogate, the home of *Lincoln Memorial University.* Founded in 1896 as a living memorial to President Lincoln, the school's charter mandated the establishment of a museum to house memorabilia of the Lincoln era. Today the Lincoln Library and Museum on the campus houses the third-largest collection of Lincolniana and Civil War items in the world.

One of the most historic items in the museum is the ebony cane the president was carrying on the night he was assassinated. A lock of Lincoln's hair is also on display. The school itself is beautiful and is a nice tribute to mountain life in east Tennessee. Take time to walk through the campus. Admission is charged to museum. (423) 869–6237.

High atop Clinch Mountain, about 5 miles out of Bean Station on Highway 25E, you'll find *Clinch Mountain Lookout Restaurant.* It's not much to look at and the signs are falling down, but don't let any of that scare you away. The eatery is home to the famous vinegar pie. What a taste sensation! The story told to me was that lemons were hard to get during the Depression, so vinegar was substituted for lemons in pie making, and some liked the taste so much, they never switched back.

Joining vinegar pie on the menu are ostrich burgers from a local farmer, hamburgers, and steaks. Breakfast is served all day. The outside tables have an astounding view of the valley and the Clinch River far below. Open seven days a week, 7:00 A.M. to 9:00 P.M. (423) 767–2511.

When Andrew Johnson came to Tennessee to establish a tailor shop, he spent a few months in Rutledge before relocating to nearby Greeneville. A reproduction of Johnson's first shop has been built and is located in front of Grainger County Courthouse, on the original site.

THE MOUNTAINOUS EAST

A few blocks away is the circa-1848 Grainger County Jail, the oldest standing brick jailhouse in Tennessee. Restored by the county's historical society, the facility now houses the society and serves as a public meeting house for the area's clubs and organizations. Inside, the original metal stairs and wall partitions are intact.

In the 1790s Davy Crockett's dad opened a small, six-room tavern near present-day Morristown. That's where little Davy spent his early years. In the 1950s a reproduction of that tavern was built on the original site, and today the **Crockett Tavern and Museum** serves as a frontier museum honoring the Crockett family and other early Tennessee pioneers. The tavern is full of period utensils and furnishings. It's located at 2002 East Morningside Drive. Open Tuesday through Saturday, 9:00 A.M. to 5:00 P.M., May through October; (423) 587–9900.

The first patented flying machine in America was developed by Melville Murrell, a Morristown preacher. Patented in 1877, a good while before the Wright brothers, the **Murrell Flyer** flew several hundred yards under bicycle-type power. Parts of the original flyer, including its wings and some of the frame, are on display at the city's Rose Center. A video presentation features interviews with some of Murrell's descendants and several photos of the plane itself.

Built in 1892 and saved from destruction in 1975 by a community action group, the **Rose Center** was the area's first school. It now serves as a community cultural center and includes a history museum, art gallery, exhibit space, and gift shop. (423) 581–4330.

Each October, the **Mountain Makin's Festival** is held on the grounds of the Rose Center and features one of east Tennessee's finest juried crafts shows. Two music stages feature various forms of local mountain music and other activities. (423) 586–6382.

Downtown Morristown is a busy business center, and there are several antiques and collectibles shops along Main Street.

ALSO WORTH SEEING IN THE MOUNTAINOUS EAST

Fun Mountain Amusement Park, Gatlinburg, (423) 430–PARK

Ober Gatlinburg Ski Resort & Amusement Park, (423) 436–5423

Great Smoky Mountains National Park, Gatlinburg, (423) 436–1200

Farragut Folklife Museum, Farragut, (423) 966–7057

James White's Fort, Knoxville, (423) 525–6514

Museum of East Tennessee History, Knoxville, (423) 544–4318

Balloons & Bluegrass Festival, Mid-May, Sevierville, (800) 255–6411

Tennessee International Wine Festival, Early February, Knoxville

Winterfest, November through February, Pigeon Forge, Gatlinburg, Sevierville

Festival of British & Appalachian Culture, Mid-May, Rugby, (423) 628–2430

Townsend in the Smokies Spring Festival, Late April/Early May, Townsend, (423) 448–6134

Cosby was settled in 1783 by a corn farmer searching for a quiet, peaceful life. Corn remained the main crop for many years, and it didn't take long before the discovery was made that it was easier to transport corn in the liquid form known as moonshine. For many years the area was known as the *"Moonshine Capital of the World."*

Today the unincorporated "downtown" of Cosby consists of a post office, bar, bank, a small grocery store, and a gas station. In the hollow bordering the Great Smoky Mountains National Park, the area is still peaceful and quiet. *The Mountain MusiCrafts,* about a mile from the post office on Highway 32, is advertised as the "kind of shop you hope to find when you visit the Smokies." The family makes and plays dulcimers, but the store also sells crafts and products from more than 100 local craftspeople.

Mountain MusiCrafts' owners Jean and Lee Schilling, now retired from touring and almost retired from making dulcimers, love their music so much they invite the world to their door every year for the Dulcimer and Harp Convention. The two-day event starts the second Friday in June and is held throughout their property, even their front porch. People from all over attend this unique event.

The couple have held the festival here since its inception in 1976. It includes daily workshops for dulcimers, harps, and various folk instruments; instrument building demonstrations; watermelon seed-spitting contests for both distance and accuracy; storytelling; and special events for kids. Miniconcerts are held throughout the day, and major concerts are held in the evening featuring the genre's top entertainers. Primitive and tent camping are permitted on-site. Admission is charged. (423) 487-5543.

Hippies to Heroes

*J*ean and Lee Schilling met at a crafts show that both were attending because of their shared love of making mountain musical instruments and playing their own creations. They fell in love and started touring and recording together in the early 1970s. Somewhere during their twenty years on the road they got married and moved back to Cosby, where Jean had been raised.

"We were called 'those damn hippies' by just about everyone when we moved in," Jean said. "We weren't accepted until people found out that the famous moonshiner Ike Costner was my father. Then we were OK neighbors. For years, I had people tell me they spent time with my daddy in prison."

Apples are now considered one of the area's biggest cash crops, and there are five or six major orchards that sell directly from their farms. Also, many smaller orchards have been planted and produce excellent crops. Look for APPLES FOR SALE signs along the roads.

One of the most popular year-round apple producers of the area is the **Kyle Carver Orchards,** located on Route 321 South, about 5 miles from I–40. The best time to visit Carvers is between mid-August and December—that's when most of the action takes place. They grow and sell many different varieties of apples on the farm, and are known widely for their fresh fried apple pies. For $1.25 you get a huge, tasty, magnificent, and hot fried treat. Forget your diet. You can't find pies of this quality just anywhere!

Along with their apples, the Carvers also sell grapes, peaches, fresh vegetables, honey, jellies, jams, apple butter, molasses, cider, and other seasonal items. There's a snack bar in the barn that sells a full lineup of snacks and light meals. Open daily year-round, 8:00 A.M. to 5:00 P.M. (423) 487–2419.

Down the road from Carver's is a historical log cabin that houses **Holloway's Country Home.** Boasting that it has the largest selection of vintage quilts in the area, the shop also features locally woven and embroidered afghans, some of which sell for as low as $12 each. If you're a quilt maker, the shop carries a full line of fabrics, quilt kits, and supplies.

Located next to the Holloway shop is **Our House Next Door,** which houses more than a dozen local artists and crafters, who not only sell their products here, but create them here as well. Located at 3892 Highway 321, both shops open daily 9:00 A.M. to 5:00 P.M. (423) 487–3866.

The **ramp** is an onionlike vegetable native to the foothills of the southern Appalachian Mountains. The odd-looking plant has been described as the "vilest-smelling, sweetest-tasting vegetable in the world." Early settlers attributed special medicinal qualities to the ramp.

Raw, parboiled, fried, or scrambled in eggs, it was regarded as a necessary spring tonic to ward off the sluggishness of winter. In the 1950s Cosby introduced the ramp to the rest of the world when it established its first annual spring festival in the plant's honor. Each May thousands come here for the annual **Cosby Ramp Festival** to enjoy activities and eat truckloads of ramps.

In the county seat city of Newport, the **Cocke County Museum** is located upstairs in the Community Center building. Among items on display are many from Grace Moore, an internationally known opera singer and movie star who was born in the southern part of the county. Downstairs are the chamber of commerce and tourist information offices. This is a good place to start a tour of the county. Free; 433 Prospect Avenue. (423) 625–9675.

How about a nice long hike through the Pisgah National Forest without having to lug a backpack around? Well, with Bob and Cathy McIntyre's llamas doing the work, there's no need for you to carry anything! Bob and Cathy own **English Mountain Llama Treks** and are able, thanks to a special-use permit, to offer one-day to multiple-day trips through the forest, with their llamas doing all the heavy work.

The sure-footed beasts of burden can each carry up to 100 pounds and are personable partners for the narrow mountain trails. There are several different treks offered, and the one-day journey starts at $60 per person, including lunch. You'll find their ranch at 738 English Mountain Road, just outside Newport. (423) 623-5274 and (800) 653-9984. Check out their Web site at www.hikinginthesmokies.com for more specifics.

Located next to the popular Lake Douglas, **Dandridge** holds the distinction of being the only town in the United States named for Martha Dandridge Washington, George's wife, and today has a well-preserved downtown historic district to be quite proud of. Self-guided tour maps are available throughout town and at the **Jefferson County Museum,** located on the first level of the circa-1845 county courthouse. One of the unique holdings of this regional history museum is **Davy Crockett's Marriage License.** Admission is free and it's open during courthouse hours. (423) 397–3800.

This community was quite the crossroads through the years. It was a regular stop for boats carrying provisions up and down the French Broad River, it was a major stage stop, and it was a road traveled by the stock traders operating between Tennessee and the Carolinas. As we know, wherever travelers gather, there will always be an abundance of taverns. Today three are still standing in Dandridge.

Almost swallowed by the waters when the Tennessee Valley Authority dammed the river to create Lake Douglas in the early 1940s, Dandridge was saved thanks to local protests and the intervention of President Roosevelt. The million-dollar dyke of native stone that holds back the waters today serves as backdrop to many of the historic buildings along Main Street. The lake dominates the outdoor activities in Dandridge as well as the entire county. The yacht club holds a July 4th boat parade, various fishing tournaments run throughout the year, and the lake is always dotted by the colorful sails of pleasure boaters enjoying themselves.

As a result of the dam and the abundance of water, the TVA built a hydroelectric plant that is still in operation today.

The **Glenmore Mansion** is considered by many architects as an almost perfect example of Victorian architecture. Built in 1869, the twenty-seven-room, five-story mansion is fully furnished with antiques of the period. In eastern Tennessee, where most historical preservation efforts are saved for pre-1850 architecture, it's good to see the preservation of the Victorian era. The mansion is located at 1280 North Chucky Pike in Jefferson City. Open Saturday and Sunday afternoons from 1:00 to 5:00 P.M. May through October; (423) 475–5014.

Great Smoky Mountains National Park

As the most visited national park in the country with ten million visitors a year, the **Great Smoky Mountains National Park** is hardly off the beaten path. But the facility is so large at 500,000 acres and has so many nooks and crannies that it isn't difficult to get away from the madding crowds.

There are established camping areas throughout the park, but camping is also permitted in the undeveloped regions as well. Special backcountry permits are needed for that.

The Sugarland's Visitors Center is located 2 miles inside the park from Gatlinburg and has maps and other information about the entire park, as well as exhibits on what one will most likely see during a visit.

Featuring more species of plants than any other area on our continent, this official International Biosphere Reserve is a true gem in Tennessee travel opportunities.

Within the boundaries there are sixteen peaks towering above 6,000 feet, including Clingman's Dome, which, at 6,643 feet, is **the highest point in Tennessee.** For information and a list of events, call (423) 436–5615.

One of the park's most unusual attractions is **LeConte Lodge,** a great place to stay while in the mountains if you enjoy walking. In fact that's the only way you can get there, and it's not the easiest walk you'll ever make. The lodge rests on top of the third-highest peak in the park, making it the highest guest lodge in the eastern United States. The shortest (and steepest) hike to the lodge is 5 ¹/₂ miles long, which is about a four-hour hike for a person in good condition. Once there you'll find no electricity, phones, or showers—just a great view and wonderful food. Rates start at $64 per adult, per night, and include dinner and breakfast. (423) 429–5704.

Cades Cove was a thriving mountain community in the 1850s, with about 685 residents and 15,000 acres of usable farmland under cultivation. Today the area is as it was then, with original buildings in original locations, so the visitor can get a true sense of the spaciousness of early mountain life. An 11-mile self-guided auto loop tour gives the best idea of the culture of the region. Most homes, churches, and stores are open to the public and are accessible by dirt paths.

It's easy to get to the scenic panoramas in the park; there are plenty of designated pull-offs and observation areas. The Foothill Parkway provides some of the best sight-seeing from your auto, and possibly the best view in the park comes after a short walk through the wilderness to the observation tower at Clingman's Dome.

Just outside the boundaries of the park, Darrell and Brenda Huskey have created one of the most unique hotels in this part of the state. The wonderfully rustic **Wonderland Hotel** is located deep in the woods and carries on the proud tradition of the Wonderland that operated in the park for decades. After operating the original Wonderland Hotel for fourteen years, the Huskey family lost its lease when the government decided to close down the facility. However, the traditions live on. In the new rustic hotel, the operators still promise "no TV, no phone in every room," and the rocking-chair bedecked porch still offers a great panorama of the mountains. The restaurant specializes in country ham and mountain trout for dinners for under $10 and is open daily. Make sure you save room for some great homemade cobbler! Room rates start at $58. Take Highway 321

Cades Cove Grist Mill
Great Smoky Mountains National Park

about 6 miles out of Pigeon Forge, turn onto Lion Springs Road, go about a mile and a half, and you'll see their sign on the right. Follow Wonderland Way into the woods and you can't miss the hotel. (423) 436–5490.

Gateway to the Smokies

The tourist destination city of Gatlinburg is located near the main entrance to the park and is considered its main gateway. Souvenir and craft shops and various attractions line the main streets, while honeymoon houses and motels line the back streets.

Among the attractions here you'll find something to please everyone.

The parkway strip is lined with fun, colorful, and often macabre things to see and do. Don't miss *Ripley's Believe It or Not!,* up from the *Guinness World Records Museum,* down from the *Mysterious Mansion,* and under the *Space Needle.*

One of the most unusual attractions in the area is *Christus Gardens.* Calling itself America's number-one religious attraction, it was created in 1960 after founder Ronald Ligon recovered from a threatening case of tuberculosis. He vowed if he were ever to regain his health, he would build "some type of significant memorial as a permanent expression" of his gratefulness to "divine Providence."

Today the attraction portrays the life of Christ in various scenes and through various stories, including the nativity and the Sermon on the Mount. Each scene has custom-crafted, life-size figures dressed in garments faithful to the originals in the Bible. It's a nondenominational message and while not totally off the beaten path, is a cool, noncommercial unique attraction. Located at 510 River Road; admission fee charged. (423) 436–5155.

There are so many craftspeople in the Smoky Mountain area that they have joined together to offer visitors a driving tour of their studios and shops. The *Great Smoky Arts & Crafts Community* tour is an 8 mile auto loop that starts and stops in Gatlinburg. An Arts & Crafts trolley leaves the City Hall Park & Ride lot on Highway 321 North every thirty minutes.

If you begin the trip at Glades Road, 3 miles on Highway 321 North from downtown Gatlinburg, you'll go past the establishments of more than seventy craftsmen as well as restaurants and inns. Detailed maps and brochures are available throughout the area.

If you continue out Highway 321 North toward Cosby, you'll pass some of the best scenery the state has to offer. You'll skirt the foothills and pass a great many gift shops, wood shops, and antiques and crafts outlets.

Since parking is at such a premium in Gatlinburg, perhaps the best deal in town is the 25-cent ride on its rapid transit system, the trolley. During peak season the entire city can become one large parking lot, so find a place to park on the edge of town or at your hotel and rely on the trolley.

The nation's first Fourth of July parade takes place on the streets of Gatlinburg each year at 12:01 A.M. July 4. Floats, bands, and huge helium balloons go by as more than 80,000 annually gather for the "Midnight Parade."

The **Hillbilly Golf Course** may well be one of the most unusual minia-ture golf courses in the world. To get to the first hole, you must ride an incline up to a point 300 feet above the city. Two 18-hole courses, with all sorts of mountaineer hazards, including a genuine outhouse and a moonshine still, are carved out of the mountainside. It's near Traffic Light Number 2. (423) 436–7470.

The **Ripley's Moving Theater** offers quite an experience! A wide screen, individual computer-controlled seat movement, and surround sound all help create a "you-are-there" sensation. Theatergoers expe-rience the jolts, bumps, and hairpin turns of adventures such as mon-ster roller coasters and dune buggy races. It's located at Traffic Light Number 8. (423) 436–9763.

With literally hundreds of nationally known craftspeople living and working around the Smoky Mountain region, you can only imagine the scope of arts and crafts, paintings, furniture making, and wood carv-ings you'll find at the **Gatlinburg Craftsmen's Fair,** held three times a year at the Gatlinburg Convention Center. The summer event runs a week in late July, a four-day show runs over Labor Day weekend, and the two-week fair runs in mid-October.

In addition to local and regional craftspeople, the best from around the country take part in these events as well, and there is always live music, from bluegrass to mountain music, being performed on the trade show floor. Admission charged. (423) 436–7479.

Head north on Route 441 out of Gatlinburg, go through a part of the national forest, and 5 miles later you'll be in Pigeon Forge, where a 25-cent trolley ride with fifty stops helps you avoid traffic congestion. Similar to Gatlinburg in its attractions, this city's main draw is country singer Dolly Parton's theme park, *Dollywood.* Country music prevails in the park, as do country crafts and good country cooking. It's easy to find: Turn east at the big Dollywood billboard at the corner of Dollywood Lane. The park's welcome center is located under the sign. (423) 428–9488.

If you see any billboards or newspaper ads while in Pigeon Forge showing Dolly Parton saying "Turn Me On," don't think she's found a new profession. What she's asking you to do is to turn on her own radio station, WDLY (105.5 FM). It provides weather, music, and a great deal of visitor information. She's even been known to drop in and talk awhile.

If you're an Elvis fan, you can get a good fix by visiting the *Elvis Museum,* where you'll see the King's last limousine, his "Double Trouble" tuxedo, and the one-of-a-kind "TCB" (Taking Care of Business, his motto) ring he designed and wore throughout his career. The ring alone is valued at more than $250,000. Of course there is a full line of the wonderfully kitsch Elvis souvenirs in the gift shop, along with plenty of CDs, cassettes, and video tapes. There is an admission fee for the museum, but none for the gift shop. Located on the Parkway, one block south of Ogle's Waterpark. (423) 428–2001. (For much more on Elvis, see the Memphis listing in the last chapter of this book.)

The *Dixie Stampede* has an interesting concept for a southern dinner theater. While eating a southern feast, patrons watch a live show in the central dirt-covered arena. The Western Show features thirty horses, Conestoga wagons, pig racing, bull riding, steer wrestling, and a bunch more good-old-boy activities. For added flavor the Northerners sit on one side, the Southerners on the other. Reservations are sometimes necessary. (423) 453–4400.

Another unique dining opportunity in Pigeon Forge is at *Mel's Diner,* where the good ole days of rock and roll are featured on the menu, on the walls, and on the jukebox. Located at 119 Wears Valley Road, one road west of the parkway, in an authentic stainless-steel diner, Mel's features a fun, tasty menu. The basket dinners are called Beach Boy Baskets, the plate dinners with side items are called The Platters, the desserts are called The Temptations, and the wonderful thick milk shakes are called Whole Lot O' Shakin Goin On.

Little Anthony's is what the kid's menu is called. For breakfast, you can choose from I Only Have Eggs For You, Blueberry Hill Pancakes, and Four Tops Breakfast Sandwiches. The three-egg omelets are called The Supremes.

Next to the vintage jukebox is a sign that reads "If music is too loud, you're too old," and over the cash register a sign proclaims "If you think you have a reservation, you're in the wrong place." This is a fun, quality eatery. Open daily. (423) 429–2184.

Along the Parkway, across the road from the red-roofed Factory Merchants Mall at stoplight number 4, you can pan for your own treasures at *The Mine.* Rubies, sapphires, and other precious stones are mixed with the dirt, and it's finders keepers. A gem shop is next door for those who want their finds mounted in earrings or rings. (423) 453–7712.

Flyaway, which bills itself as America's "most unique" sports attraction, is the country's only skydiving simulator. You suit up and ride in a vertical wind tunnel with speeds up to 115 mph. You're never more than 5 or 6 feet off the ground, but you're actually floating and flying on the air current! This is a great experience. Located at Traffic Light Number 5, 3106 Parkway. (423) 453–7777.

At the Bavarian Haus in Bell Tower Square, located next to the Pigeon Forge Welcome Center, a **Giant Cuckoo Clock,** billed as the world's largest, goes into action every fifteen minutes. Five-foot-tall wooden musicians play while a 3-foot-tall cuckoo bird makes its presence known. Inside the clock a shop sells clocks, Hummels, and other old-world gifts. (423) 453–0414.

Busy, Busy, Busy

"Action-Packed Pigeon Forge" is what the chamber of commerce here calls their community, with a year-round population of less than 4,000. Another 35,000 stop by during the summer to enjoy:

• *47 Family attractions*

• *144 Craft, gift, and specialty stores*

• *202 Outlet and factory-direct stores*

• *91 Restaurants*

• *76 Motels*

• *14 Campgrounds*

At *Carbo's Police Museum,* along the Parkway, you'll see the 1974 Corvette in which Tennessee's *Walking Tall* sheriff, Buford Pusser, was killed. (For more on Buford Pusser, see the McNairy County entries in The Western Plains chapter.) Also at Carbo's are displays featuring police badges, uniforms, weapons, and other police items from around the world. (423) 453–1358.

Elvis Presley's Mercedes-Benz is just one of the thirty cars on display at the **Smoky Mountain Car Museum.** Al Capone's bullet-proof Cadillac is here, as is Sheriff Buford Pusser's Oldsmobile patrol car. Open seasonally, daily during summer peak periods. 2970 Parkway, next to Mountain Breeze Motel.

Applewood Farms is located just off Route 441 at 230 Apple Valley Road, right where Pigeon Forge and Sevierville meet. A working apple orchard, the barn was converted into a cider mill in 1981, just in time to attract people from forty-five different states and ten foreign countries who were in the area visiting the 1982 World's Fair in nearby Knoxville. Owners Bill Kilpatrick and Bon Hicks knew they had something going and started to expand.

Giant Cuckoo Clock, Pigeon Forge

Today, in addition to the cider mill, they have a bakery, a winery featuring apple and fruit wines, an apple butter kitchen, a fudge kitchen, a candy factory, an ice-cream factory specializing in apple-flavored ice cream, a smokehouse, and a gift shop featuring crafts, gifts, and souvenir items. In 1987 their old farmhouse home was turned into the **Applewood Farmhouse Restaurant.** On the menu you'll find traditional items such as prime rib and steaks, but you'll also find local favorites, including fried biscuits and fresh Smoky Mountain trout. One of the favorites is trout cake, made from crumbled trout mixed with cheese and onions. But save room for some wonderful apple dessert. The homemade apple pies are always a favorite, but the apple fritters, accompanied by homemade apple butter, are also high on the list for apple lovers. Located across the road from the Little Pigeon River, there are plenty of huge shade trees to sit under while you wait your turn. There was such a demand for their food that the owners decided to build a second eatery on the property in 1995, so that they wouldn't have to turn so many hungry friends away. Now, the **Applewood Farms Grill** offers the same menu, plus some lighter options for those who want to sample the different foods without digging into a full meal. Open daily for breakfast, lunch, and dinner. There are special meals and hours for Thanksgiving and Christmas. (423) 453–9319.

Finding a unique, funky, fun, and quality shelter to spend the night is difficult for the person with an off-the-beaten-path-type attitude. If you're in this area, look beyond the myriad hotels and motels along the strip and stay at the **Hidden Mountain Resorts,** down the road from the Apple Mill. This is a cool, classy place.

There are condos, cottages, and log cabins, but I highly recommend the cabins. Individually placed along the sides of the mountains, most of the cabins have a whirlpool bath and/or a hot tub, gas grill, and eating areas on the back screened-in porch as well as wide-screen television, fireplaces, and a full kitchen inside. All have linens, towels, cooking utensils, and central heat and air.

The cabins all have a theme, and all are relatively new, clean, and easy to get to. It's quiet, and plenty dark at night up here. No big porch lights blocking your views of the stars or the cities far below. There's a large clubhouse and two swimming pools.

Cabins of various sizes offer from one to seven bedrooms and range in price from $125 to $450 per night. The welcome center, offices, and check-in are at the bottom of the mountain, at 475 Apple Valley Road. Call for more information or reservations. (423) 453–9850 or (800) 541–6837.

About 4 miles north on Route 441, or the Dolly Parton Parkway as they call it around here, is the downtown section of Dolly's hometown, Sevierville. Stop and ask about her and you'll be amazed at how many "good friends" this lady has. Less commercial than the other communities along Route 441, the downtown section has retained most of its small, mountain atmosphere. On a walking tour of twenty-six historic landmarks you'll get to see a bronze, life-size statue of Dolly.

Sevierville's **Maplewood Farms** is located in the largest post-and-beam wood structure in the eastern United States and houses an amazing

8,000 Marriages

*J*immy Temple owns **Temple's Feed & Seed** store in Sevierville and he serves the area as county commissioner and is an ex-mayor of the city. He also holds the record for marrying more people in Tennessee than any other person! In fact, he has married more than 8,000 couples over a thirty-year period.

The fun part to this story is that most of the weddings have taken place in his feed store. Dressed in his khaki pants and worn work boots, he'll take time to marry a couple between serving his

customers. His "real" business comes first, so you might have to wait a bit. A friend of Jimmy's told me that Jimmy loves to perform marriages and he still gets cards and letters from couples he married decades ago.

With all the "romantic" wedding chapels in the Smoky Mountain area, Jimmy does more than his share of marriages, without advertising. He won't accept any money, but if you insist, he'll take it and turn it over to his church. 106 West Bruce Street. (423) 453–3341.

collection of country store memorabilia and local specialties. Actually, there are seven different stores within the huge structure, all owned by the same person: The Farmers Market; Country Peddler General Store; Root Beer Brewery; Apple Press & Cider Mill; Candy Store; Bakery & Old Fashioned Ice Cream; Southern Gentleman Tobacco Shop; and the Tennessee Christmas Store. This is the type of mountain store you'd expect in this area, without a lot of souvenirs and gaudy trinkets.

The Farmer's Market features locally grown, fresh vegetables and fruits, gourmet jams and dressing, smoked meats, and homemade dairy products. A separate barn houses the McIntosh Grist Mill. All open at 10:00 A.M. every day, year-round; 2510 Winfield Dunn Parkway, Highway 66, next to the Lee Greenwood Theater. (423) 932–7637.

Heading to Knoxville from Sevierville on Highway 441/411, you'll pass an abundance of antiques and craft shops, potteries, and souvenir and gift shops. When the highways split, continue on Highway 441 into Knoxville until you cross the Tennessee River. That big golden ball you see high in the air to your left as you cross the river is the *Sunsphere,* the 300-foot-tall centerpiece of the 1982 World's Fair.

Visitors can ride to the observation deck for free and survey the fair site and the downtown section of the city. The sphere is open Monday through Saturday, 10:00 A.M. to 3:00 P.M. The adjacent amphitheater and parklike settings are used several times during the year for festivals, concerts, and all sorts of arts-related activities.

Adjacent to the fair site is an area known as the *11th Avenue Artists' Colony.* All four floors of the restored 1910 Candy Factory building and a row of Victorian homes behind it house various galleries and art workshops. Products available for purchase by the public range from ceramic mugs to textile hangings. The city's welcome center is located in the first-floor lobby of the Candy Factory and is open 10:00 A.M. to 5:00 P.M. Monday through Saturday. (423) 525–8195. Next to the factory building, in its new $10 million home, the *Knoxville Museum of Art* is open six days a week and offers music, lectures, and twelve exhibitions annually. (423) 525–6101.

Down the hill from the World's Fair site is the main campus of the *University of Tennessee,* where the Volunteers play their football games in the 95,000-plus-seat Neyland Stadium. It's only natural that tailgate partyers would adapt to the unique position of the stadium next to the Tennessee River. The Volunteer Navy, as it is called, starts gathering as early as the Thursday before a Saturday game, and by game time as many as 300 boats have tied up. The only traffic these folks have to contend with is walking across the street to the stadium. Washington State is the only other major college stadium in the nation accessible by water.

Colorful "Big Orange" football is king in the fall, but the pinks and whites of flowering dogwood dominate the city's attention each spring. City officials estimate that about a million such trees bloom in their city each year. A Dogwood Arts Festival is held annually during late April with arts, crafts, and other activities. There are six designated "dogwood trails" in the city for self-guided tours. Free bus tours leave from the festival grounds at Market Square Mall.

You won't find any chain stores or nationally known restaurants in the *Old City area* of Knoxville. What you'll find is a several-block area of one-of-a-kind shops, restaurants, bars, and music clubs that feature everything from jazz to reggae.

The hub of the Old City is at the junction of Jackson Avenue and Central Street in the northeastern section of downtown Knoxville. The area is a product of the period when the railroad made the city a center for commerce by delivering merchandise to the many huge brick nineteenth-century warehouses in the neighborhood.

The headquarters for JFG Coffee are located here among the art galleries and boutiques and all the roasting, packing, shipping, and administrative aspects of the business takes place in three major buildings. Across the street is the *JFG Coffee House.* It's not associated with the coffee company, but it does brew and serve only the JFG brand.

In addition to the great coffee, light meals, sandwiches, soups and salads are served. For breakfast, baker Kara Kemp creates an amazing lineup of coffee cakes, cookies and muffins. Make sure you try her special blueberry coffee cake. It's an amazing taste treat. Open 9:00 A.M. to 10:00 P.M. Monday through Thursday; 9:00 A.M. to midnight Friday and Saturday; 132 West Jackson. (423) 525–0012.

In Morningside Park, near downtown, is the largest statue of an African American in the United States. The 13-foot-tall bronze statue honors Tennessee's own Alex Haley, author of numerous novels, including *Roots.* Designed for interaction, the statue depicting Haley with an open book as if he's reading to children is a popular setting for photos.

Another monument of sorts will be open to the public by mid-1999. *The Women's Basketball Hall of Fame* is being designed and constructed as the "spiritual home of women's basketball." It's only fitting that the building be in the home city of one of the most dominant college woman's basketball forces of all times, the University of Tennessee's Lady Vols. It

Sampling of African American Cultural Events in Tennessee

Tennessee Black Heritage Festival,
February, Memphis
(901) 427–9676

Memphis Cotton Makers Jubilee,
May, Memphis
(901) 774–1118

Black Family Reunion Celebration,
September, Memphis
(901) 753–0308

African-American Street Festival,
September, Nashville
(615) 299–0412

Black Family Heritage Conference,
October, Nashville
(615) 399–7604

Kuumba Festival,
June, Knoxville
(423) 637–5049

Artfest,
August-September,
Knoxville (423) 523–7543

will be constructed in downtown Knoxville at Volunteer Landing, the new waterfront development in the city. (423) 522–3777.

If you enjoy sampling local and regional food items as well as enjoying regional arts and crafts, *The Knox County Regional Farmers Market* is a good stop to make while in Knoxville. You'll find everything from in-season fruits and vegetables to gourmet herbs and specialty produce. Local honey, molasses, jams, jellies, Amish butter, farm-made ice cream, and breads are also available daily. Among the crafts you'll find brooms, pottery, wreaths, quilts, and rocking chairs. Open daily 8:00 A.M. to 7:00 P.M., Sunday, noon to 6:00 P.M., hours may vary seasonally, so call first. Exit 8 off I–640 to East Town Mall, northeast of downtown. (423) 524-FARM.

East Tennessee's preeminent fair, the *Tennessee Valley Fair,* takes place in early September each year in Chilhowee Park, 4 miles east of downtown. There's top-name entertainment, livestock and agriculture show, carnival rides, and plenty of great old-time fair flavor. Admission charged. (423) 637–5840.

Another fun event to attend is the *Foothills Craft Guild Fall Show and Sale,* held during mid-November at the Exhibition Center at World's Fair Park. It's a juried show that features more than 130 exhibitors displaying both traditional mountain crafts and contemporary crafts. Admission charged. (423) 483–6400.

East of Knoxville on Campbell Station Road, just off exit 373 of I–40, among the commercial clutter of a typical suburban area, rests an oasis of country style. The *Appalachian Log Square* is a showcase for the Appalachian Log Homes company, but it is also a unique shopping area. Containing upscale country shops, a few offices, and the Apple Cake Tea Room restaurant, the complex not only shows off the workmanship of the log home company but also brings in money and provides a peaceful setting for a few shopkeepers. The tea room is a very country-oriented eatery that specializes in soups, sandwiches, and quiches. Open for lunch only, 11:00 A.M. to 2:30 P.M. Monday through Saturday. (423) 966–7848.

Another example of the old-time company town is found along Highway 129 south of Knoxville. Incorporated in 1919, the city of *Alcoa* was created by the Aluminum Company of America (ALCOA). Corporate offices are in Pittsburgh, but the southern plant opened in 1913 in a town called North Maryville. Six years later, with the financial help of the corporation, the city was created and its name changed.

Sam Houston, Davy Crockett's good friend and commander at the Alamo, came to Blount County with his family when he was fourteen years of age and in due time developed a fascination for the lifestyle of the neighboring Cherokee Indians. Soon he was adopted by the Cherokees, who called him "The Raven."

He left the Indians to take a teaching position in a one-room schoolhouse near Maryville. He had little formal education but had read every book he could get his hands on, had won every spelling contest he entered, and could recite large portions of Homer's Iliad from memory. His teaching career lasted one term. In March 1813 he gave up teaching to enlist in General Andrew Jackson's army to fight the Creek Indian War.

The schoolhouse where he taught still stands and is considered the oldest original schoolhouse in the state and the only building left having a close association with this famous soldier and statesman. Built in 1794 the school now houses many of Houston's artifacts, including a pair of lead knuckles with his name carved in the soft metal. The guide at the *Sam Houston Schoolhouse* speculates whether he used them to keep order in the classroom.

The site also includes a visitors center and museum exhibits. It's located 6 miles north of Maryville on Sam Houston Schoolhouse Road, off Highway 33. Open year-round; admission for adults, 50 cents; children under 18, free; (423) 983–1550.

Before the Smoky Mountains became a national park in 1935, the little community of Townsend was a major lumbering center. The *Little River Railroad and Lumber Company,* headed by Col. W. B. Townsend, set up mills and harvested logs from the rich, fertile forests that are now federal lands.

Today very little of that heritage exists. Townsend is a gateway to the Smokies, and tourism is the major industry. In the center of town on Highway 321, *Cartwright's Roadhouse* specializes in chicken and steak dinners and homemade chicken and dumplings on Sunday. (423) 448–6881. Out back, the *Little River Railroad and Lumber Company*

Museum features a restored Shay Engine No. 2147 that was used locally during the early 1900s.

A restored train depot serves as a museum that's filled with memorabilia and photos of early railroad and lumbering industries. It's open daily during the summer, weekends during April, May, and September. Admission is free.

Sandy Headrick is the president of the group that runs the museum, and she can be found across the street at the resort facility she owns and operates with her husband, Don. The Tudor-style *Highland Manor Motel* has a classy country inn atmosphere. The views from the balconies offer a spectacular vista of the Smokies, and several rooms have private whirlpool baths. It's located up on a hill, off Highway 321, near the center of town. Room rates start at $49. (800) 213–9462.

The *Dogwood Mall,* on Scenic Highway 73 near the Cades Cove entrance to the park, features a variety of shops specializing in handmade mountain items, crafts, and artwork. Such items as brooms, wooden toys, quilts, stained glass, and fine art and prints from more than thirty local artisans are available.

Country Lifestyle

Sequoyah was an uneducated, crippled Cherokee half-breed who was shunned by his peers for much of his life until, in 1821, he introduced an alphabet to his people. It was so easy to learn that soon thousands were using it. Before long the Cherokees were more literate than most of the white men living in the area.

Sequoyah is the only man to single-handedly develop and perfect an alphabet. In doing so he endowed an entire nation with learning. The story of Sequoyah is told in the *Sequoyah Birthplace Museum,* which is located south of Vonore on Highway 360 and is owned and operated by the Cherokee people.

The museum is dedicated to this brilliant Native American, but it also tells a great deal about the Cherokee Indians as a nation. Displays range from Indian artifacts to a present-day Blondie comic book written in the Cherokee alphabet. An adjacent gift shop offers a wide variety of Cherokee crafts, works of art, and related books. Open daily, year-round; admission for adults, $3.00; children under 12, $1.50; (423) 884–6246.

Along Highway 11 a few miles from Sweetwater lies the little town of *Niota,* which you may remember from national news reports a few years back. It was put on the map when the town was run by an all-female government. Coincidentally, this was the home of Harry Burn, the Tennessee legislator who cast the deciding vote to ratify the amendment to the U.S. Constitution that gave women the right to vote.

The main attraction here is the **Niota Depot,** the oldest standing railroad depot in the state. Built in 1853, the building now houses the town offices. If you'd like a tour, stop by and someone will take you on a guided walk through the historic building. (423) 568–2584.

Along Highway 68, just outside of Sweetwater, you'll find something quite amazing "under the beaten path." It's **The Lost Sea,** an attraction the *Guinness Book of World Records* calls **"America's largest underground lake."** It's a four-and-a-half-acre "bottomless" lake 300 feet underground.

The fifty-five-minute tour is an easy walk down to the lake. There's not a single step to concern yourself with, since all paths are sloping and include handrails. Glass-bottomed boats take you out onto the water, and white trout will gather around the boat as you approach their end of the lake. The tour guides are local and have quite a few interesting stories to tell. They might even try to scare you a few times as you walk along. Make sure you ask about the cave's nightclub, complete with a wooden dance floor.

Lost Sea has been designated as a Registered Natural Landmark by the U.S. Department of the Interior because of the lake phenomenon and the abundance of rare crystalline formations throughout the cavern system. Open year-round; admission for adults, $9.00; children six to twelve, $4.00; (423) 337–6616.

Eugene Morgan is in the museum business now and he loves it. The **"Museum from the Past"** is his creation and is regularly open on the weekends and during the week by chance. On display is his personal collection of 20 years' worth of acquiring everything from South American pottery to a 5.3-foot-long chain saw to a genuine Tennessee moonshine still.

Most of his collection of 1,300 items is out on tables and shelves, and he encourages you to touch them or pick them up. He'll even show you how the thing worked.

"I had to get special permission from the government to put up the still. I think they thought I might want to put it in action," he laughed as he told me the story of how he acquired it. The permission letter is tacked to the door of the still, located down a short path from the museum in deep woods. Morgan is a cordial host and he'll be more than happy to spend time with you explaining every item inside and outside his main building. A blacksmith shop has just been completed, and he has devised an old-time round pump to pump water out of the creek up to his bathrooms.

Located 4 miles south of Madisonville, on Highway 68. Watch for the signs along the road and the old stoplight in his front yard. (423) 442–4833.

It all began back in 1958 when members of the Tellico Plains Kiwanis Club started talking about the lack of roads from Monroe County across the mountains into North Carolina. That put plans in motion, and in 1996 *The Cherohala Skyway*, also known as the Ribbon in the Sky, opened as a $100 million, 51 mile scenic stretch of pure, uninterrupted mountain beauty. It runs along the ridge for a portion, down into the valleys for a while, and provides amazingly colorful vistas from 5,000 feet up, from the dogwoods and redbuds in the spring to the oranges, reds, and browns of the fall.

> **Here We Come**
>
> *Tennessee earned its nickname, the Volunteer State, by its remarkable record of furnishing volunteers in the War of 1812 and in the Mexican War.*

The road is one of only twenty National Scenic Highways in the United States and gets its unusual name from a combination of the two national forests where it begins and ends, the *Chero*kee in Tennessee, and the Nanta*hala* in North Carolina.

In Tellico Plains, enter the Skyway via Highway 162. There are plenty of brochures out about the road, and it even has its own newspaper, *The Cherohala Skyway News.* (800) 245–5428.

It may be wise to fill up your tummy before heading to the mountains, and in Tellico Plains, the popular *Tellicafe* is the place to do it. They offer an enormous selection, but if you're stopping for lunch, try the country-ham sandwich or the chicken-fried steak. You'll find them on the menu under "Luncheon Favorites." Located at 228 Bank Street. Open daily for lunch and dinner. (423) 253–2880.

The people of the Coker Creek area are still shouting, "There's gold in them thar hills!" The community has been celebrating the *Autumn Gold Festival* each October since 1968 to highlight the area's two forms of gold—the golden color of the leaves as they turn each fall and the gold that can still be found in the creeks of the area. The festival salutes the gold-mining heritage of the region, which goes back to the late 1820s.

Organizers bring down a few truckloads of dirt from the mountain gold mines so festival-goers have a better chance of finding some real gold when they participate in one of the major events, panning for gold. There are also board splitting, syrup making, gospel and country music, and arts and crafts. The festival is held at *Coker Creek Adventure Center and Mountain Ranch,* a family resort area a few miles out of town.

The 300-acre resort village is located on Highway 68 a few miles from North Carolina in the Cherokee National Forest area. Downtown consists of the post office in Mamie Murphy's house. She's the postmistress and ran the postal business out of the general store until 1988 when it burned down.

Coker Creek Crafts Gallery is located 1 block off Highway 68 on Hot Water Road. Turn onto Hot Water across from the fire station in town. Owned by Ken and Kathleen Dalton, the business specializes in high-quality crafts and visual arts. The Daltons' baskets are widely known and are in craft collections and museums all over the country. (423) 261–2157.

The *Crosseyed Cricket* advertises that it's more than "just a place to stay." Located on Paw Paw Road a few miles from exit 364 on I–40, about 20 miles southwest of Knoxville, the Cricket is a restaurant/public fishing/camping complex in a beautiful rural setting.

The restaurant is located in a 150-year-old operating gristmill and an adjacent 50-year-old log cabin overlooking the lake. The specialties are rainbow trout and channel catfish, both caught and cleaned fresh every day from the lake. Hush puppies, coleslaw, homemade pies, and fried chicken round out the menu.

There are two fish-out lakes, one for the trout and one for the catfish. Public fishing is allowed, and you pay by the pound for what you catch. They'll provide everything you need, including bait, for free if you didn't bring your own. If you wish they'll clean your catch and send it over to the restaurant, where it will be cooked to your taste. Otherwise they'll pack it in ice and you can take it home with you. There are forty-seven campsites on the far side of the lake. There's no need to have a fishing license either; they have one that covers anyone who fishes their lakes.

In October you can climb aboard a hay wagon and take a ride up to the top of the hill to the pumpkin patch, where you can pick out your choice from the thousands growing in the field. There's a flat fee for the ride, which includes your choice of a pumpkin. From Thanksgiving through Christmas, the Christmas Tree Plantation is open. You'll pay $28 to take a ride on the hay wagon to the tree lot where you can choose from several thousand trees to cut down. After your trip back to the camp, you'll be invited to enjoy a big bonfire and a cup of hot chocolate. Fishing privileges and the restaurant are closed December through February, but camping is open year-round; everything is closed on Sunday. (423) 986–5435.

Roane County is dominated by the Tennessee Valley Authority's (TVA) Watts Bar Lake. With 783 miles of lakefront, water-oriented activities are quite popular. Numerous marinas with boat rentals are scattered throughout the county. Once on the lake, island hopping is a popular activity. Hundreds of small islands make perfect secluded areas for picnicking and swimming.

Watts Bar Lake is one of several TVA lakes throughout the state that make up the chain called the The Great Lakes of the South. Many families live on the lake in houseboats. One colony is located just west of Kingston off Highway 70.

The TVA steam plant in Kingston has free tours. There's no way you can miss it; just follow the roads to the big stacks. Elsewhere, a driving tour of the county has been developed, as has a backcountry trail driving tour. Brochures and maps for both are available from the Roane County Visitors Bureau, 119 Court Street, Kingston, inside the historic Roane County Courthouse. (423) 376–5572. The Old Courthouse Museum is also located here. It features local and state history from prehistoric time to World War II. Open Tuesday through Friday; free. (423) 376–9211.

Fort Southwest Point in Kingston is the only fort in the state that has been reconstructed on its original foundation. The completed sections of the fort so far include the barracks, blockhouse, and more than 250 feet of palisade walls. A separate building houses the welcome center and the *Fort Southwest Point Museum.* Work began on the site in the early 1970s, with a lot of work still to do, according to officials.

The fort is located on a thirty-acre hill overlooking Watts Bar Lake. Take Highway 58 south out of town; go 1 mile and the fort is on your right. (423) 376–4201.

East of Rockwood off Highway 70, high atop "the mountain" (as locals call it), is a forest service–run fire tower. While visitors are not supposed to climb to the top of the tower, the picnic area around the bottom offers a magnificent bird's-eye vista of Rockwood and Watts Bar Lake. There are several shaded picnic tables and barbecue grills for the public to use. Open daily during daylight hours only. If you're driving through Rockwood during the Christmas season and see a huge star shining brightly to the east, this is where it's plugged in.

In Rockwood, the old business area is replete with antiques shops and older businesses. One of the oldest still in existence is **Hickey's 2,** a small store at the corner of Rathburn and Chamberlain. A red neon OPEN sign hangs above the front door of the old building, which was built in 1924 by Gordon Hickey to house a grocery store. Old, worn wooden floors and a high tin ceiling greet customers as they walk in. Georgia Hickey, wife of Gordon Hickey Jr., will also be on hand to greet you.

"I became a Hickey in 1945 and started working here with Gordon shortly after," she said. "My husband is one of three brothers and at one time they all had similar stores in town. They were called Hickey's one, Hickey's two, and Hickey's three."

Gordon sold bikes and had a bicycle shop in back for decades, but when he became ill several years ago that part of the business was closed down. In-stock bicycle parts are still available, however, in addition to groceries, ceramics, and gift items. Georgia is most cordial and is quite the star herself. She was on the state championship girl's basketball team in 1941. Ask her to show you the photo.

Open Monday through Saturday but closed on Wednesday and Saturday afternoons. (423) 354–9391.

The Dream Counties

ot Byrd is a celebrity in the Back Valley area, near Coalfield. She once had the distinction of operating **America's Smallest Library.** She's been on the Johnny Carson Show, and film crews from throughout the world have found the Back Valley Public Library, located in the front yard of her home. In 1989 she was the grand marshal of Coalfield High School's homecoming parade.

Once a part of the county system, the library is now independently owned by Dot and her husband, Samuel. When a new library was built in town in the early 1990s, taking away the need for Dot's little literary contribution to the community, she decided to fill the 5-x-6-foot building with donated books and keep it as a library in the front yard of the house she has lived in for more than forty years. The small structure is centered in a well-kept flower garden and is never locked. Today withdrawals are on the honor system. "People can come in any time they want, take a book or two, and return them whenever they finish," she told me, adding that people very seldom stop by anymore. The library is located about 4 miles from Oliver Springs off Highway 62 on Back Valley Road. (423) 435–7819.

If it's rugged wilderness and wild white water you're looking for, follow Highway 27 north to Wartburg and the ***Obed Wild and Scenic River.*** The area is managed by the National Park Service and the Tennessee Wildlife Resources Agency and consists of four streams within the same watershed. Through the years they have carved their way through the landscape and have created beautiful gorges, some as deep as 500 feet.

During the rainy season, from December through April, the streams provide some of the finest, most technical white water in the nation. Some primitive camping is allowed. The visitors center for the area is located at 208 North Maiden Street, next to the Federal Building in Wartburg. (423) 346–6294.

Yearning for something naturally sweet? Well, come on out to the ***Scott County Sorghum Festival,*** held the third week of September each year. Coming here is certainly a trip back in history. This is a cool festival! Sorghum is a grass that is cultivated as grain and forage or as a source of syrup resembling molasses. During the festival, men from the local Mennonite community provide an old-fashioned stir-off event. Horses pull the mill that squeezes the juice from the stalks, which are boiled, gradually turning the stalks into a thick, golden-colored syrup. Great tasting stuff.

There are all sorts of entertainment and plenty of crafts booths, providing a lot of locally made items, including baskets, honey, and apple butter. Held in Oneida City Park.

Of the three utopian experiments in Tennessee during the late 1800s, Rugby's was the largest and has left us with the most evidence of the dreamers' struggles.

Today seventeen of the seventy original buildings of

America's Smallest Library

Rugby's Utopian Community still stand and have been preserved or restored. A few are still inhabited by descendants of the original settlers.

In 1880 English author-reformer Thomas Hughes launched this colony with the dream that it would be "a centre in which a healthy, reverent life shall grow." At its peak in 1884, population was about 450. Today Rugby has about seventy residents.

Hughes's vision of a utopian existence in the wilderness of Tennessee brought a taste of British culture along with it. Most of the settlers were young British of good family, and today their colorful Victorian legacies line the streets, making Rugby one of the most unusual communities in the state.

A journey through town should begin at the old Rugby Schoolhouse, which now serves as a museum and visitors center. In addition to the school, historic buildings open to visitors include the Christ Church, Episcopal, with its original hanging lamps and 1849 rosewood reed organ, and the *Thomas Hughes Free Public Library,* which still contains what is regarded as the best representative collection (7,000 volumes) of Victorian literature in America.

Two historic structures have been restored and now offer overnight accommodations with historic accuracy. The Pioneer Cottage and the Newbury House Inn are available with prior reservations.

If you're into ghosts and stories of haunting, you'll get your fill during your tour of Rugby's historic district. If your guide doesn't talk about the various sightings through the years, make sure you ask. Rugby is located on Route 52 a few miles west of Highway 27. Structures are open year-round except for Thanksgiving Day, Christmas Eve, Christmas Day, and New Year's Day; during January tours are by appointment. Housing, shops, and a restaurant are open year-round. (423) 628–2441.

Approximately 1 mile west of Rugby on Highway 52 is the *Grey Gables Bed and Breakfast Inn.* The magnificent home was built in 1990 for the purpose of setting up a classy inn that would combine the best of Victorian English and Tennessee country heritage. Decorated with country and Victorian antiques, the inn reflects the grace of the English and the cordiality of the country.

Innkeepers Bill and Linda Brooks Jones, along with their daughters, not only have a great eight-bedroom inn, but you'll have to loosen your belt a few notches after you've eaten a couple of meals with them. In fact, Linda's cooking has gone over so well, and so many people were asking for her recipes, that she is in the final stages of writing her own cookbook, called *The Table at Grey Gables.* She was born and raised in the area, and the cookbook will have not only recipes, but historical narrative about Rugby and her relationship with the locals through the years.

If you look around, you'll see a few photos of former President Jimmy Carter and his wife, the inn's most famous boarders to date. They stayed here on June 17, 1997, and Linda has some great, fun stories about the visit. If it's available, she may let you have the bed the famous couple slept in.

In addition to the great hospitality and the yummy cooking, the hosts offer a full array of activities and themed events. Rates include an elegant evening meal and a hearty country breakfast. Reservations are required; rates are $115 double occupancy, $80 single occupancy. Call Linda or Bill and they'll send you a calendar that highlights their special themed weekends. (423) 628–5252.

In addition to their bed-and-breakfast duties, Bill and daughter Tiffany run the *R.M. Brooks General Store,* on Highway 52 just west of Grey Gables. Linda's grandparents started the store in 1930 and it has remained in the family since. The village post office is tucked away in a corner of the store and Bill serves as postmaster. The family wants to keep it a "typical, working country general store" where you can buy sandwiches, hoop cheddar cheese, mouse traps, soup, and just about anything else. Plus they have a selection of antiques and local crafts on sale. As in most establishments of this type, you'll find a good supply of local characters sitting around the potbellied stove just about any time you drop in. If Bill is in, ask him to show off a few of the antiques he won't sell you, including the rare "Icyball," a contraption used to make ice years before real refrigeration. The general store is open Monday through Saturday 7:00 A.M. to 6:00 P.M. (423) 628–2533.

During the 1880s and 1890s, *Oliver Springs* was a central railroad town for the local coal miners. The area was booming by 1895 when the Oliver Springs Hotel opened and created a strong passenger rail service to the area. As a result, the town built a new rail depot in 1896 to serve the increased needs.

That depot still stands today and is the home to a museum that highlights the area's growth to fame and fortune. The hotel burned in 1905 and was never replaced, and the town hasn't had passenger service for decades. The town's library is located in the restored depot as well. A reconditioned caboose sits out back, as does several other large pieces of local memorabilia. Located on the corner of Winter's Gap Road and Walker Avenue; free admission. (423) 435–2509.

In 1942, as World War II was raging, President Franklin D. Roosevelt approved the proposal by Albert Einstein to proceed in making a secret weapon. The Army Corps of Engineers chose an isolated 60,000-acre site here in Anderson County; within one year, three defense plants were built and a *"Secret City"* of 75,000 was cut out of the wilderness.

Throughout the war years, Oak Ridge, the name given the community, remained under direct supervision of the government and was surrounded by a tall barbed-wire fence. Only a handful of the workers knew the true nature of the project, and all were sworn to secrecy. It was not until the dropping of the first atomic bombs in 1945 that the inhabitants behind the fence learned that they had been members of an important team of the famed Manhattan Project. Oak Ridge produced the uranium 235 and plutonium 239, the fuel necessary for the atomic bomb.

The fences went down in 1949 and the city was incorporated. Today more than 4,000 buildings exist as a link to this era of secrecy. All three plants are still there, but the main emphasis in Oak Ridge now is energy research.

The original graphite reactor, the oldest continuously operated nuclear reactor in the world, is open to the public and is located in the Oak Ridge National Laboratory. A map of the 38-mile self-guided motor tour of the entire area is available at the visitors center, 302 South Tulane Avenue. (423) 482–7821.

Next to the visitors center, the U.S. Department of Energy has developed one of the world's largest energy exhibitions. The *American Museum of Science and Energy* includes interactive exhibits, live demonstrations, computer displays, and filmed interpretations. All forms of energy and their relationship to humanity are explained. One favorite demonstration, especially of the young, makes a person's hair stand straight up on end. Open daily year-round, 9:00 A.M. to 5:00 P.M., closed Thanksgiving Day, Christmas Day, and New Year's Day. Closing time is extended by one hour in June, July, and August. Admission is free (423) 576–3200.

The story behind the creation of the living areas of Oak Ridge is an amazing one. Five home designs were created and assigned to workers according to family size and job importance. Neighborhoods centered on the Town Site, which was designed to offer shopping and recreation. The high school, multifamily housing, and the hospital were also built near the Town Site. Now known as Jackson Square, a walking-tour of that original town site is available. You can get information on the tour at the visitors center.

Within Oak Ridge's city limits on Highway 62 the University of Tennessee has established a forestry experiment station. The arboretum is open to the public and has three designated nature walking tours. More than 800 species of plants grow here naturally, and most of them are labeled for easy identification by visitors. Specific information about the experimental work being done is available at the visitors center. (423) 483–3571.

The *Community Crafts Center and Shop* is located on Highway 61 about a mile after it crosses I–75. The center was started in 1970 to "enrich the souls and pocketbooks of low-income people." Today the nonprofit organization that runs the center works with local people to preserve traditional Appalachian crafts and techniques. All types of crafts are available. The center is open 9:00 A.M. to 5:00 P.M. Monday through Saturday and 1:00 to 5:00 P.M. Sunday. (423) 494–9854.

Less than a mile down the road from the crafts center is the *Museum of Appalachia.* Founded by John Rice Irwin in 1960, the museum is considered one of the most authentic representations of early Appalachian mountain life. Dozens of cabins and buildings have been moved here and preserved in the spaciousness of their original locations. More than 250,000 items are on display. Live music and demonstrations abound as employees go about living and working in a mountain village. Roots author Alex Haley said he loved the museum so much that he "built a home in sight of it." He lived across the street until his death in February 1992. Open daily, year-round; admission for adults is $7.00; children six to fifteen, $4.00. (423) 494–7680.

If you can, plan your visit during one of the three "authentic" annual events: July 4th Celebration; Tennessee Fall Homecoming, October; and Christmas in Old Appalachia.

The nearby city of *Norris* is a great little community. Planned and built by the Tennessee Valley Authority (TVA) in 1934 as a demonstration of sound community development, the town features a greenbelt; a town forest, which protects the city's water supply; and houses placed in a parklike atmosphere. Now an independent municipality, Norris has preserved its original look. Brochures and information are available at the police and fire departments.

The Tennessee Valley Authority Act was signed into law by President Franklin Roosevelt on May 18, 1933, and within a few weeks the TVA's first flood-control project, the Norris Dam, was started. As the oldest TVA facility, the dam is open to visitors on occasion, although the entire operation is now run by remote control. (423) 494–0610.

The dam and the lake make up a part of the Norris Dam State Park, as does the **Lenoir Family Museum.** Made up primarily of Helen and Will G. Lenoir's "junk" collection, items in the state-run facility date from prehistoric times to the present. The place is filled with artifacts that visitors are encouraged to pick up and touch. As the guides walk visitors through, they tell stories that bring the items to life. Many of the stories are more fun than the items themselves. To get the full benefit here, take the tour first and listen to the stories, then go back through and look at the displays at your own pace.

The museum's most treasured artifact is a European barrel organ with tiers of hand-carved wooden figures. Research shows it was made in Germany in 1826 and probably brought to America by a traveling showman. Admission is free. (423) 494–9688.

Outside, the TVA has gathered two additional buildings. The **Cosby Threshing Barn,** built in the early 1800s, was one of the first threshing barns to be built in the United States. It's full of pioneer machinery,

Fiddling Around in the Gift Shop

*J*im Russell has been playing the fiddle since 1930. He practiced daily even when he was a full-time architect. He also volunteered his fiddle and his time to play at the Museum of Appalachia, owned by his longtime friend John Rice Irwin. His doctors made him retire early from his business and told him to stop going to the museum every day because he had to drive 6 miles to get there, and in his condition it could be dangerous.

"I sat at home for a while, and I really have nothing against talking to the walls, but I realized I had to do something before the walls started talking to me," Russell said. Now he goes to the museum almost daily and walks around the gift shop playing his fiddle for guests, or sits in front of the huge fireplace taking requests from the schoolchildren.

"After a couple of years of doing this, John (the owner) wanted to start paying me, but I wouldn't accept anything. If I got paid, that means this is work, and I certainly don't see it as such!"

Sit down and talk with Jim, he's got some great stories and I bet he'll know every song you ask him to play! Take a close look at the big Hall of Fame building next to the parking lot. Jim designed that many years ago and is more than willing to tell you all about it.

including a wooden treadmill made in 1855. Across the field from the barn is a 1798 gristmill where corn is ground during the summer months. A gift shop is on the upper level. The entire setting is very rustic and just a short distance from the dam and a picnic area.

There are several caves within the park, but only one is open to the public. A tour of **Hill Cave,** which can be reached only by boat, is led by a park naturalist. The cave features many formations and is not equipped to handle large crowds, unlike nearby commercial caves. A few safety devices have been added, but the rest is as wild as it was when discovered. Reservations must be made in advance. (423) 426–7461.

Forests and Cliffs

he 667-acre *Cove Lake State Recreational Area* is located on the banks of Cove Lake, near *Caryville.* Established in the 1930s as a recreation demonstration area by the TVA, the National Park Service, and the Civilian Conservation Corps, the lake is home to more than 400 Canada geese each winter. Surrounded by the towering Cumberland Mountains, the park is perhaps more popular with visitors in the winter than the summer. The *Cove Lake Restaurant* has a full menu of country cooking favorites and seats about 115. Open daily year-round, nearly one million people visit the park each year.

The restaurant and the ranger's station and the masonry fences around them were built by the Civilian Conservation Corps.

Christmas in the Park is an annual event that county residents look forward to. The celebration features all sorts of music, lights, and decorations throughout the park. The walkways and roads are lined with candles. In the summer the park offers an Olympic-size swimming pool, tennis courts, and 4 miles of paved hiking trails. (423) 566–9701.

This entire county has been described by many as one big natural museum. Ruggedness is the key word here, and one access to that ruggedness is through the *Big South Fork National River and Recreation Area.*

Authorized by Congress in 1974, the park has been frequented mainly by those who have been willing to explore the wilderness on its own terms. During the last few years, more roads, overlooks, and river access sites have been built, opening up the 100,000-acre park to less adventurous visitors.

The Big South Fork River cuts a course through one of the most spectacular chasms east of the Mississippi. The gorge is rimmed by towering bluffs of weathered sandstone rising as high as 500 feet. It's considered to be one of the best white-water rivers in the East. In all, there are more than 80 miles of prime canoeing waters within the park.

Camping is permitted just about anywhere in the park, and mountain bikes and four-wheeled off-road vehicles are permitted on designated trails and roads. There are three developed campgrounds and the **Charit Creek Hotel,** which offers dormitory-style housing with bunk beds. There is no electricity here and no vehicular traffic is allowed. (423) 429–5704.

The most comfortable way to see the rugged terrain and the river is aboard the **Big South Fork Scenic Railway.** The three-hour narrated trip leaves from the historic coal-mining town of Sterns, Kentucky. The 7-mile trip takes you down gently to the bottom of the gorge, through a massive tunnel, and along high rock ledges. It then hugs the banks of the river, where you might catch a glimpse of white-water aficionados. (800) 462–5664.

One of the most scenic highways in this part of the state connects Jellico with LaFollette. Although it seems much longer, Highway 25W curves and twists for 29 very interesting miles. The road offers some spectacular views as it follows the canyons through the mountains. This route is a great alternative to interstate driving, but you'll need to adjust your speed to the road conditions, and you'll probably want to pull off a couple of times to enjoy the scenery. Several bitter skirmishes were fought around here during the Civil War.

Since 1760, treasure hunters have searched this area for the legendary Swift's Silver Mines, where John Swift and his crew mined silver, minted coins, and took it all back to the colonies. The operation ended during the Indian Wars and several years later Swift came back, but due to his failing eyesight was unable to locate his mines, which he insisted were still full of silver. Nobody has found that mine yet.

Now, during September, the folks around here celebrate the history and the legend of the mines during **John Swift's Lost Silver Mine Weekend.** There are lots of metal detectors, organized treasure hunts, field trips to see the area's unusual rock formations, arts, crafts, music, and of course, good ole mountain cooking. (423) 784–3275.

Over in Newcomb on Highway 297, the **Crazy Quilt Friendship Center** is a nonprofit outlet for the craftsmanship of the area's women. There are some great mountain treasures here, including quilts, cornshuck dolls, wooden toys, and other area folk art gems. As a nonprofit outlet, the prices here are amazingly affordable. Located next to the railroad tracks; admission is free. (423) 784–6022.

PLACES TO STAY IN THE MOUNTAINOUS EAST

CARYVILLE
Cove Lake State Park (Camping)
Highway 25 West
Restaurant, hiking trails, lake, fishing
(423) 566–9701

CUMBERLAND GAP
Ramada Inn
Highway 25E
Restaurant, pool, lounge
(423) 869–3631

DANDRIDGE
Tennessee Mountain Inn
531 Patriot Drive
Restaurant, pool, fireplaces, cable TV
(423) 397–9437

GATLINBURG
Great Smoky Mountains National Park (Camping)
Camping in undeveloped areas
(423) 436–5615

LeConte View Motor Lodge
929 Parkway
Fireplaces, indoor & outdoor pool
(423) 436–5032

Mountain Stream Cabins
Call for location
Secluded cabins, hot tubs, fireplaces
(423) 436–5838

KNOXVILLE
Yogi Bear Jellystone Park (Camping)
9514 Diggs Gap Road
Grocery, pools, showers, phones
(423) 938–6600

LENOIR CITY
Crosseyed Cricket
Paw Paw Road
Restaurant, fishing, camping (year-round)
(423) 986–5435

PIGEON FORGE
Creekstone Outdoor Resort (Camping)
304 Day Springs Road
Pool, river tubing, pool, laundry room
(423) 453–8181

RUGBY
Grey Gables Bed and Breakfast Inn
Highway 52
Great food, themed weekends, Country/Victorian decor
(423) 628–5252

SEVIERVILLE
Oak Tree Lodge
1620 Parkway
Private balconies, fireplaces, pools
(423) 428–7500

Hidden Mountain Resorts
Condos, cottages, and log cabins
(423) 453–9850

Wonderland Hotel
Wonderland Way
Rustic, no phones or TVs, restaurant
(423) 436–4059

TOWNSEND
Highland Manor Motel
Tudor-style, balconies, private whirlpools available
(800) 213–9462

PLACES TO EAT IN THE MOUNTAINOUS EAST

BEAN STATION
Clinch Mountain Lookout Restaurant
Highway 25E
At the Summit
Vinegar pie, ostrich burgers, breakfast all day
Open daily 7:00 A.M. to 9:00 P.M.
(423) 767–2511

COKER CREEK
Village Inn Restaurant
Highway 68 at Coker Creek Village
Regional foods, country buffet, BBQ ribs
Open Monday through Saturday for lunch
Open Saturday for breakfast buffet
Open Saturday and Sunday for country buffet
(423) 261–2310

OFF THE BEATEN PATH

COSBY
Kyle Karver Orchards
On Route 321 South, 5
miles from I-40
Fried apple pie,
cider, snack bar
Open daily year-round,
8:00 A.M. to 5:00 P.M.
(423) 487-2419

CUMBERLAND GAP
Ye Olde Tea & Coffee Shop
Colwyn Avenue, downtown
Voted one of five best
restaurants in
East Tennessee
Fine dining, indoor and
outdoor seating
(423) 869-4844

GATLINBURG
Burning Bush Restaurant
Highway 441, Entrance to
Smoky Mountains
National Park
Great view of the Smokies,
country rustic atmosphere
Bountiful breakfast served
until 2:00 P.M.
Open daily for breakfast,
lunch, and dinner
(423) 436-4669

KNOXVILLE
Great Southern Brewing
Company
424 South Gay Street
Microbrewery,
seafood, steaks
Monday through Saturday,
lunch & dinner
(423) 523-0750

Shrimp Shack Restaurant
& Oyster Bar
8027 Kingston Pike
City's most untraditional
seafood experience
Open daily for lunch
and dinner
(423) 539-1700

PIGEON FORGE
Dixie Stampede
Located on the Parkway
Watch a live show while
eating a southern feast
(423) 453-4400

Mel's Diner
119 Wears Valley Road
Rock and roll featured on
menu, walls, and jukebox
(423) 429-2184

Old Mill Restaurant
2934 Middle Creek Road
Southern cooking, fish,
chicken, steak
Next to 1830 Old Mill
attraction
Open daily for breakfast,
lunch, dinner
(423) 429-3463

SEVIERVILLE
Applewood Farmhouse
Restaurant
230 Apple Valley Road
Fried biscuits, fresh trout,
trout cake, apple pie
Applewoods Farm Grill
offers lighter options across
the street
(423) 453-9319

SWEETWATER
Dinner Bell
I-75 and Oakland Road
Home cooking, nightly
buffet, country atmosphere
Open daily at 6:00 A.M. for
breakfast, lunch and dinner
(423) 337-5825

TOWNSEND
Carriage House
Family Restaurant
8310 State Highway 73
Big country-style
breakfasts, biscuits,
country ham
Open daily for breakfast,
lunch and dinner
(423) 448-2263

Cartwright's Roadhouse
In center of town
on Highway 321
Chicken and steak,
dumplings on Sunday
Opens at 8:00 A.M.
Closing varies; call first.
(423) 448-6881

Plateaus & Valleys

Upper Cumberland

I n a valley surrounded by the Cumberland Mountains a few miles from the Kentucky border, Sergeant Alvin York, one of America's most celebrated military heroes, was born and reared. Except for the two years he spent in the war, Sergeant York spent his entire life in these mountains. But those two years put York in the history books and this part of the state on the map. Today the *Alvin York State Historic Area* commemorates his life and career.

York's one-man firefight with the German Army in France's Argonne Forest on October 8, 1918, is now legendary. As a patrol leader, he killed twenty-five German soldiers and almost single-handedly captured another 132. As a result he received more than forty Allied decorations and worldwide publicity.

His modest upbringing here in the Tennessee mountains and his refusal to cash in on his popularity by selling out to the media won the hearts of millions, and he returned to the valley as a bona fide hero.

York died in 1964, and four years later the state bought a large portion of land that included his family farm and the mill that he once operated. The exhibits are fine, but the real reason to visit this area is the park ranger, York's son, Andy York. He'll be more than glad to spend some time with you and tell you all sorts of stories about his famous father and the family's ties to the area. It's not too often that you get to meet a genuine hero's son whose business it is to talk about his father's life. It's a unique opportunity to put history into perspective.

The area is about 9 miles north of Jamestown on Highway 127 and is open daily. (931) 879–4026.

In Pall Mall, an interesting stop is the *Beaty family farm,* where *Tennessee Branch Water* is bottled. The family's historic spring was a source of fresh water for the Indians and early pioneers, now, thanks to the family, we can all enjoy it by purchasing it from our favorite retail store. The bottling plant and a small nature area on the farm are open to the public, but call (931) 864–3223 first for specific directions and hours.

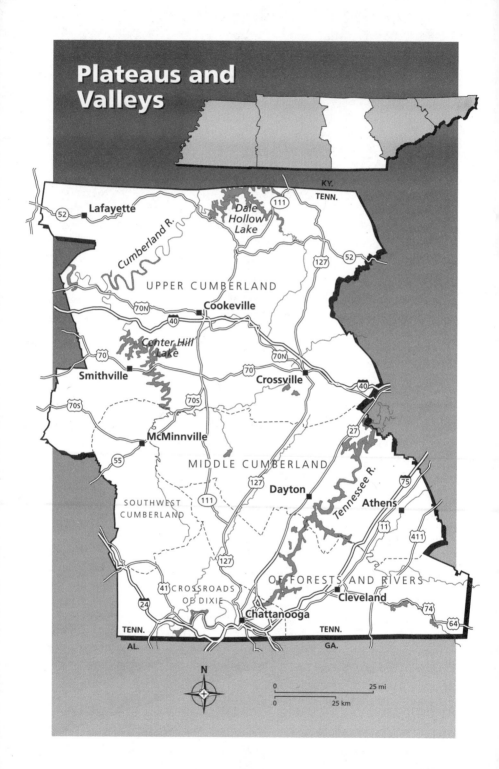

PLATEAUS & VALLEYS

TIM'S TOP TEN PICKS
THE PLATEAUS AND VALLEYS

Highland Manor Winery

Muddy Pond

Homesteads

Russell Stover Candy Factory Outlet

Dutch Maid Bakery

Wonder Cave

Tennessee's Badlands

Ocoee Whitewater Center

International Towing & Recovery Museum

Scopes Monkey Trial

Jamestown was popular with the Indians and early travelers because of the many freshwater springs that came up through the sandy soil. In fact the original name of the community was Sand Spring. One of the early settlers here was John M. Clemens, the father of Samuel Clemens, better known as Mark Twain. On Main Street, just off courthouse square, the **Mark Twain Spring Park** is on land adjacent to the Clemens homestead and still has a small spring that was once the source of water for the early residents. Although there is no evidence that Samuel Clemens ever visited here, he was conceived here. Five months after his parents moved to Missouri, he was born.

Three miles south of Jamestown on Highway 127 is the **Highland Manor Winery,** which has the distinction of being the oldest licensed winery in the state and the first American winery to be awarded the International Gold Medal for Quality in Madrid, Spain. Currently this is one of the seventeen commercial wineries in the state. (See Grundy County later in this section and Montgomery County in the Heartlands section for additional fruit-of-the-vine experiences.) The winery is open Monday through Saturday and on selected Sundays for tours and tasting. (931) 879–9519.

In the heart of the Upper Cumberland region, **Livingston,** the county seat, is rapidly becoming known for its quality crafts outlets. The downtown area around the historic courthouse is known as Court Square and is the home of many retail shops, antiques stores, and crafts stores.

Counted among the antiques stores in downtown is **The Antique Market,** at 116 North Court Square. Inside you'll find more than fifty booths and two large rooms full of everything from fabulous antique jewelry to postcards to oak furniture. It's open seven days a week; (931) 823–4943. Hungry? The Apple Dish, with a nice selection of soups, salads, and sandwiches, is located inside The Antique Market and offers not only great home cooking, but tremendous home-baked desserts, including Italian cream cake. (931) 823–3222.

Mayhue Masters has been a shopkeeper since 1948 at his **Masters General Merchandise,** up in the northern part of the county on Highway 85, 2 miles west of Hilham. "I bought a little store in 1948 and built this new building in 1952," Mayhue reminisces. "I was hardly ever in any type of store before I bought one. Nobody ever showed me how to do it [run a store], so I do things my way up here." And he does it seven days a week, twelve hours a day. Retire? "I'll have to when I kick the bucket," he predicts.

He considers United States Vice President Al Gore and his family among his friends as well as everyone else up in this part of the state. A potbellied stove in the back of the store attracts the locals, who spend just about as much time there as does Mayhue. He sells "just about everything. No sense in being here if I don't have what people want," he professes. There are gas pumps out front, hardware and plumbing supplies out back, cement and horse feed in a side room, and he's ready to make you a fresh bologna or ham sandwich anytime you need one. (931) 823-6388.

With a state as full of outdoor recreational facilities as Tennessee, it's difficult to call one facility unique, but the *Bend of the River Shooting Center* could well be. Located on Highway 136 about 10 miles north of Cookeville in the county's southwest section, the 100-acre center offers pistol and archery shooting ranges, a high-power-rifle range, and skeet and trap fields. In the rustic lodge, a variety of classes in shooting and firearm safety are held.

Owner Charlie Pardue welcomes shooters, "wanna-be" shooters, and spectators. If you don't have any weapons with you, you can rent a bow or gun for $3.00 a day, and shoot all you want for an additional $4.00. Ammunition is extra, of course. It's free if you just want to watch, and Charlie will lend you a pair of ear protectors. Open Saturday only; (931) 498-2829. Charlie also owns the *Bend of the River Shooting Supply* store, 115 W. Broad Street in nearby Cookeville, where supplies can be purchased during the week. (931) 526-1136.

Down in the southeast corner of Overton County is *Muddy Pond,* a small Mennonite community that happens to be way off the beaten path. Entrance to the community is off Highway 164, about halfway between Crawford and Monterey, or off Highway 62, 1 mile west of Clarkrange. In either direction you'll have a nice paved road for several miles before the gravel road begins.

There are several retail shops located back here, plus several of the farmers sell fresh eggs and bread out of their homes. A horse-powered mill creates the product at the Sorghum Mill, where the owners also sell homemade bread and fried pies. Country Side Quilts features handmade quilts, fabric, and crafts; the Muddy Pond Variety Store makes its own sorghum and carries produce and vegetables as well; the Baken Haus is a homestyle bakery with great breads and pies; and the Muddy Pond General Store has sorghum, cheeses, meats, quilts, pottery, outdoor furniture, and a large variety of gift and household items. Most of the businesses are open daily and closed on Sunday.

Grady Wilson has been a taxidermist for more than twenty years and it was his dream to some-day own a small museum where he could display some of his work. His dream is now known as **Wilson's North American Wildlife Museum,** located in Monterey just north of I–40.

There are nearly 400 mounted animals ranging from small hummingbirds to full-size bison and Rocky Mountain elk in eighty-five different scenes and displays, all behind glass. For a pri-vate museum, this is a first-class place. Grady built the exhibits himself with absolutely no dis-play or museum experience and has been able to capture the essence of the wildlife. Yes, these are dead, stuffed, beautiful animals, but there is nothing dark or upsetting about the place.

Grady's wife Janet runs an antique shop in front of the museum. Located 9 blocks north of Main Street at 914 North Chestnut Street. Open Mon-day through Saturday 9:00 A.M. to 5:00 P.M. Admission is charged. (931) 839–3230.

If you're into Hank Williams, Jr., make sure you stop by the **Hank Williams Jr. General Store and Tourist Information Center,** just off I–40 at the Highway 127 exit. To be more exact, it's near Crossville, 110 miles east of Nashville and 70 miles west of Knoxville. It's located on the north side of I–40 in a funky-looking, western town lineup of buildings.

ALSO WORTH SEEING IN THE PLATEAUS AND VALLEYS

Creative Discovery Museum, Chattanooga, (423) 756-2738

IMAX 3-D Theater, Chattanooga, (800) 262-0695

OOH Ostrich Ranch, Cleveland, (423) 472-9785

Cumberland County Playhouse, Crossville, (931) 484-5000

Fort Blount, Gainesboro, (931) 268-0971

Key Park Log House, Lafayette, (615) 666-5885

Deep Valley Trout Farm, Livingston, (931) 823-6053

Virgin Falls, Sparta, (931) 836-3552

Riverbend Music Festival, Mid-June, Chattanooga, (423) 756-8687

RiverRoast, Mid-May, BBQ cook-off, Chattanooga, (423) 756-8687

Cherokee Days of Recognition, First weekend in August, Cleveland, (423) 478-0339

Talk about an eclectic, you-won't-find-this-stuff-anywhere-else selection of things to buy! There are literally thousands of things here emblazoned with Bocephus's name (Hank Junior's nickname), picture, or logo. Key-chains, mugs, shirts, back scratchers, hats, kerchiefs—you name it! It's a real hoot to walk among the items and wonder what kind of a person would buy such things. The customized "Bocephus Truck" is on display in the back of the store. A large portion of the shelf space is dedicated to fire-works. A nice selection is presented at what appear to be good prices.

They also have snacks and a lot of tourist information that you'll find especially helpful if you're heading toward Nashville. It's open daily, year-round; 8:00 A.M. to 8:00 P.M. (931) 484–4914.

There are a great many houses, fences, walls and buildings around Crossville made of the famous Crab Orchard stone, a brownish-beige stone that is quarried along Highway 70 in the small community of Crab Orchard. The quarries are located along the north side of the highway and show years and years of mining operations.

Chances are you'll find a few of the workers eating breakfast or lunch at the *S&H General Store,* along Highway 70, across from the quarries. The store is the area's restaurant, hardware store, grocery store, plumbing supply store, and gathering place. Open seven days a week.

A few miles east on Highway 70 is the *Ozone Falls Natural Area,* where old-growth forest dominate. The highlight here is the magnificent 110-foot-high waterfall where Fall Creek cascades into the deep gorges below. Park in the pull-out area along the highway, and you'll only have about a fifth of a mile walk to the top of the falls. *Be very careful.* There are no guardrails or railings. If you follow the path, you'll walk right over the edge! Also, be wary of slippery stones that you might step on as you lean over to take a look.

Looking for some great cheddar cheese? *Simonton's Cheese House,* located behind the chamber of commerce on West Avenue North in Crossville, is known throughout this part of the country for its three-pound hoop of cheddar, made from grade A milk. It's sold here along with other specialty cheeses, jams, jellies, teas, candies, and hams. Simonton's Cheddar even has a cheer: "Red as an Apple, Yellow as Gold, I am Delicious, I am Told. . . . TRY ME!" Simonton's is open seven days a week. (931) 484–5193.

South of Crossville, where Highways 127 and 68 split, is the planned community of *Homesteads.* The area, with its quaint little stone houses lining both highways, is often referred to as the "showplace of the New Deal."

In January 1934, following several years of hard times in the area, the local farm agent submitted an application to the government for one of the subsistence projects formulated by the Roosevelt administration. The application was accepted and work began on the 10,000-acre project.

The plan was to build 250-plus homesteads, each of about twenty acres. The homesteaders were selected following a series of intense background checks and interviews of about 4,000 applicants. Cooperatives were established for the community, and family members went to these to make their family's mattresses, can their family's food, or weave at a loom house.

Today 218 of the 255 houses built are still standing. At the base of the 85-foot-tall octagonal tower that originally served as a water tower is a sandstone building that housed the administrative offices of the project. Today those offices serve as a museum depicting Roosevelt's homesteading project. If you want you can climb the ninety-seven steps to the top of the tower.

Of the 102 New Deal projects, the Cumberland Homesteads was considered one of the most successful of all. Open daily March through December. A small admission is charged. (931) 456–9663.

In addition to the museum, tower, and original homesteads, the area also has an interesting country store right across the street from the tower. Claiming to sell "Goods in Endless Variety for Man & Beast," the *Cumberland General Store* specializes in new old-fashioned items for the modern-day homesteader. One of the best areas of the store, however, is a book section that sells how-to books on such lost arts as hog butchering, building a stone fence, and hand digging a well. Open daily; (931) 484–8481.

Cannon County is known throughout the state for the number of fine craftsmen it has within its borders. Just about every craft you can think of is created here by a superb artist. From potters to folk artists to basket weavers to chair makers, a great many craftsmen call Cannon County home.

Unfortunately, most of the gifted craftspeople don't like you to visit their home workshops unless they know you, preferring instead to sell their crafts through various shops and at craft shows throughout the Southeast. Once you do business with them at a show, they'll probably let you do business directly with them from their home.

The county's craftspeople come out in force for the local *White Oak Country Fair,* held the second weekend in August. Artists from other counties are invited to participate as well, making this a wonderful place to buy unique items you won't find in too many locales. The fair is held at the Arts Center of Cannon County on John Bragg Highway 70–S.

This is a juried show in its infancy, and as it grows the date and location may change accordingly. Check statewide crafts show calendars or write the Arts Center of Cannon County, P.O. Box 111, Woodbury 37190. (800) 235–9073.

The New Deal Homesteads Tower

Up off Highway 96 at the very top of the county is the little community of **Auburn-town,** which claims to have the *"Best Little Fish Fry in the South."* A tradition that started in 1978 to raise money for the local Lion's Club, the event is the social highlight of the area. Held the first Saturday night of each month in the community center, the dinner is just about the best bargain around, especially if you're hungry.

The Lion's Club outing was so popular that the local fire department decided to fry up some fish on their own. Held the third Saturday of each month, the firefighters' fry offers fish as well as shrimp and chicken at the same price, in the same location. Business is brisk both nights.

For $7.00 you get all the great northern white bass you can eat, along with hush puppies, coleslaw, and iced tea or coffee. There's a huge repeat business from month to month from a five- or six-county radius. It's a great place to catch up on all the gossip.

There are several bed-and-breakfast facilities in the state that are also bona fide tourist attractions, and **Evins Mill** in Smithville is one of them. James Lockhart built his mill on this spot in 1824 and soon had a burgeoning business through the late nineteenth century. Tennessee State Senator Edgar Evins purchased the property in 1937, renamed it, and had a 4,600-square-foot lodge built on the bluff overlooking Fall Creek and the mill.

Today the lodge, along with four other rustic cabins built along the bluff, serve as a bed and breakfast. The restored mill, still with all its workings in place, serves as a full-service, state-of-the-art conference center. The kitchen of the lodge has been turned into a modern operation with a full-time chef who provides lodging guests as well as conferencing business folks with gourmet meals. The huge stone fireplace and the original wood flooring add a neat homey feeling to the environment. Off Highway 70 on Evins Mill Road, 1 ¹/₂ miles east of the junction of Highways 70 and 56; (615) 597–2088.

The internationally famous ***Old-Time Fiddler's Jamboree and Crafts Festival*** is held on the Smithville Square early each July, and for a country and Appalachian music fan it's truly a piece of heaven. There are twenty-eight categories of traditional music and dancing, including old-time bluegrass, clogging, buck dancing, old-time fiddle bands, five-string banjo, dulcimer, Dobro, fiddling, and flat-top guitar, all for top prizes. The fiddle players have a fiddle-off to determine the grand champion fiddler. There are also seven categories for musicians under the age of twelve. In addition, there are more than 300 traditional crafts booths, food stands, and other fun things to do and see. This is a great educational experience as well as a fun, unique event to visit. The festival is free. (615) 597–4163.

Back when this part of the state was known as the New Frontier, the Wilderness Trail (Highway 70) was the main route through the state, connecting the frontier settlements to the west and the more civilized areas to the east. The Rock House stagecoach inn and tollhouse were strategically built at the point where an early railroad connection crossed the trail. Built between 1835 and 1839 of Tennessee limestone, the inn soon became a gathering place for the "Who's Who" of the American frontier.

Preserved through the years by caring friends, this piece of Americana is now open to the public, usually every Saturday afternoon, year-round. The Rock House chapter of the Daughters of the American Revolution is the caretaker of the property, now known as the ***Rock House Shrine*** state historic area. Located on Highway 70, 4 miles west of Sparta. (931) 836–3552.

The good old days of logging are brought back to life each year at Edgar Evins State Park, just north of Smithville on Highway 96. The event is ***Log Jam,*** and you won't find too many events around like this one. It's a three-day competition based on the events common in old Tennessee logging camps. There are seventeen different competitions, including axe throwing, bowsawing, cross-cut sawing, log rolling, pole climbing, rope climbing, log toss, and a favorite of all the women who attend, a Paul Bunyan look-alike contest.

Anyone can enter the competition—no experience or equipment are needed, and there are trophies and other prizes awarded. Last weekend in July. Free for entrants and spectators. (931) 858–2446.

Cookeville, DeKalb County's seat of government, had two early surges of commerce that resulted in two distinctive downtown sections. The town had already established its square and business hub long before the railroads came through. When the rails came to town in 1890, they came through a residential area on the west side of town. That area soon became less residential and more commercial as business shifted from the established area around the courthouse to the new, prospering area around the depot. A large hotel was built, and warehouses and stores soon followed.

By 1910 a new passenger depot had been built, and the area was considered the "Hub of the Upper Cumberland." Passenger service was terminated in 1955, but the locals were able to save the depot, which is now on the National Register of Historic Places and the site of the *Cookeville Depot Museum.*

Inside is one of the best re-creations of an early depot in the state. Original fixtures, desks, time schedules, and the like have been preserved through the years. There are four rooms of exhibits, plus a caboose out back with more displays. Open Monday, Wednesday, and Friday 11:00 A.M. to 2:00 P.M. and Sunday 1:00 to 4:00 P.M. Admission is free; location is Broad and Cedar Streets; (931) 528–8570.

Across the street from the museum, high atop an old dairy, you'll see a big, old-fashioned neon sign advertising Cream City Ice Cream. Atop the sign is a giant ice-cream sundae whose cherry bounces up and down (in neon) when the sign is turned on. The people who bought the location when the dairy closed chose to not only save but restore the sign to its 1950s beauty. Now, several times each year, the sign is lit, much to the delight of local photographers and nostalgia buffs.

The Scarecrow Country Inn is a classy place to dine. The wood from fourteen log cabins was used to build the inn, which served as a private home for more than twenty years. Owner Wanda Fitzpatrick oversees the kitchen, which puts out some of the best prime rib and filet mignon in this part of the state.

The house specialty is the Scarecrow hickory ham cooked in hickory bark syrup, a family recipe that dates back to the late 1700s. The syrup, which is made on the premises, is also used in the inn's homemade butter. Seafood, chicken, and vegetable dishes are also on the regular menu. Dinner is served nightly from 4:00 to 10:00 P.M. Take exit 290 off I-40 and go 1 mile north. Turn right onto Whitson Chapel Road and look for the signs on your right. (931) 526–3431.

CHOCOLATE ALERT! CHOCOLATE ALERT! The Russell Stover candy factory, located on Chocolate Drive in Cookeville, also has an outlet store. A great selection of Russell Stover candies are offered at less than retail prices. WOW! There are three levels of prices. The first quality level is the exact candy you'd buy at a retail store, but for a little less. The intermediate level is for overstocked items that exceed the company's strict peak of freshness standard, but are still of top quality. The seconds are imperfectly shaped or are lacking the standards necessary for them to be included in regular packaging. (Yes, they do give out free samples!) The *Russell Stover Candy Factory Outlet Store* is open daily 9:00 A.M. to 6:00 P.M. Take the Cookeville/Algood exit off Highway 111, 3 miles north of I–40, and turn toward Cookeville. Almost immediately take a right onto Chocolate Drive. The store is on your left about a half-mile down the road. (931) 528–6434.

Looking for some truly off-the-beaten-path, funky, laid-back outdoor fun? Cookeville's *Hidden Hollow* fills that bill. The place is hard to explain and is certainly something you don't see every day. Back in 1972 Arad Lee retired in order to live out his childhood dream and transformed an old, eighty-six acre discarded farm into a fun place to picnic. Among its offerings now are a small petting zoo with deer, rabbits, and birds; a dandy beach complete with kiddie swimming pool; and cane-pole fishing in the pond.

There's a gingerbread house for the kids to play in, a covered bridge, a waterwheel, a wedding chapel, rock gardens and fountains. But the real uniqueness shows up between Thanksgiving and Christmas when Lee transforms the place into a winter wonderland, most of the time without snow. The 50-foot high windmill is lit to resemble a Christmas tree, and the hills are alive with thousands of lights and figurines. Located at 1901 Mt. Pleasant Road, Hidden Hollow is open daily year-round. Admission is $1.00; swimming and canepole fishing are each $1.00 extra. Call Lee at (931) 526–4038 and he'll be glad to tell you all about his dream come true.

There's definitely artistic magic in a remote hollow in the beautiful hills of northern Jackson County. About 3.3 miles west of Whitleyville, along Highway 56, you'll find North Fork Lane. If you follow that gravel road for about a mile, you'll discover the hideaways of three nationally known potters: Tom and Sally Freestone of *Freestone Pottery* and Ann McFather of *Annie's Pottery.*

Tom and Sally moved here from New England in 1986 and established Freestone Pottery. They had met in early 1985, got married, and decided to start a new life and lifestyle in Tennessee. Tom, an Englishman, was a well-known gristmiller and had earned a reputation for restoring old mills throughout England. Sally was a potter and an art teacher. They both are now full-time potters and can barely keep up with their orders.

They specialize in functional pottery, and what makes their stuff so unique is that each piece has a short Bible verse on it. "They are all happy love and faith verses. None of this doom, gloom, and damnation for us," Sally says with a smile, adding that this work combines her three loves: clay, words, and God. Their property, which houses their showroom, home, and studio, has a waterfall and a lot of room to "come on out and have a picnic," Tom adds. Located at 707 North Fork Lane; (931) 621–3456.

Right down the holler, Annie has her studio, showroom, and home. She was a banking officer in Atlanta and a restful weekend trip to nearby Red Boiling Springs changed her and her husband Bob's lifestyle forever. "We fell in love with the area and decided to move," she said. They met the Freestones, bought a farm nearby, and moved. Annie and Bob got jobs as bankers, but in 1993 Annie's desire to become a potter led to her leaving corporate life forever. She took lessons and was soon throwing functional stoneware pottery. She went to a couple of shows, won several "best of" kudos, and can now barely keep up with all the orders. Her items are bedecked with colorful flowers and are made to be used

What the Heck is Poke Sallet?

*T*here are only three poke sallet festivals in the United States, and downtown Gainesboro is home to one of them. That distinction is something to be proud of, even though this is basically a festival to celebrate a weed. Poke sallet grows wild in the south and is cooked the same as (and tastes something like) turnip greens and mustard greens.

Events that you won't want to miss include the poke sallet–eating contest, continuous country music, and the outhouse races. (No, not a race to the outhouse, but rather a race of outhouses.) The terrapin (turtle) races are also a highlight. Found locally in the countryside, the terrapins are placed in a circle by up to sixty contestants, and the first turtle to cross the outer line of the circle wins. There are also crosscut saw contests, a hay bale roll, and the Miss Poke Sallet Festival contest. Held during early May each year for more than 22 years; proceeds from the festival fund the Rescue Squad. (931) 268–0971.

in the kitchen; all are microwave and dishwasher safe. The address is 547 North Fork Lane; (931) 621–3302.

Gainesboro is the seat of Jackson County and has several antiques stores on the main square in the downtown area. It also has two drug-stores, Anderson & Haile Drugs and Gainesboro Drugs, which still have the old-fashioned soda fountains in operation. A nice selection of Free-stone Pottery is carried at Gainesboro Drugs.

If you think marbles are just for kids, then you haven't met the gang of marble players in Celina. For the group of dedicated players around here, the simple ring marble game is unheard of. What they play in "these here" parts is called Rolley Hole.

The game is a team sport, played on a 40-by-20-foot field called a mar-ble yard. There are three holes evenly spaced down the middle. The object of the game is for each team of two to get their marbles into each hole in succession, down the court, back and down again, three times.

The top players make their own marbles or buy them from other local players. The best of the best was Dumas Walker, who died in 1991. He was the world champion Rolley Hole player, and people would come from miles to watch him play.

In his memory the *Dumas Walker (King of Marbles) Tournament* is held each September in conjunction with the county's Homecoming Day celebration. Players from other Rolley Hole hotbeds, namely Kansas City and parts of New Jersey, come to Celina to compete in that tourney. In September the national championships are held at the nearby Standing Stone State Park. Several English players usually show up for that one as well. (931) 823–6347.

No one seems to know why this type of marble playing is so popular around here, but you'll see marble yards all over town, and just about every night there will be at least one game going on. If you happen to come through town during the day, drop by the Hevi-Duty Electric shop, just outside of town. The boys working here are champion shoot-ers and practice out back during breaks. (931) 243–3113.

The *Dale Hollow National Fish Hatchery,* just north of Celina on Highway 53, produces yearly about 300,000 pounds of 9-inch rainbow trout, which are used to restock public waterways. They also hatch and ship about 500,000 fingerlings each year.

Most of the public waterways in the Southeast are too warm for trout to breed, hence the need for this facility. Trout fishing is allowed and encouraged on most dam and river sites owned by the government, so periodic restocking is necessary.

The hatchery offers self-guided tours, but there are plenty of workers around to answer any questions. The long greenhouse-type building is where the eggs are hatched, and then the small trout are taken outside to spend the rest of their time here in one of the one hundred and four 8-by-100-foot concrete raceways.

Feeding times, early morning and late afternoon, are probably the best times to visit. The larger fish are fed food pellets from a truck. A certain amount of food drops down onto a base and then is blown across the water by a current of air. The smaller fish are fed by hand. Open every day year-round; admission free; (931) 243–2443.

During the first half of this century, **Red Boiling Springs** was a bustling health and vacation resort known for its medicinal waters. The resort enjoyed its heyday in the years between the world wars, when as many as six large hotels and ten boardinghouses were in business. Today the spa resort feeling hasn't totally vanished. The springs are still here, as are three of the hotels, and you can still get a mineral water bath. A major flood in the sixties wiped out much of the old-time charm, but the community has rebuilt and has restored much of that ambience.

Brenda Thomas realized back in the early 1990s that Red Boiling Springs still had a life to it and that some of the charm and history of the area could be brought back. She and her husband, Bobby, both born and raised in the area, bought and renovated **Armour's Red Boiling Springs Hotel,** built in 1924. Based on her hard work and the resulting success, two other old hotels have been purchased, renovated, and are now open for guests. Ironically, the owners of the two operating hotels are related. Brenda's facility is the only one that still offers mineral baths. There are twenty rooms with private baths, and the rate per person, per room is $40, which includes dinner and breakfast. An hour-long treatment consisting of a steam bath, mineral bath, and a massage is $40. Located at 321 East Main Street; (615) 699–2180.

Just down the street is the two-story brick hotel, *The Thomas House.* Owned by Evelyn Thomas Cole, who was born and raised in the area, the hotel differs in style from the others in that it has a courtyard and a European feel to it. Evelyn houses her extensive antique collection in the house. The Christmas room is decorated to the hilt and contains her large Santa Claus collection. The next room is full of her antique doll and toy collection. Another room is dedicated to antique clothing. Thank heavens she has so many rooms!

One of the guest rooms has the bedroom suite that was once owned by her friends, Tipper and Vice President Al Gore. Family portraits and photos donated by local residents line the walls. She also has the town's only swimming pool. It's open free to hotel guests and for $3.00 to the public. Rooms without meals start at $30. Rooms with two meals are $45 per person, per night. At 520 East Main Street; (615) 699–3006.

The town was famous for four types of water: black, red, double and twist, and free stone. Each is quite different in its mineral analysis and each was considered a "cure" for different ailments. A self-guided-tour brochure of the area is available at the small log cabin visitors center on East Main Street.

Over in **Lafayette,** the county seat, you don't have to have a map to find the biggest loafers in the county. On any fair-weather day, be it in January or June, you'll find a group of men of indeterminate age sitting under an old oak tree on the southeast side of the Macon County Public Square. With knife in hand, these whittlers have become part of small-town life around here. The chamber of commerce likes them because of their almost unlimited knowledge of the area. But you don't have to have kin in the area to ask after; just walk right up and start talking with them. But, of course, you'll always walk away wondering whether the directions they gave you will really take you where you want to go or whether these good ole boys have played another trick on a city slicker.

Al Gore, vice president of the United States, is from the small town of **Carthage,** the county seat of historic Smith County. In addition to seeing Gore's house, there are many interesting sites in the county, including the 1879 courthouse, the old city cemetery and many historic churches and buildings. The Smith County Chamber of Commerce can point you in the right direction. Call them at (615) 735–2093.

If Civil War history fascinates you, here's an unusual chance to find out quite a bit about General John Hunt Morgan and the Battle of Hartsville. A seventeen-stop, self-guided tour starts at the site where General Morgan, known as the *"Thunderbolt of the Confederacy,"* crossed the Cumberland River with his troops the night of December 6, 1862, and ends at the Hartsville Cemetery, where more than fifty Confederate soldiers are buried.

The general and his men seized the Hartsville *Vidette* newspaper while raiding the town, and they ended up publishing it themselves when they could find the opportunity and paper. The newspaper still publishes and still bears that historic name. The tour brochure is available from the chamber of commerce, 200 East Main Street, Suite 111. (615) 374–9243.

Middle Cumberland

I t's hard to believe that Dayton, a small city 40 miles north of Chattanooga, was probably a household word from coast to coast during the long, hot summer of 1925. That's when the silver-tongued orators, William Jennings Bryan and Clarence Darrow, engaged in a legal battle in the *Rhea County Courthouse.* The Scopes "Monkey Trial" let the world know that a Dayton outside of Ohio actually did exist. Although John Scopes, a schoolteacher, didn't reach the heights that the Wright brothers of the other Dayton did, he earned himself a place in history.

The Romanesque Revival–Italian Villa style courthouse was built in 1891 and has been restored to its 1925 vintage. The Scopes trial courtroom is on the second floor and contains the original judge's bench, four tables, railing, jury chairs, and spectator seats.

The *Rhea County Museum* is housed in the courthouse and contains exhibits, photos, and actual newsreel footage of what many still call the first major trial treated as a media event.

Scopes was accused of teaching the Darwinian theory of evolution to a high school biology class in violation of a recently passed Tennessee statute making it unlawful "to teach any theory that denies the story of the divine creation of man as taught in the Bible."

Scopes wasn't even the school's regular biology teacher, but a math teacher filling in. He was fined $100, a fee he never paid. Open Monday through Friday during courthouse hours; admission free; (423) 775–7801.

The Scopes Trial Play and Festival takes place each summer in mid-July when a special drama, *The Scopes Trial: Destiny in Dayton,* is acted out in the courtroom where the trial took place. The play is adapted directly from the trial transcript and is presented by Bryan College. A historic homes tour, a crafts fair, an antique car show, and traditional music are all a part of the festival. Of course, there's plenty of great Southern cooking available as well.

Like strawberries? If so, plan your visit to the Dayton area during the first week of May. That's when the annual *Strawberry Festival* takes place, featuring the "World's Longest (line of people eating) Strawberry Shortcake" and ten days of eclectic fun.

Other events include a carnival midway full of rides, a formal ball, various sports tournaments, an arts and crafts show, and the Strawberry Jam, a music festival. (423) 775–0361.

Out on Highway 30 is the small community of Meigs, the county seat of Decatur, where a historic town square will attract your attention. Unlike many of the older courthouse squares, this one is a bit barren and free of large trees.

But in the shadow of the courthouse, you'll find the area's version of the **Spit and Whittle Gang,** a bunch of old-timers who gather each day to—well, you guessed it.

Over behind the post office, on tiny Smith Avenue, is the **Meigs County Historical Museum.** Housed in an 1880s Gothic building, the interior has been restored to its natural wooden glory. In 1948 the last of several attorneys who practiced their trade here hung his shingle over the front door.

Dudley Culvahouse served the area for many years before retiring. After his "official" retirement, he still worked with a few clients and wrote wills and other documents for those who needed them. He became famous for the sign that hung in his doorway for years. It read: OPEN WHEN I GET HERE. CLOSED WHEN I GET TIRED.

That sign is now hanging in the museum. Upon his death in 1989, his widow sold the building to the historical society. "The building was built by a Smith, and it's located on Smith Avenue," said one of the volunteers who runs it. "So we refer to our museum as the Little Smithsonian."

Full of local memorabilia and artifacts, the museum is open Wednesday through Saturday. (423) 334–4424.

Outside of town, in the middle of the Tennessee River, is **Jolley's Island,**

The Work Has Been Done For You

*T*hree "Heritage Trails" have been created through Tennessee. Each allows the traveler to delve deep into the rich heritage of Tennessee. Follow the Music Trail to the sites where the state's diverse style and influences have been developed. The Arts and Crafts Trail will lead you from small-town craft commissaries to urban fine arts galleries and outdoor drama performances. The History Trail explores all the sites where people and events have shaped the course of the Volunteer State. A book outlining the trails is available free of charge from the Tennessee Tourist Development, Fifth Floor, Rachel Jackson Building, 320 Sixth Avenue North, Nashville 37243. (888) 243–9769.

where Sam Houston lived with the Cherokee Indians for several years and earned his Indian name, "The Raven." The National Park Service plans to make the island an official part of the Trail of Tears.

The island, which can be seen from the Blythe Ferry, will house several historical exhibits, including a marble wall with the names of the Native Americans who left on the Trail of Tears journey.

Codfish dinners are the specialty of the house at **Lee's Restaurant,** 11 miles south of Decatur off Highway 58. The popular eatery attracts people from all over, mostly by word-of-mouth recommendation. The "secret ingredients" in the light batter are what give the fish its great, memorable taste. A children's menu is also available. Other items include steaks, seafood combination plates, and a special vegetable plate for Sunday dinner. Open Wednesday, Thursday, and Friday 4:00 to 9:00 P.M., Saturday noon to 9:00 P.M., and Sunday noon to 8:00 P.M. (423) 334–5695.

In Athens, just off Highway 30, rests **Tennessee Wesleyan College,** a liberal arts school established in 1857. The first building on campus, appropriately called the "Old College" building, is still standing and up until 1989 housed the county's heritage museum.

The structure, built in 1854 and also used as a hospital during the Civil War, faces the quad grounds of the school. Behind Old College on Dwain Farmer Drive, you'll find a marker explaining one of the most poignant legends in Tennessee history.

A wounded English officer from nearby Fort Loudon was befriended by an Indian chief and nursed back to health by Nocatula, daughter of the chief. The soldier, given the name of Connestoga (the oak), was accepted into the tribe and married Nocatula. A jealous suitor attacked Connestoga with a knife. As he lay dying, Nocatula confessed her eternal love for him and plunged a knife into her breast.

The pair were buried together, and the chief placed an acorn in Connestoga's hand and a hackberry in Nocatula's hand, symbolizing undying love. From these there developed two trees that grew intertwined on this spot for more than 150 years.

After these two original trees died in 1957, two others were planted. Those have since died, and today the stumps are all that remain.

The **McMinn County Living Heritage Museum** is located in the city's old high school building, about a half mile from downtown at 522 West Madison Avenue.

The museum's collection of nineteenth- and twentieth-century quilts is one of the finest in the state. In addition to the permanent display of quilts, a nationally known quilt show is hosted by the museum each February, March, and April.

There is also a great children's collection that includes china and bisque-head dolls, toys, and clothing, along with school desks, books, and maps dating from 1850. Admission is charged; open daily; (423) 745–0329.

The *Mayfield Dairy* has been serving the folks in this part of the state for more than seventy-five years with fresh milk products and some of the best ice cream you've ever sunk your teeth into. The dairy now offers fun tours, which conclude at a gift shop and dairy bar where you can sample (for a price) some of the products you saw being made. (423) 745–2151.

The annual Arts in the Park festival is held the third week of September each year and, among other offerings, has one of the most respected juried arts and crafts show in this part of the state. Held on the campus of Tennessee Wesleyan College. (423) 745–8781.

Out on County Road 52, 8 miles west of I–75, Dave and Vicki Rhyne make "fruitcakes for people who don't like fruitcakes." Really, that's their slogan. Dave told me his pecan fruitcakes don't have the raisins or citrus peeling that the others do, and that his are 25 percent pecans by weight. Their *Sunshine Hollow Bakery and Exhibition Gardens* pumps out about 10,000 pounds of the holiday treat each year.

When they aren't making fruitcakes, they are out in their greenhouse hybridizing daylilies and hostas. Right now they grow and sell 1,000 varieties of daylilies and 100 varieties of hostas. They sell them at the farm as well as by mail order. They have a two-and-a-half acre shade garden and a seven-acre daylily garden, displaying many of their varieties. The public is invited to come out and visit the bakery operation October through December, and their plant business May through July. The store sells other items as well, including pecan pralines, jams, and jellies. Free; (423) 745–4289 and (800) 669–2005.

At the turn of the century, the site of present-day Etowah on Highway 411 was muddy farmland. Then news came that the Louisville and Nashville Railroad (known as the L&N) was to build a new railroad line between Cincinnati and Atlanta. The land was purchased to build a rail center. Named Etowah, a boomtown soon sprang up, and the *L&N Depot* was built in 1906 and became the community's central point from which social, economic, and cultural activities evolved for many years.

By 1974, passenger travel had declined to the point that the depot was abandoned and sat empty until the town purchased it in 1978. It was restored and placed on the National Register of Historic Places. It now houses a railroad museum that examines what it meant to be a railroad town in the "New South."

You've never seen a railroad depot like this one! As you drive up, the elegant Victorian structure looks more like a hotel or an elegant private home than a railroad depot. It's made of yellow pine and has fifteen rooms. The depot is also home to the Etowah Arts Commission Art Gallery and the Depot Gift Shop.

The grounds around the depot remain a community gathering spot and are the site of several fairs, festivals and weddings during the year, including a popular old-time July 4th celebration. The train yard is still active and can provide rail buffs a fun time watching all the switching and maneuvering. Located on Highway 411 in downtown Etowah. (423) 263–7840.

The city fathers of Etowah have also purchased the circa-1918 *Gem Theater* and are restoring it to its cultural splendor. At one time, the Gem was considered the largest privately owned theater in East Tennessee. Today, it has a full schedule of filmed and live stage presentations. Located at Seventh and Tennessee Avenues. (423) 263–7840.

There aren't too many museums around that spotlight women in industry, but in the little village of Englewood you'll find such a place. This area of the state is unusual in that it was built on textile manufacturing, the one Appalachian industry that employed large numbers of women. *The Englewood Textile Museum* traces the area's textile industry from 1850. Exhibits present examples of different textiles and machinery from 1890 and emphasizes the role of the working-class women in the mills, their home life, and their role in the development of the community. Located at 17 Niota Street. Open Tuesday through Saturday noon to 5:00 P.M. Free admission, but help them out by throwing a couple bucks in their donation bucket. (423) 887–5224 or (423) 887–5455.

Southwest Cumberland

In *Tracy City* you'll find *Dutch Maid Bakery,* the state's oldest family bakery. Along with its baked goods, the store sells a nice selection of local crafts, a sampling of local honey, and other cottage industry products made in this area of the state.

Founded by John Baggenstoss in 1902, the bakery is still owned and run by family members. Through the years all of Baggenstoss's six sons have been involved in the family business, but today the operation is in the hands of a close family friend, Lynn Craig.

The bakery resembles a museum. Everything but the baked goods is at least sixty years old, and most of the baking is done in a circa-1923 converted stoker oven.

In addition to their famous applesauce fruitcake, the bakers also create salt-rising bread and other "regular" bakery items. Informal tours are given whenever someone drops in and wants one. Open daily; (931) 592-3171. Make sure you get on the mailing list so you can order by mail.

A few doors down from the bakery, **Henry Flury and Sons** general store has had "staple and fancy groceries" for sale since 1905. The proprietors like to call their little establishment the "living museum of mountain life and the gathering place for friends."

Along with the groceries the store offers fresh meats, hoop cheese, produce, deli sandwiches, deli trays, and hand-dipped ice cream. Call ahead and they'll pack a picnic for you. The old wooden floors and the high ceilings are just what you would think you'd find in a store like this. There are feed bags hanging from the ceiling, baskets line the top shelves, and old-time items are sitting around the shop. The local folk use the store as a handicraft outlet for their home-made products. Located on Highway 41 in Tracy City. (931) 592-5661.

Stay on Highway 41 and head to Monteagle, where, just across I–24 on Highway 64/41A, you'll find one of the best places for pit barbecue and hickory-smoked meats in the state. *Jim Oliver's Smokehouse* complex offers a great country store, meeting rooms, a lodge, a motel, and his famous restaurant. In all, he has twenty acres full of all sorts of things to do. The motel's swimming pool is a sight in itself; it's in the shape of a ham. (931) 924-2268.

Across the highway is the *Monteagle Wine Cellars,* which offers tours and wine tasting. The establishment of the winery here represents what is hoped to be a revitalization of the area's grape growing and wine making that was started by a group of Swiss immigrants who settled nearby in 1870. Monteagle is at an elevation of 2,100 feet. Open daily year-round; (931) 924-2120.

If you're heading toward Monteagle, make plans to stay at the *Edgeworth Inn,* located on the grounds of the historic Monteagle Assembly. The inn, owned and operated by Wendy and David Adams, is a first-class, thirteen-bedroom bed and breakfast. Built as a boardinghouse in 1896, the structure has been completely renovated to its Victorian splendor and offers guests a respite from the real world.

Each morning you'll find Wendy and David in the kitchen baking the day's breakfast, which includes carrot muffins, spoon bread, sausage casserole, and a selection of the Adams's specialty breads. While here you'll eat from Wedgwood china, cover up with heirloom quilts, and get a chance to enjoy the family's extensive art collection located throughout the house.

The Adamses accept no pets, and they ask you to call ahead and make arrangements if you'll be bringing children. Rooms start at $95. A five-course candlelit gourmet meal is served each evening for an additional fee. (931) 924–4000.

Back in 1897 three Vanderbilt University students were exploring the foothills of Monteagle Mountain when they followed a cool stream, went through a small, dark opening in the hillside, and discovered the magnificent *Wonder Cave.* Soon the cave was opened to paying customers and became a popular tourist attraction. Luckily the owner back then didn't modernize the attraction by stringing electric lights throughout. He believed electricity would spoil the environment and the sense of discovery as guests walked through the cavern.

Today the owners feel the same, and Wonder Cave remains the only commercial cave in the state that has not been wired for electricity. Instead, each guest is given a flashlight or a gas lantern to carry during the hour-long tour. You'll be led along a river and through the three levels as the guide stops and points out some great rock formations, including the priest at the altar and the onyx goat. The water temperature remains a constant 46 degrees, while the air temperature remains at 56 degrees. Tours are given on the hour 9:00 A.M. to 4:00 P.M. Tuesday through Sunday during the summer season. After Labor Day the cave is open by chance or appointment. Adults pay $7.50; children under 12, $4.50.

An adjacent log house, built in 1929, now serves as a bed and breakfast; rates start at $65 per couple, per night. Julia Born operates the family-owned complex and has turned it into a true off-the-beaten-path gem. Located off Highway 41 in Pelham; (931) 467–3060.

Grundy County is gaining a national reputation as a mountain crafts center thanks to several artisans whose works are known and in demand from coast to coast. Many of these craftspeople have settled in the center of the county and have established homes and local ties.

In Altamont, folk artist Ron Van Dyke bought the town's old mill, rebuilt a couple of its buildings, and has plans to restore as much as possible. *Greeters Mill* pumped water for the town, ground its corn, cut its wood, and was a major operation until 1968.

Today, one of the buildings serves as the home for the **Cumberland Craftsman,** a shop specializing in Van Dyke's work as well as that of other local artists. The old wood kiln is now Van Dyke's workshop. Out front, the old steam engine that was used in this operation has been put back together and painted. It's a good landmark for the establishment. Van Dyke specializes in taking old "farm junk" and turning it into "all kinds of creature sculptures." Open mostly on weekends; (931) 692–3595.

On the other side of Beersheba Springs, Phil and Terri Mayhew live and work in an 1850s log cabin. Phil's work with high-fired, functional porcelain pottery is represented by sixteen galleries in twelve states. Terri creates porcelain and handwrought silver jewelry. Phil, a former arts professor, has developed a porcelain that will fuse at a higher temperature, thus making it more durable and giving it a unique color range. Phil and Terri both will show you their work, which is usually displayed on the front porch of their house during the warmer months. Their business is called **Beersheba Porcelain.** (931) 692–2280.

Beersheba Springs was a bustling resort area during the last half of the 1800s, and its grand hotel, which was built in 1850, is still standing. Down the road a couple of blocks from the Mayhews, the building is now owned by the United Methodist Church and used as a summer meeting facility. The view from the front of the hotel is nothing less than breathtaking.

When the hotel was active, stagecoaches would stop at the foot of the mountain and sound a horn once for each guest they had aboard for the hotel. By the time they reached the top, the hotel's band was ready to greet them. Dinner and a clean room had also been prepared.

The hotel grounds are the site of an annual arts and crafts show held in late August.

Cumberland Caverns, located about 7 miles southeast of McMinnville just off Highway 8, is the second-largest cavern system in the United States, after Kentucky's Mammoth Cave. Unless you happen to be an expert in this sort of thing, most of the tour through the cave reminds you of just about any other cave journey.

One room here, however, is impressive no matter what your interests are. The "Hall of the Mountain King" room is 600 feet long, 150 feet wide, and 140 feet high. It is the *largest cave room east of the Mississippi River.* The room's man-made amenities are built alongside the natural formations. Of these constructed features, the most amazing is the dining room, which will seat 500 for a banquet. High above the tables is a 15-foot, 1,500-pound chandelier from a theater in Brooklyn, New York. And all this is more than 300 feet below the hustle and bustle of the real world! (931) 668–4396.

Historic Falcon Manor, in McMinnville, is both an elegant bed and breakfast and a tourist attraction. In fact, owners Charlien and George McGlothin had so many requests for tours of the house, that they now have a standing tour at 1:00 each afternoon for $5.00 per person. The hour-long tour, peppered with local color and anecdotes, is a great way to learn the personal history of this magnificent Queen Anne Victorian mansion, built in 1897 by entrepreneur Clay Faulkner for his wife, Mary.

Faulkner promised Mary that he would build her the finest house in Warren County if she would move next to their woolen mill, then 2 1/2 miles from town. She agreed and a year later the couple moved in with their five children. In 1946 the 10,000-square-foot mansion was converted into a hospital and nursing home. By the mid-1950s the building had been added onto and named the Faulkner Springs Hospital. Today bloodstains can still be seen on the floor in a couple of spots, and the nursing station now houses some of the modern kitchen equipment.

In his tour of the house, George proudly points out that this was the first house built with central heat and air-conditioning in the county, and that its foundation goes 17 feet below ground to solid bedrock. George was born and raised locally, and he points out that his sister was born in this house when it was a hospital. As a bed and breakfast, the mansion offers five guest rooms lavishly furnished with period antiques. Rates are $105 per room, per night with a full breakfast. A honeymoon suite, complete with brass bed, has been built in the old kitchen. At the end of Faulkner Springs Road, off the Highway 70 bypass; (931) 668–4444.

Warren County, which McMinnville serves as county seat, is known as the *Nursery Capital of the World.* More than 500 commercial nurseries throughout the county produce trees, shrubs, and plants, many of which are located along the major highways and provide miles of flowering beauty for you to observe as you drive along. Many are open for tours and several have small retail outlets. For a listing of those open to the public, call the chamber of commerce at (931) 473–6611.

Of Forests and Rivers

I f you happen to be in this part of the state and are tired of beautiful, lush mountains and forests, trek on over to the Ducktown area, a portion of the state often referred to as *Tennessee's Badlands.* Here you won't be surrounded by lush, green vegetation. In fact, you'll be surrounded by a 56-square-mile area of barren red hills, stunted pine trees, and washed-out gullies. This area of raw landscape is similar in looks to the famed badlands area of the Dakotas.

The story about this area, known officially as the *Copper Basin* area of Tennessee, Georgia, and North Carolina, is a fascinating tale of hard work and inadvertent destruction of the environment. The area is steeped in the history of copper mining. Copper was first discovered in 1843 near Potato Creek, between Ducktown and Copperhill, and by 1860 copper mining was in full swing and dominated and dictated the lifestyle of the basin for generations until the last mine closed in 1987.

By the time the industry called it quits, there was a 56-square-mile area of denuded red hills shimmering with glowing colors ranging from soft pastels to dark copper hues. The area stood out because of the otherwise lush green of the Cherokee National Forest. From space, NASA photos show the area looking like a moonscape.

Through vigorous reforestation programs, most of the area now has some vegetation growing, and it will only be a matter of years before the Copper Basin blends in with the rest of the area. However, some historians are hoping to keep a part of the area barren as an example of their active copper mining heritage.

The copper mining story is told through numerous methods at the *Ducktown Basin Museum* on the Burra Burra Mine site, now on the National Register of Historic Places. Founded in 1978, the museum is located on seventeen acres that include the buildings, mining structures, and mechanical operations of the mine site just as they were when it went out of business. The state purchased the museum in 1988, making it the first state-owned historic industrial site.

This is a fascinating part of the state that few residents even know exists. It's also an industry that isn't much talked about in the state. Your visit here should begin at the museum. You'll learn about the industry, why the area looks as it does, why the social life was affected so drastically by the industry, and what part Native Americans played. You'll also get a chance to tour the mine site, but you are not permitted to go underground.

Hoist House, which housed the equipment used to pull men and ore from the mines, is now used as a theater and is where the annual Halloween Ghost Stories storytelling festival is held. This structure and the steam boiler building were two of the first structures built at the turn of the century by the Tennessee Copper Company. Hoist House is open Monday through Saturday, year-round. Adults are $3.00; seniors, $2.00; children 12 and under, 50 cents; (423) 496–5778.

In the quaint little village of Ducktown, around the corner from the museum, is the ***Company House Bed & Breakfast.*** Built in 1870 by the mine company's doctor, the building has had a colorful past. After standing empty for nearly a decade, the building was purchased by Margie Tonkin and Mike Fabian, who dove in and undertook 90 percent of the massive renovation project by themselves. That was 1994. "It took us two weeks just to figure out where to start and we did it one room at a time," Mike told me. Now, the structure is listed on the National Register of Historic Places.

Ask Margie and Mike about the renovation and they'll pull out a volume of "before" and "after" photos that will astonish you! They'll also show you photos of the Italian Olympic white-water team that stayed here during the Olympic trials that took place on the nearby Ocoee River.

The six bedrooms, all with private baths, are named after area mines and are quite nice, as is the marvelous hearty breakfast the couple puts out every morning for their guests. All rooms are non-smoking and well-behaved children over ten years of age are welcome, Margie notes. Rates are from $70 to $75 per room. 125 Main Street. (423) 496–5634.

A great many residential and industrial structures within the Copper Basin are listed on the National Register of Historic Places. More than 200 are listed as part of the ***Copper Basin Historic District.*** Copperhill, across the Ocoee River from Georgia, was another major town during the copper days. It was the corporate headquarters for the Tennessee Copper Company in 1904 and still resembles the company town that it was.

The storefronts along Ocoee Street and the stone steps that lead to the houses on various levels of the hill above the town offer a glimpse of early life there. As in any company town, the workers lived at street level, closest to the factory or mine. Other employees lived further up the hill in order of importance, most often with the president at the top, so he could overlook the entire operation. Many of those houses are still in use today and are a part of a walking tour of Copperhill's residential area. Maps are available throughout the town.

Lisa and Joe Jacobi are outdoors-type people, and they are pretty savvy business owners as well. They own and operate *The Lodge,* an English-style bed and breakfast here in Copperhill. Lisa was the manager of the 1996 U.S. Olympic Canoe & Kayak Team, and Joe was the two-man canoe gold medalist in the 1992 Olympics and he is training for the 2000 Games.

They have five guest rooms in their historic home at 12 Grande Avenue, and the rate is $20 per person including a bountiful breakfast. At any one time, you might find everyone from a fly fisherman to an international white-water athlete to an old-time musician staying here. Lisa also runs an educational program called Taproot. Several times a year she sells a two-day weekend package that includes a room and two days of instruction from an expert in a Southern Appalachian skill. In the past, programs have included fly fishing, fiddling, and wildflower walks. They've even had a moonshine workshop. (423) 496–9020.

In 1911 the Grand Avenue Bridge was built across the Ocoee and connected the mining town of McCaysville, Georgia, with Copperhill. Take a walk across the bridge and look for the spot where you can stand with one foot in Tennessee and one in Georgia. For more information on these two historic mining towns, write the Ocoee Region Information Center, P.O. Box 1094, Copperhill 37317.

Farther down Highway 64, between Ducktown and Cleveland, you'll find yourself driving along the Ocoee River, one of the top ten white-water rivers in the country. You'll also find numerous business establishments that will be more than happy to rent you a raft, canoe, or kayak so you too can experience an adventure of a lifetime. The river is such a good area for white-water events that it was chosen as the site of the 1996 Summer Olympics white-water competition held in nearby Atlanta.

The *Ocoee Whitewater Center,* located a few miles northwest from Ducktown along Highway 64, was the site of the 1996 Olympic Slalom Canoe/Kayak events, and following the games became a visitor center and a hub for both land and water-based recreation activities in the Cherokee Forest and Ocoee River areas. Open daily 9:00 A.M. to 5:00 P.M. (423) 496–5197.

Now open to the public, the center houses a gift shop, the Olympic Legacy exhibit, and a conference center. Outside, a native flower garden and a magnificent pond have been created. A path has been built along the whitewater channel where the races took place, and you can hike or bike the Old Copper Road, of which a section has been restored adjacent to the center.

A walk along the 2.4-mile-long section of the **Old Copper Road** takes you across four footbridges from the 1850s era. Built in 1851, the 33-mile-long road was used to haul copper ore from the mines in Ducktown to the railhead in Cleveland. Most of the original section was destroyed when the adjacent Highway 64 was built in the 1930s, and this is the only original section still intact.

If you're not of the adventurous variety or don't have the time, there are several pull-offs where you can experience the danger and the excitement of the white water vicariously. The mostly two-lane road is very busy here, so be careful to pull off the road completely before looking.

If you do choose to be adventurous (and you really should), a good place to stop is the **Ocoee Adventure Center,** located on Highway 64, 3 miles east of the Ocoee Whitewater Center. The proprietor of this outpost has worked the river for decades for other people and when he decided to go off on his own, he brought along some of the best river guides in the area.

You'll get a lesson on how to best combat the white-water adventure awaiting you, then you'll be told how you must respect the river itself. "It's a wild, unpredictable ride, and you must be ready to handle everything. This is not an amusement park ride," our guide told us.

With life jackets and helmets in place, you'll climb aboard a school bus for a 4-mile trip down to the river's entry point. There you'll be launched for one great ride through areas of the river with such ominous names as Grumpy's Ledge, Hell's Hole, Tablesaw, and Double Trouble. Call (888) RAFT−OAC for up-to-date schedules, special events, rates, and prices. The cost here and at most outfitters along the river usually depends on the day of the week you choose for your trip, with Saturdays during peak season costing approximately $42. No one under twelve years of age is permitted.

Look closely through the trees on the other side of the river and you'll see the largest wooden flume known to exist in the United States. The **Ocoee Flume** is 5 miles long, 11 feet wide, and 14 feet tall. Originally built in 1912 by the Tennessee Valley Authority (TVA), it was closed for a few years in the late 1970s and then rebuilt.

Its major function is to divert water from the river to help produce hydroelectric power, but recently it has also been a savior of the river for the white-water aficionados. With the diversion the flume creates, the TVA can produce their power and the river can still run to the point of whiteness.

The Webb Bros. Float Service in Reliance, along the Hiwassee Scenic River, is not only a professional outfitter, but the **Webb Brothers Store,** in which it is located, is a fun and funky general store to visit.

If it's a peaceful, easy journey down a scenic river you're looking for, here's the place. They rent one- or two-passenger rubber "duckies" that are self-bailing and hard to flip over. Resembling a kayak, they cost from $18 to $20 per person, including the 5-mile trip up the river where you're dropped off. You then paddle and float the current back down river and get out at the store, where you began your journey.

The trip can be direct, or you can stop and swim, rest, or just sit and watch the other boats go by. If you like, pack your lunch and take it along. This is a great first river adventure for smaller children and the weak at heart, and it's a beautiful journey as well.

In addition to its river services, the store sells groceries, prepared foods, snacks, gasoline, and just about anything else you'll need while you're in the area. The Reliance Post Office is located inside, and the great-grand-daughter of the first "keeper of the mail" still works there. The store, built in 1955, also serves as the town museum and has photos and memorabilia of early Reliance. Free; (423) 338–2373.

Webb's Store is a good starting place for your tour of the **Reliance historic district,** listed on the National Register of Historic Places. You can pick up information and quite a few stories about the area that will make your visit a lot more fun. The district, off Highway 30 along the river, has five principal buildings, including a hotel and the first house to have indoor plumbing. None of the restored structures is open to the public on a regular basis, but they are beautiful to look at. The area is still quite underdeveloped, so a drive through can give you a good idea of what life was like along the river at the turn of the century.

For a spectacular view of the Hiwassee River, you'll want to walk all or part of the **John Muir Trail,** an 18.8-mile-long trail that meanders along the river. Not only are the views of the river fantastic, but you'll see a tremendous amount of wildlife and native plants. Watch for the beaver activity all along the trail. In addition you'll have the oppportunity to view ruby-throated hummingbirds, mink, raccoons, and great blue herons. What are those things sunning themselves on the flat rocks in the river? Chances are they are North America's largest salamander, the hellbender.

The trail begins at Childers Creek, near Reliance (follow the signs), and ends near Highway 68 at Farner. If you have your entire family to watch out for, you might want to stick to the first 3-mile section of the trek; it has been designated as an easy walk, but still covers some beautiful terrain.

Mention mountain forests and fantastic views, and most people think of the Smoky Mountains. That's why the 620,000-acre **Cherokee National Forest** here in the southeast portion of the state remains virtually untouched by crowds.

More than 1,100 miles of roads have been cut through the dense forest, opening up all sorts of opportunities for outdoor enthusiasts or for those who simply enjoy driving and looking. Take your time; there's a real good chance that no one will be honking and trying to get around you. The Forest Service maintains twenty-nine camping areas, horse trails (bring your own horse), and 105 hiking trails. This area is every bit as beautiful as the Smokies, making it a great alternative that most locals are hesitant to tell too many people about. The supervisor's office can give you more specifics; (423) 338–5201.

When you're in **Cleveland,** you're deep in Cherokee country, and history abounds. This was the geographic center for Native American culture in the Southeast and there are reminders of that fact throughout the city and county.

The historical area of Cleveland is known as the Downtown Historic Greenway and Johnson Park, in the heart of downtown, is a great place to start a walking tour of the city. There are twenty different historic sites on the tour, including restored churches and buildings. While in Johnson Park, stop by and marvel at the Cherokee Chieftain, a wonderful sculpture of an Indian chief carved from a tree by internationally known Native American artist Peter Toth.

To get a better idea of the role the county played in the everyday life of the Cherokee, two self-guided tours have been developed, with maps and additional information. They are available at the Cleveland Convention and Visitors Bureau, 2145 Keith Street, (423) 472–6587. The Cherokee Heritage Wildlife Tour points out the best locations in the area to view wildlife and allows you to get a good feel for the Cherokee heritage. The Cherokee Scenic Loop Tour begins and ends in Cleveland and takes you throughout the county, where you'll visit many of the areas mentioned in this chapter, including Red Clay and the Ocoee River. Both maps offer a well-organized way to see the best the county and the region have to offer.

About 6 miles outside Cleveland on Highway 64E, hidden behind the hustle and bustle of a busy highway and myriad antiques shops and flea markets, is a neat little living-history museum called the **Primitive Settlement.** Here a collection of nineteenth-century log cabins from the area has been moved and rebuilt to show life the way it was. The owners claim that they have the area's largest collection of primitive antiques.

When you enter the gates, the settlement appears to be a small attraction, but once you start talking with the employees and sticking your head into the various corners, a visit can turn into a very interesting couple of hours. Each cabin, with the oldest being more than 150 years old, depicts a different mode of frontier life.

During the summer live country music is offered every Saturday night. Open daily March through October; admission is charged; (423) 476– 5096.

If you're looking for some great food and want to have a little fun at the same time, head out to the **Apple Valley Orchard,** 351 Weese Road, 10 miles southeast of Cleveland. There you'll visit a farmer's market and bakery that offers a variety of foods. Take my advice on this one. Fresh-baked apple goods don't get any better than this! Open daily from the end of August through December; free; (423) 472–3044.

The **Morris Winery and Vineyard,** 352 Union Grove Road, about 10 miles out of Cleveland, offers more country family fun. The winery is known not only for its fine Tennessee wines; it also lets visitors pick their own fruit. Blueberries are ready in July; grapes from July through October. Open daily during picking season. It's wise to call first to make sure they have the fields open on the day you want to visit; (423) 479–7311.

About 12 miles south of Cleveland, off a series of back roads, you'll find the historic **Red Clay** area. Red Clay was the site of the last council ground of the Cherokee Indian nation before their forced removal in 1838. It was the site of eleven general councils, national affairs attended by up to 5,000 Indians each.

The U.S. government wanted the Cherokees to surrender their eastern lands and move the entire tribe to lands in Oklahoma. The Cherokees fought it for quite a while, but controversial treaties resulted in their losing the land. Here at Red Clay, the journey to Oklahoma, known today as the Trail of Tears, actually began.

The march, often referred to as the Great Removal, was a wintertime, cross-country journey that covered more than 1,000 miles. Reportedly, 4,000 of the 18,000 who were forced to leave perished during the walk. That was almost one-fourth of the entire Cherokee nation.

Today people can drive that same path across the state on the Trail of Tears State Historic Route. It's marked quite well, and maps that explain the various historical activities along the way are available here at Red Clay. About 80 percent of the original trail is now covered by modern highways.

Here where it all began a 275-acre state historic area has been developed. The only original part left is the council spring, locally known as the "blue hole." It was this pure running spring that probably attracted the Cherokees to this site in the first place.

Also on the grounds are various reproductions of early Indian homesteads and an interpretive center with displays and historical exhibits.

It's not an easy place to find. Take Highway 60 south out of Cleveland and follow the signs. They are good signs, but often understated in size and can be easily overlooked if you happen to be looking at the cows and horses along the way. If you see a sign that reads WELCOME TO GEORGIA, you've gone about a half-mile too far. Open daily; admission free; (423) 478–0339.

Crossroads of Dixie

hattanooga, the state's fourth-largest city, with a population of less than 155,000, is located along a 7-mile bend in the Tennessee River. The deep ravine along the river is often referred to as the Grand Canyon of the South.

Lookout Mountain is probably the best known of the three major "ledges" that loom over the city. And, as in any major tourist destination, the beaten path and the unbeaten path catch up with each other here, with the same attraction often offering different things to different people.

A lot of states have large public aquariums, but none can beat the *Tennessee Aquarium* here in Chattanooga at One Broad Street next to the Tennessee River. The location is quite appropriate for the theme of this beautiful facility, which opened in late May of 1992.

Billed as the "world's first major freshwater life center," the aquarium salutes the state that has more species of freshwater fish than any other state. Few of us will ever have the chance to personally explore the entire length of the magnificent Tennessee River, but here's your chance, and it will take less than two hours.

Through exhibits of live and luxuriant flora and fauna, you can take a journey from the river's source in the Appalachian High Country through its midstream and finally to the Mississippi Delta. A visit to the aquarium is an enjoyable experience for the entire family. Open every day except Christmas and Thanksgiving. Admission charged; (423) 265–0695.

The city is obviously quite proud of its river heritage. To prove that point, the city fathers have created the **Tennessee Riverpark** along the mighty Tennessee River, adjacent to the aquarium. Beware, there are some steep grades and a lot of steps, but it does appear to be handicapped accessible via a series of ramps. The area includes parks, fishing piers, a riverside amphitheater carved out of the bluff under a highway overpass, and playgrounds. A scenic walk takes you from the aquarium to the really cool **Bluff View Art District,** where The Hunter Museum of American Art, several restaurants, gardens, terrace cafes, working art studios, and the Bluff View Inn Bed and Breakfast are located. The bed and breakfast consists of three turn-of-the-century restored homes, all offering spectacular bird's-eye views of the river. (423) 265–5033. Make sure you take in the River Gallery Sculpture Garden, which overlooks the river. An amazing area for outdoor sculpture! (423) 267–7353.

Along the Riverwalk you'll come upon the 2,370-foot-long **Walnut Street Bridge.** Spanning the river, the circa 1891 bridge is considered the longest pedestrian walkway in the world. Once the only way across the river in the city, the structure underwent a $4 million renovation in 1993 and is now a fun place to walk, jog, or sit upon one of the benches and enjoy a fantastic view of the river far below and the Ross's Landing area of the city.

A fun event takes place on the Walnut Street Bridge in late September each year. The **Wine Over Water Festival** is a wine-tasting event that offers a fine selection of wines, entertainment, and activities.

The popular **Riverbend Festival** takes place along the river each June and usually attracts about a half million people during its nine-day run. It's so spread out; however, you don't usually feel crowded. More than 100 musical artists perform on five different stages, offering up everything from rock, country, and blues to jazz and folk. Of course, there are all kinds of food and drink and other festival-style activities. (423) 265–4112.

Along with all its Civil War history, the area around Lookout Mountain contains a lesser-known fact about an earlier war. History books usually tell us that the American Revolution started at Lexington and ended with

Cornwallis's surrender at Yorktown. Actually, historians currently say that the last engagement between official forces of the war took place on the slopes of Lookout Mountain on September 20, 1782, a year after Yorktown.

The National Park Service must agree with these historians, because they have marked the spot, just off Highway 148 near the foot of the mountain, with a historical marker, calling it the *"Last Battle of the Revolution."*

Farther up the mountain, one of the Civil War's most famous battles was fought. Known today as the "Battle Above the Clouds," the fight at Chickamauga Creek and the Battle of Chattanooga are immortalized in the nation's first and largest national military park. The huge ***Chicka-mauga–Chattanooga National Park,*** established in 1890, contains more than 400 markers on the battlefield that outline the series of events that claimed 34,000 casualties. In addition the park also contains 666 monuments honoring the men who fought on the grounds.

The visitors center is a good place to start your education on the area's Civil War history. It's located at the top of the mountain across from the entrance to Point Park, the site of the Battle Above the Clouds. (423) 821–7786.

As you climb the mountain, you'll pass several other well-known attrac-

See Rock City

*T*hat's a phrase you've seen painted on the roofs and the sides of barns throughout America. Have you ever wondered who painted most of those barns? Clark Byers can be given that credit. As the Depression grew to a close in the 1930s and more and more tourists began hitting the nation's highways once again, Rock City Garden's owner, Garnet Carter, enlisted Byers to paint the barns as unique billboards. Legend has it that when Byers asked what he was supposed to paint, Carter gave him a slip of paper with three words: See Rock City.

Farmers welcomed the new paint job

on their barns, and Carter enjoyed the increased business the signs brought to him. Being a creative person, Byers often added mileage and the best route to the attraction on his own. Today, the barns can still be seen as far north as Michigan and as far west as Texas. The barns became legendary, and today, bird-houses can be purchased with See Rock City on their roofs, and modern billboards for the attraction are in the shape of a barn (or birdhouse) with the famous words on top. There are also several new books that feature the barn art. For more information, visit their Web site at www.seerockcity.com

tions, including the incredible **Ruby Falls.** They are very much on the beaten path but shouldn't be overlooked just because you don't like crowds or don't want to visit a place where everyone else in the world has been first. Open every day but Christmas. Admission charged; (423) 821–2544.

The **Mountain Memories** gift shop is located on the Scenic Highway, less than a mile up the mountain from Ruby Falls, and if you're looking for some funky stuff, this is the place to stop. The outside of the building is covered with advertising signs, and the porches are overflowing with rustic crafts. They offer the best price around on "See Rock City" birdhouses and bird feeders, and they have one entire area dedicated to Coca-Cola collectibles.

A Rock City Barn

Located next to the incline tracks, the store is open daily, year-round. (423) 821–6575.

Many Tennessee natives don't realize that one of the most popular attractions on Lookout Mountain, **Rock City,** is actually across the state line in Georgia.

"See Rock City" birdhouses and painted barn roofs throughout the Southeast have made this attraction a genuine piece of Americana. There's nothing like it anywhere else. Ten acres of natural rock gardens, some with formations looming twenty stories high, and a barren spot called **Lover's Leap,** where seven states can be seen, are the highlights of the attraction. Twisting paths take you through wonderfully landscaped gardens and narrow crevices. One such crack is thoughtfully named "Fat Man's Squeeze."

The founder, Garnet Carter, first built a hotel on the property and in early 1928 developed a recreational outlet that changed leisure-time activities from coast to coast. Using the natural hills, rocks, hollow logs, and pools of water as hazards, he created a miniature golf course for his guests who didn't want to take the time to play a complete round of regulation golf.

Within a short time various other hotels in the country asked him to design courses for them, and *"Tom Thumb Golf"* took the country by storm. By 1930 about 25,000 miniature golf courses were operating in the United States, many of which were Carter's courses.

The original course and the hotel are now gone, but several of the small characters that were placed around the course are a part of the Fairyland portion of Rock City. Admission is charged; (706) 820-2531.

Less than a mile from Rock City, at the very top of the mountain, **The Castle in the Clouds** resort hotel was built in 1928. Today the old hotel, since restored, is the main building for Covenant College, a small liberal arts school. Other buildings on the campus also have historical as well as nostalgic appeal. Drop by and look up one of the school's officials, who love to give tours. (706) 820-1560.

If you're a little leery about driving up the mountain, there's a solution. Built in 1895, the **Lookout Mountain Incline** is now a part of the city's transit system. Billed as the "World's Steepest and Safest Incline Railway," it has a 72.7-percent grade near the top. At the top of the mile-long ride, the upper station has been developed into a small retail village, which happens to have some of the best ice cream in the Chattanooga area. (423) 821-4224.

At the foot of the "other side" of the mountain, the west side, at 400 Garden Road in Lookout Valley, the **Chattanooga Nature Center** is an environmental education facility. This is a great place for your family to learn about the wonders of nature through interpretive activities. It features passive solar-designed buildings that house a wildlife diorama, a touch and feel discovery room, and interactive exhibits.

The center is also home to the region's only federally licensed wildlife rehabilitation hospital, which cares for injured and orphaned wildlife with the goal of releasing them back to the wild. They won't let visitors inside the hospital, but they often have a few of their patients on exhibit. There's a 1,200-foot boardwalk out over the wetlands, with interpretive signs along the way.

Next to the nature center, the **Reflection Riding** is a 300-acre nature preserve and botanical garden that is absolutely beautiful during the spring. That's when all the wildflowers are in bloom. A 3-mile loop meanders through the area and you can either drive, walk, or ride a bike along the path. You might spot some deer or wild turkeys as you enjoy the flora of the park. Both facilities are open year-round. Admission to both for adults is $3.00, children ages four to twelve, $2.00; (423) 821–1160.

The first franchised Coca-Cola bottling plant in the world was built in Chattanooga in 1899 by two local attorneys, who bought the franchise bottling rights for $1.00 each.

Pardon me boy, but isn't that the **Chattanooga Choo Choo**? Down in the city, the Choo Choo is one of the most unusual shopping areas in the state. Located at the old Terminal Station, 1400 Market Street, the complex features a Holiday Inn with rooms in restored train cars, landscaped gardens, and myriad Victorian-era shops and restaurants. All play on the train theme. (800) TRACK–29.

If sleeping in a vintage railroad car sounds romantic to you, here's an opportunity to give it a shot! The forty-eight sleeper cars offer a nice nostalgic touch to the journey of an off-the-beaten-path road warrior. Several of the cars overlook a formal garden area, which offers a nice selection of plants and shrubs. In early summer the roses are wonderful! A bandstand in the garden features free live entertainment several nights of the week during the summer months. This is a huge complex. In addition to the sleeper cars, the hotel consists of three buildings of hotel rooms, one indoor and two outdoor swimming pools.

The hotel's lobby, the original railroad terminal, was built in 1909 and is considered an architectural wonder. The 85-foot-tall freestanding brick dome is the largest of its type in the world.

The city was one of the country's earliest and largest railroad centers, and this station was the hub of that activity. On the top floor of one of the terminal buildings, one of the world's largest model railroad layouts showing the area as it was during its heyday has been created by a local model railroad club. During the week it can be seen running under automated control, but on weekends members of the club come out and "play" with their creation.

The entire display is 174 feet long and contains more than 3,000 square feet of space. The HO-gauge layout has about 100 locomotives and several hundred passenger and freight cars on about 100 miles of track. Admission is charged but is usually included in the various hotel packages.

Several stores sell copies of Glenn Miller's version of the Chattanooga Choo Choo song. The phrase itself was coined in 1880 when a reporter took the first train ride out of Cincinnati on the new Cincinnati-Southern Line. Since the tracks only went as far as this city, he called the train the

"Chattanooga Choo Choo." The original recording is framed and hanging in the old terminal, now the hotel lobby.

In downtown Chattanooga the historic Radisson Read House Hotel & Suites has undergone a $2 million renovation and now has much of the same charm it possessed through the years when five U.S. presidents, Winston Churchill, and Eleanor Roosevelt were numbered among its guests. The building is listed on the National Register of Historic Places.

What makes the historic hotel unique today is that each of its thirteen floors is dedicated to a different battle of the Civil War. As you walk off the elevator, you'll see a 40-by-60-inch framed print that depicts the battle and a framed parchment next to it explaining the skirmish. There are at least nineteen additional prints, which show many of the generals who took part in that particular battle, along the corridors.

You don't need to be a guest to enjoy the exhibits. Stop by the front desk and you'll receive a brochure explaining what you'll see on each of the floors. The Radisson Read House is at the corner of Martin Luther King Boulevard and Broad Street. (423) 266–4121.

Do any of your kids have a passion for dragons? Well, Barbara Newton turned her special love for the critters into a dragon museum called

Tow Truck Heaven

*T*he towing industry was born in 1916 in Chattanooga, after Ernest Holmes helped a friend retrieve his car with three poles, a pulley, and a chain hooked to the frame of a 1913 Cadillac. After patenting his invention, Holmes started manufacturing wreckers and towing equipment. Today, that humble beginning is featured in the International Towing and Recovery Hall of Fame and Museum, located 1 block away from Holmes's original shop.

There are nearly twenty tow trucks on display, and the museum offers a fun and educational view of this unheralded industry, which we have all probably depended on at least once during our lifetime. Several early wreckers,

which were built on the back of cut-off automobiles, are on display, as are trucks from various periods of history.

For a fun gift, wouldn't your friends love a wrecker T-shirt? There's a nice selection of shirts and other souvenir items in the gift shop, including a coloring book of the World's Greatest Tow Trucks, and ink pens that proclaim "I LOVE MY WRECKER."

Several signs, including the one warning that CHILDREN LEFT UNATTENDED WILL BE TOWED AWAY are also for sale.

Located at 401 Broad Street, just 2 blocks away from the Tennessee Aquarium. Open daily, admission charged. (423) 267–3132.

Chattanooga Choo Choo

Dragon Dreams. Her collection of more than 2,000 dragons spans eight rooms. The dragons are awake and ready to greet you Wednesday through Sunday except for major holidays. "Even the dragons need a day now and then to visit their friends and family," Barbara told me. At 6724-A East Brainerd Road. Adults are $5.00, children thirteen and under, $2.00; no charge to enter the dragon-filled gift shop. (423) 892–2384.

Before leaving the city, another interesting stop is the ***National Knife Museum.*** Owned and operated by the National Knife Collectors Association, the 8,000-square-foot museum was created to provide a showplace for the work of the association's 16,000 members. Private collections from members are on display, as is the museum's growing permanent collection. Handmade blades and knives from most of the 360 American cutlery firms are featured. By the way, one thing you'll find out here is that a knife collector is technically known as a *machairologist.* The museum is located at 7201 Shallowford Road, at I–75. Admission is charged. Open Monday through Saturday; (423) 892–5007.

Leave Chattanooga via Highway 41/64/72, also known as Will Cummings Highway, and you'll be in the Raccoon Mountain area, on the "other" side of the city. Follow the signs to the ***Alpine Slide*** and the ***Raccoon Mountain Caverns & Campground,*** quite a fun complex tucked away in the mountains.

The Alpine Slide is one of the best of its kind in the country. First, you'll take a scenic chairlift ride to the top of the mountain, then you'll slide down 2,350 feet on a bobsled-type cart on which you can control your own speed. WOW, what a rush! These slides are not only unique in the state, but they are great, safe fun for the entire family! The Grand Prix of Chattanooga go-kart track, a video arcade, and a batting cage are also a part of the Alpine Slide complex.

Outside the entrance to the Raccoon Mountain Caverns you can pan for your own gemstones just like the old-timers did. Entrance to the caves is through the gift shop. During the forty-five-minute guided tour, you'll meander past many beautiful formations and squeeze and duck through many small passages.

Don't miss the unique shield formation toward the end of the tour. There are only twenty such formations known to exist throughout the world, our guide told us. A map of Tennessee can also be seen outlined by formations on the ceiling in one of the rooms. On a hot day, the wonderfully cool cave can be a fun treat. Admission charge; open daily. The campground has a full-service RV camp as well as tent camping sites.

Located 1 1/4 miles north from I–24 at exit 174. Cavern and campground; (423) 821–9403; Alpine Slide, (423) 825–5666.

In Dunlap there's a developing historic site that most overlook mainly because it was the illegal town dump for decades. Through the dedication of volunteers, headed up by Carson Camp, history is being uncovered on the sixty-two-acre *Coke Ovens Historic Site.*

A huge coal industry was present in this area at the turn of the century, and in this Dunlap industrial complex coal was turned into coke for use in the iron and steel foundries in nearby Chattanooga.

When the company went out of business in 1917, there were 268 beehive-shaped coke ovens in operation. Through the years, the ovens were forgotten, covered up, and neglected. During the past few years, Camp and his crew have uncovered a lot of the area's heritage that had almost been forgotten.

The park has been listed on the National Register of Historic Places, and a museum has been built on the original foundation of the old commissary building. Excavation is continuing; meanwhile the park is open, and on some days you might find Camp or one of his volunteers over in a corner with a shovel in hand. They'll tell you the story. The museum is open on weekends during warmer months. (423) 949–3483.

Farther up Highway 41 just across the county line you'll see the sign for the *TVA's Raccoon Mountain Pumped Storage Facility* on your right. It is the most unusual of all the Tennessee Valley Authority's operations.

This hydroelectric plant uses more power than it generates. The safety officers who take you on an amazing hour-long tour of the plant will usually agree with that arguable fact, but they will quickly tell you that the plant is very cost-effective.

The visitors center is located at the top of the mountain, about 9 miles from the front entrance, and what a view of the Tennessee River Valley it offers! Also at the top is a 528-acre lake. Deep inside the mountain is the mammoth power plant, totally protected from the elements and enemy attack.

At night, during off-peak hours, the extra energy produced at TVA coal-burning plants is used here to pump water from the Tennessee River up a 1,100-foot pipeline to fill the reservoir above. This is cheaper than shutting down and restarting those plants, and the electricity that would be wasted is now used to stockpile water that will, in turn, create more power.

During the day, when the demand for electricity is greatest, the water is released from the reservoir and tumbles down the 35-foot diameter intake tunnels to turn the four large generators, thereby producing electricity.

During the free tour, the guide will take you through some of the 2 1/4 miles of bored-out tunnels within the mountain. You'll also visit one of the cavernlike rooms, each large enough to hold twelve tennis courts and with ceilings 80 feet tall. The statistics recited to you will boggle your mind.

There are fewer than two dozen pumped storage facilities in the United States, and this is the only one that is completely underground. There are several scenic pull-offs on the drive to the top and quite a few picnic areas. At the foot of the mountain, there are fishing areas along the river, all courtesy of the federal government. Tours are given daily; admission is free. (423) 825–3100.

As you pull back out onto Highway 41, take a right and head toward the best catfish dinner or lunch you've ever had. About 6 miles from the TVA, and in a different time zone, you'll find the **Riverside Catfish House** on Highway 41 North on the right next to the river.

The family-run business was established in 1959 and is owned today by Miss Hattie Massengale. Daughters Linda Turner, Sharon Graves, and Donna Caradine work there, as does Turner's daughter. The place seats 230, with many of the tables in front of big windows overlooking the river. "We don't take reservations, so you'll have to get here early if you want a window seat," cautions Turner.

Although they also serve items other than fish, Turner said that 95 percent of the people order the grain-fed catfish dinner, which comes with coleslaw and hush puppies. (In the lobby there's a picture of a cow and a pig, both begging the patrons to "Please eat Fish.") If you enjoy a cold beer with your catfish, you're out of luck here. "We used to sell it, but the church people complained," Turner said. For dessert, Miss Hattie's famous buttermilk pie is a favorite, as is the coconut cake.

They're open Thursday through Sunday, and although they are on central time, they run by eastern time since most of their customers come from "that side of the line." (423) 821–9214.

**PLACES TO STAY IN
PLATEAUS & VALLEYS**

CHATTANOOGA
Bluff View Inn Bed
and Breakfast
412 East Second Street
Spectacular view of river
from restored homes
(423) 265–5033

Radisson Read House
Hotel & Suites
At corner of Martin Luther
King Boulevard and
Broad Street
Each of thirteen floors
dedicated to a
Civil War battle
(423) 266–4121

Shipp's Yogi Bear
Jellystone Park
6728 Ringgold Road
200 sites, fishing, showers,
grocery, pool
Open year-round
(423) 892–8275

Sky Harbor Bavarian Inn
2159 Old Wauhatchie Pike
Great views of Tennessee
River from private balconies;
whirlpool tubs, kitchens,
cable TV, hardwood floors
(423) 821–8619

CLEVELAND
Hampton Inn
185 James Asbury Drive
Close to Ocoee white-water
rafting
Continental breakfast
buffet
(423) 559–1001

COPPERHILL
The Lodge
12 Grand Avenue
Bed and breakfast offering
outdoor workshops
(423) 496–9020

CRAB ORCHARD
Cumberland Gardens
Resort
Highway 70E
Kitchen, pool, tennis, golf
(931) 484–5285

DUCKTOWN
Company House Bed
& Breakfast
124 Main Street
On National Register
of Historic Places
(423) 496–5634

LIVINGSTON
Cornucopia Bed
& Breakfast
303 Mofield Street
Historic home,
antique furnishings
Full breakfast, cable TV,
video library
(931) 823–7522

McMINNVILLE
Falcon Manor
At end of Faulkner
Springs Road
Bed and breakfast in Queen
Anne Victorian mansion
(931) 668–4444

MONTEAGLE
Edgeworth Inn
On Assembly grounds
Victorian bed
and breakfast
(931) 924–4000

Jim Oliver's Smokehouse
Highway 64/41A
Motel with swimming pool
in shape of a ham
(931) 924–2268

MONTEREY
The Garden Inn
1400 Bee Rock Road
An atmosphere
of relaxed elegance,
Mountain and
garden views
(931) 839–1400

RACCOON MOUNTAIN
Raccoon Mountain Caverns
& Campground
1 1/4 miles north from I–24
at exit 174
Full service RV camp
and tent camping sites
(423) 821–9403

RED BOILING SPRINGS
Armour's Red Boiling
Springs Hotel
321 East Main Street
Mineral baths, steam baths,
and massages available
(615) 699–2180

The Thomas House
520 East Main Street
European feel, courtyard,
antiques, pool
(615) 699–3006

SMITHVILLE
Evins Mill
Evins Mill Road
Lodge and rustic cabins
serve as a bed and breakfast
(615) 597–2088

WATERTOWN
Watertown Bed & Breakfast
116 Depot Avenue
Restored 19th century
railroad hotel
Private baths, non-smok-
ing, breakfast
(615) 237–9999

**PLACES TO EAT IN
PLATEAUS & VALLEYS**

CHATTANOOGA
Adams Hilborn
801 Vine Street
Fine dining in 1889
mansion
Steaks, lamb, chicken,
pork, salads
Open Monday through
Saturday, 5:30 to 9:00 P.M.
(423) 265–5000

Big River Grille
& Brewing Works
222 Broad Street
Microbrewery,
sandwiches, snacks
Open daily at 11:00 A.M.
(423) 267–BREW

Rib & Loin
5946 Brainerd Road
Considered the city's best
rib restaurant
Open daily at 10:30 A.M.
(423) 499–6465

CLEVELAND
The Gondolier
3300 Keith Street
Greek and Italian cuisine
Open daily for lunch
and dinner
(423) 472–4998

COOKEVILLE
The Scarecrow Country Inn
Hickory ham cooked in
hickory bark syrup
Whitson Chapel Road
Dinner nightly from 4:00
to 10:00 P.M.
(931) 526–3431

DECATUR
Lee's Restaurant
Highway 58
Fish in a light batter
Wednesday–Friday
4:00 to 9:00 P.M., Saturday
noon to 9:00 P.M., Sunday
noon to 8:00 P.M.
(423) 334–5695

LIVINGSTON
The Apple Dish
116 North Court Square,
inside The Antique Market
Great home cooking
and desserts
Hours vary, call first.
(931) 823–3222

McMINNVILLE
Pish-La-Ki Restaurant
208 Pish-La-Ki Circle
On top of mountain; great
views of valley
Steaks, seafood, ribs,
catfish, prime rib
Open Tuesday through
Sunday, 11:00 A.M.
to 10:00 P.M.
(931) 668–2010

MONTEAGLE
Jim Oliver's Smokehouse
Highway 64/41A
Pit barbecue and hickory-
smoked meats
Open Sunday through
Thursday, 6:30 A.M. to
9:00 P.M.; Friday and Satur-
day, 6:30 A.M. to 10:00 P.M.
(931) 924–2268

PIKEVILLE
Vaughn House & Tea Room
233 Main Street,
Highway 127
Restaurant, antiques shop
Open daily for lunch, by
reservation only
(423) 447–2678

RACOON MOUNTAIN
Riverside Catfish House
On Highway 41 North on
right next to river
Buttermilk pie and
coconut cake for dessert
Open Thursday through
Sunday. Hours vary, call
first. (423) 821–9214

WATERTOWN
Snow White Restaurant
Highway 70
Famous for biscuits,
breakfast, and burgers
Open daily 5:00 A.M.
to 10:00 P.M.
(615) 237–9715

The Heartland

Heart of the Heartland

No matter where you go in the world, mention **Nashville** to anyone and you'll get a smile of understanding. Ah, country music—that's what most people associate with the state's capital city.

Nashville is one of the areas where the unbeaten path crosses the well-traveled path and merges for a few miles and a dozen or so attractions.

There's no place like Nashville (a.k.a. Music City or Twangtown). Its maternal relationship to country music has created quite a few unique attractions and events. Since the majority of visitors come to see the music-associated attractions, many of the other attractions are ignored to a greater extent than they would be in just about any other city. Five of the region's top ten attractions are country music related.

A hint about getting around: There's a lot of traffic in the downtown and Music Row areas during peak summer periods, and parking spots can be hard to find. Find one and leave the driving to the Nashville Trolley Company. It's 50 cents a ride, or you can buy a book of ten tickets for $2.00. Unfortunately, the trolleys don't offer service to the outlying areas.

In the northeast quadrant of the city, home to the mammoth **Opryland USA,** make sure you visit the **Nashville Palace,** across the street from the entrance to the Opryland Hotel. The Palace, owned by the friendly Johnny Hobbs, is where country superstar Randy Travis was discovered while working as a dishwasher. Live music nightly and a delicious menu that includes "the best catfish in town" are featured. (615) 885–1540.

Opryland Hotel is a huge, amazing place. With 2,879 guest rooms, 222 suites, 15 restaurants, 10 lounges, and 30 retail stores, *all inside,* you can start to realize why. Add to that five ballrooms, eighty-five meeting rooms, nearly one million square feet of exhibit space, and you have one of the unique hotels in the world. It's worth a visit, but make sure you wear your tennies, you'll be doing a lot of walking!

The fun thing to see and do here is to visit the three different atrium areas, which are under nearly nine acres of skylights. The Conservatory and the Cascades are each two-acre atriums featuring tropical gardens,

The Heartland

THE HEARTLAND

TIM'S TOP TEN PICKS
THE HEARTLAND

Hatch Show Print

NunBun at Bongo Java

Harvey Washbanger

Manuel's Cajun Country Store

Cannonsburgh Pioneer Village

Jack Daniel Distillery

Elephant Sanctuary

Bell Witch Cave

Earl's Fruit Stand

Mule Day Festival & Parade

running streams, and multi-level viewing areas. The newest area, the Delta, is a four-and-a-half-acre interiorscape with a flowing river and twenty-five-passenger flatboats that take guests on a voyage through the area.

The best beignet north of New Orleans can be found on Delta Island, inside the hotel, at the Beignet Cafe. Other fresh-baked pastries are available as well. Open daily 7:00 A.M. to 9:00 P.M.

Christmas at the hotel is especially fun. Nearly two million lights decorate the exterior of the hotel, and inside there are holiday-themed dinner shows, an arts and antiques show, and other seasonal activities. (615) 889–1000.

If you'd like to park your car here and get to downtown Nashville in a convenient, stress-free way, take the **Opryland River Taxi** down the Cumberland River. From April through December, the taxis offer a shuttle service between the Opryland USA complex and downtown's Riverfront Park.

Once downtown, it's less than a 2-block walk to **The District,** a row of renovated nineteenth-century warehouses that now house restaurants, bars, clubs, and shops. Mere Bulles, 152 Second Avenue, offers live jazz (615–256–1946) and the Bourbon Street Blues & Boogie Bar, 220 Printers Alley, offers up live blues in a New Orleans atmosphere (615–24–BLUES). Other District clubs offer bluegrass, country, and rock and roll.

Also a short walk from the river is the lower Broadway area, where you'll find genuine hillbilly honky-tonks, left over virtually untouched from the 1940s and 50s. Inside each, country music, cowboy hats, and cold beer prevail.

Situated among the honky-tonks and shops is **Hatch Show Print** at 316 Broadway. Open to the public, this is one of America's oldest surviving show poster printers. Founded in 1879 by two brothers, the business printed posters for the circus, sporting events, and vaudeville shows. It won the Grand Ole Opry account and printed not only the Opry's posters but the show posters for most of country music's greatest legends. Thousands of posters printed from the original cuts are available for purchase. Free; (615) 256–2805.

At the foot of Broadway in Riverside Park is one of the most unique carousels in the world. Known as the **Tennessee Fox Trot Carousel,** it was designed and carved by well-known Nashville artist Red Grooms and is part history, part art, and part amusement ride. Instead of riding horses, riders climb aboard figures of renowned people and places that are a part of Nashville's history. Among those you can ride are Davy Crockett, President Andrew Jackson, Minnie Pearl, Roy Acuff, Olympic athlete Wilma Rudolph, and the Everly Brothers. You can also ride on a Purity Dairy Truck and a Tennessee chigger. Open daily; small charge to ride.

The world famous **Music Row,** near downtown, offers two atmospheres. First there's the touristy strip where the stars have their own museums and souvenir shops. Then there's the music-related businesses and studios located along a series of streets with such names as Music Circle and Music Square.

For the person who wants to stay away from the souvenir shoppers, a stop at the **Country Music Hall of Fame** is a must. Located at 4 Music Square East, the museum covers the genre from its beginning. Run by a foundation, the facility offers a low-key alternative to the other hubbub along Music Row. A tour of RCA's Studio B complex, the site of early recordings by Elvis and other country icons, is also offered by the museum. Admission is charged; (615) 256–1639.

Songwriting is a revered occupation in Nashville. No other city pays attention to its writers the way Music City does, and radio announcers are just as apt to say who wrote a song as who performed it. "Writers'

The Performing Arts Are Alive!!!

*T*he Tennessee Performing Arts Center (TPAC) is an oasis of the arts in downtown Nashville. Its three separate theaters are home to the Nashville Ballet, Tennessee Opera Theatre, Circle Players, Tennessee Repertory Theatre, Nashville Opera, and the Nashville Symphony. The building also houses the Tennessee State Museum. In addition to the resident groups' activities, the management of TPAC promotes a quality Broadway Series each year, as well as the New Directions Series, which features other touring shows and performers. 505 Deaderick Street; (615) 782–4000. Most tickets are available through Ticketmaster.

Other performing arts venues in Middle Tennessee include Nashville's Sarratt Student Center at Vanderbilt University, (615) 322–2471; Austin Peay University, Clarksville, (931) 648–7876; Roxy Community Theatre, 100 Franklin Street, Clarksville, (931) 645–7699; and Chaffin's Barn Theatre, 8204 Highway 100, Nashville, (615) 646–9977.

Also Worth Seeing in the Heartland

The Hermitage,
Home of Andrew Jackson,
4580 Rachel's Lane, Hermitage,
(615) 889–2941

Ryman Auditorium,
Home to Grand Ole Opry for
thirty-one years, 116 5th Avenue
North, Nashville,
(615) 254–1445

Cumberland Science Museum,
Sudekum Planetarium, 800 Fort
Negley Boulevard, Nashville,
(615) 862–5160

Cheekwood Gardens & Art Museum,
1200 Forrest Park Drive, Nashville,
(615) 356–8000

Smith-Trahern Mansion,
First and McClure, Restored
1851 mansion, Clarksville,
(931) 648–9998

Rattle & Snap Plantation,
Mt. Pleasant Pike, Restored Greek
Revival structure, Columbia,
(931) 379–5861

Arts & Crafts Fair,
Montgomery Bell State Park,
mid-September, Highway 70,
north of I–40, Burns,
(615) 797–2569

Annual Irish Picnic,
St. Patrick's Church, Last weekend
in July, McEwen,
(931) 582–3417

African Street Festival,
Middle Tennessee State University,
mid-September, Nashville,
(615) 299–0412

Main Street Festival,
Crafts, food, entertainment,
Late April, Franklin,
(615) 791–9924

Old Timer's Day,
Crafts, flea market, quilt show, First
weekend in May, Dickson,
(615) 446–2349

Nights" are held in various locations on a regular basis and are great places to get right down to the basics of country music. Hearing a popular writer singing his or her list of hits that others made into million-sellers is like listening to an oldies jukebox.

Perhaps the best-known cafe in the city, **The Bluebird Cafe,** is also one of the best places to attend a writers' night. The food is good, the talent is excellent, and chances are good that you might be sitting next to a country superstar. They hang out here a lot, especially during writers' shows. Several of today's superstars were regulars here on their way up the ladder, including Garth Brooks and Kathy Mattea. The Bluebird is located in the Green Hills area of the city, about fifteen minutes from downtown at 4104 Hillsboro Pike; (615) 383–1461.

Bagel shops are everywhere, but there's only one **Alpine Bagels & Brews.** Located in the Vanderbilt University area at 422 21st Avenue South, this is one funky and fun place. The perfect bagel was discovered by Marc, Jeff, and Chris, who, in their hopes of finding clarity and the meaning of life, meditated and contemplated for several days. The only thing they discovered, however, is that they were famished.

Inspired by their enlightening experience and motivated by their savage hunger, they set out to create the Zen of snack. From deep within they found the answer, but it was more than just a bagel—it was a way of life, the Alpine way of life.

The bagel boys not only created a great bagel, but they also developed twelve of the smoothest, creamiest, most delicious bagel toppings on the planet! Costa Rican and Colombian coffees are ground and brewed fresh all day. A wild bunch of bagelwiches are offered for lunch and dinner, including the Hootie & the Tuna Fish Sammy, the Hummus Is Among Us, the Pilgrim's Pride, and the Presidential Pardon.

With the slogan that their bagels are "so fresh they should be slapped," the eatery is open Monday through Friday 7:00 A.M. to 6:00 P.M.; Saturday 8:00 A.M. to 4:00 P.M.; and Sunday 8:00 A.M. to 3:00 P.M. (615) 327-0055.

Remember when coffee was just another cuppa joe? Those days are now

Immaculate Confection

*T*he Bongo Java Coffeehouse is home to the world-famous NunBun. Baker Ryan Finney decided to eat one of the rolls he was baking one morning and he caught a divine image just before taking a bite. The roll possessed an uncanny likeness of Mother Teresa. It was indeed the immaculate confection, Finney said. "I was horrified because I almost ate this religious piece of dough," he was heard to say.

It was stored in a freezer for a week, then became the center of a nine-minute video documentary titled: "A Music City Miracle: The Story of the NunBun." The local papers and television stations ran stories, and before long it appeared on David Letterman, Paul Harvey, BBC, Hard Copy, the Cal-

cutta Times, and other media across the world.

Properly preserved, the NunBun is on display at the coffeehouse so the masses can take a look for themselves. There's also all sorts of Bun souvenirs, including T-shirts, bookmarks and prayer cards, coffee mugs, and copies of the documentary. Go online to see for yourself at www.qecmedia.com/nunbun/index.html. Located at 2007 Belmont Boulevard, across from Belmont University; (615) 385-5282.

P.S. Don't forget to eat while you're here, they have some great nontraditional food items. But take a look before you bite and you may discover something cool. Open daily for all three meals.

gone forever. Less than a mile south on 21st Avenue, down in Hillsboro Village, the Bongo Java Roasting Co. shares the old Jones Pet Shop with **Fido,** a cafe named after the dog who discovered coffee. The cafe opened when the pet shop closed in 1996, after fifty years in business. The funky neon pet shop sign has been restored and sits upon the roof. Sean Ray is the roastmaster, and he roasts all the coffee beans used in the shop. His usual roasting days are Monday, Wednesday, and Friday. Watch him and talk with him—he loves his job!

Fido features a breakfast menu until 11:00 A.M., with such items as Spuds McFido, Egg McFido, and if you're real hungry, there's the Bubba Breakfast Burrito. During the rest of the day, there's a full menu of sandwiches, soups, snacks, bagels, and full meals, including a veggie paella, homemade ratatouille, and a veggie lasagna. A popular sandwich is the Yummy Hummy Pita, a mixture of roasted vegetables and hummus stuffed in a pita.

There are plenty of specialty coffee drinks, and the desserts are great, especially the Dog Bowl, a pint of Ben & Jerry's ice cream cut in half and topped with homemade mocha sauce, whipped cream, and other sweet stuff. Open daily until 11:00 P.M.; opens Monday through Friday at 7:00 A.M. and on Saturday and Sunday at 8:00 A.M. 1812 21st Avenue South; (615) 385-7959.

The State of Tennessee turned 200 years old in 1996, and as a present to itself, officials created the **Bicentennial Mall,** down the steps and across James Robertson Parkway from the state capitol. In addition to being a nicely appointed park and gathering place, the mall has permanent state historical exhibits and a great view of Capitol Hill.

- *The world's first night airplane flight took off from Cumberland Park on June 22, 1910.*

- *Theodore Roosevelt coined the phrase "good to the last drop" while drinking coffee at the old Maxwell House Hotel.*

- *The Grand Ole Opry House is the world's largest broadcast studio.*

- *Iroquois, a Nashville horse, was the first American horse to win the English Derby. The Iroquois Steeplechase race held here each May is named after him.*

- *While visiting the Belle Meade Plantation, President Taft got stuck in the bathtub. The owners then installed a stand-up shower for his next visit.*

- *With more than 800 churches, synagogues, and temples, the city is known as the "buckle of the Bible belt."*

- *The driveway at the Hermitage: Home of President Andrew Jackson, is shaped like a guitar.*

- *Elvis Presley recorded more than 200 songs at RCA's Studio B.*

The nineteen-acre state park and outdoor history museum features an amphitheater, a 200-foot-long granite map depicting every city in the state, thirty-one fountains representing each of the state's rivers, a botanical garden, and a 1,400-foot wall engraved with images of Tennessee's historic events. Free; open 6:00 A.M. to 10:00 P.M. daily.

Adjacent to the Bicentennial Mall is the new *Farmers Market.* Moved and rebuilt to the tune of $6.2 million in 1995, the market consists of outdoor, year-round sheds and an indoor marketplace. You'll find fresh produce from apples to zucchini, plants, flowers, and trees outside, and two restaurants, an international market, a hot sauce vendor, and fresh fish and meat peddlers on the inside. Early morning crowds consist mostly of buyers from local restaurants coming in for their fresh-picked produce. Open year-round, with peak operating hours during the summer growing season from 5:00 A.M. to 9:00 P.M. Shorter hours during the winter months. A flea and crafts market takes place here each weekend, year-round. Located on Eighth Avenue North, just off James Robertson Parkway; (615) 880–2001.

In the heart of downtown lies the *Tennessee State Capitol.* Finished in 1859, it was designed by William Strickland, who also helped design the U.S. Capitol. The beautiful building is being renovated in stages, and it is undervalued by tourists. Strickland loved the place so much that he requested to be interred in its walls. President James K. Polk is also buried there. Admission is free. For tour information call (615) 741–2692.

Down the street from the Capitol is the *Arcade,* which is being restored to its finest. It was built in 1903 as a two-tiered shopping mall, an identical copy of one in Milan, Italy. Today it is occupied by specialty shops, including several restaurants and the mandatory roasted-nut store, whose aroma pervades the entire complex.

LOOK! UP IN THE SKY. At 632 feet, the Bell South Building, fondly known locally as the *Batman Building* because of its uncanny resemblance to the caped crusader, is the tallest building in the state. It has twenty-seven floors of office space and above that several other storage, mechanical, and open floors. At the very top, two spirals go heavenward from either side, hinting of Batman's pointed ears. The behemoth makes quite a statement.

"That's what the architect wanted to do," said Bell South official David May. "The design philosophy was to be unique, be distinctive in the Nashville skyline, and avoid being another boxy skyscraper." He noted that while not planning to make it look like Batman, the design "does evoke that image, and others as well. Many people think it looks like a phone receiver and handset at the top," he said, adding that he has been told the nine-level underground parking garage was the largest building construction excavation ever in the state; (615) 214–5907.

When the *Westin Hermitage Hotel* was built in 1910, it was the city's first million-dollar hotel, and it became a symbol of Nashville's emergence as a major Southern city. It flourished for more than fifty years, only to start deteriorating with the rest of the downtown area in the 1960s. Now, as the downtown area has gained a new life, so has the Westin Hermitage Hotel, thanks to a $3.5 million renovation. From its Beaux Arts design, the only commercial example of it in Tennessee, to its magnificently ornate lobby, the hotel is once again a symbol of pride for downtown Nashville. Located across from the Tennessee Performing Arts Center, across from the State Capitol, at Sixth Avenue and Union Street, it's a comfortable, classy place to call home while exploring Music City. (615) 244–3121.

Several decades before the city was known for its music, it had a reputation as a regional center of culture and education. Numerous colleges advanced the learning of the classics, and it wasn't long before the city was known as the Athens of the South. In 1896 it was only natural for planners of the state's centennial celebrations to elaborate on this classic theme.

Batman Building

An exact replica of the **Greek Parthenon;** with a tolerance of less than $1/16$ of an inch, was built for the huge exposition, held in what is now known as **Centennial Park,** just a few miles out West End Avenue from downtown. The Parthenon now houses art exhibits and serves as a backdrop for various cultural events in the park. A 42-foot replica of Athena Parthenos has been sculpted and now is on display in the main hall. Open Tuesday through Saturday 9:00 A.M. to 4:30 P.M. Admission is charged. (615) 862–8431.

Over at the Tennessee State Fairgrounds, on Nolensville Road near downtown Nashville, the **state's largest flea market** takes place the fourth weekend of each month. There are nearly 2,200 vendors on any particular weekend, with 600 of them located indoors. They are open from 6:00 A.M. to 6:00 P.M. on Saturday and 7:00 A.M. to 4:00 P.M. on Sunday. *Hint:* Vendors can set up any time after 3:00 P.M. on Friday, and most will sell to you if you drop by as they set up their booths. That's when they all wheel and deal with each other, and it's when you'll definitely get the best choice. (615) 862–5016.

The *Tennessee State Fair* is held on these same grounds the second week of September. Lots of carnival rides, great-tasting (albeit fatty) foods, and plenty of farm animals are on hand for the entertainment and the education of guests. There's also a circus and a major country concert held during the event. A village with log cabins and working craftsmen provides a glimpse into the early days of the state. (615) 862–8980.

One of the funkiest and unusual shops in Nashville is *Karmal-Skillington.* It's hard to describe, but here goes: It's a unique furniture and accessories store for those who want quality and class but not pedestrian or vanilla items. The prices are reasonable, and it's a fun store to browse to get your decorating juices flowing. The store's buyers must have a ball! Among the 4,000 square feet of merchandise: mirrors, iron furniture, chandeliers, aromatherapy candles and supplies, pots, picture frames, decorative pieces, and pine, mahogany, and teak furniture. Located at 2019 8th Avenue South. (615) 460–7197.

OK, here's the dilemma. You're hungry for a burger, you're thirsty for a beer, but you also have to do your laundry. What's one to do? Easy answer. Visit *Harvey Washbanger* in the Vanderbilt University area. The establishment's slug line of "Eat, Drink, Do Laundry," tells you everything you need to know. Load up your wash and belly up to the bar. A light panel keeps you informed of the status of your wash. When the light goes off, you're done.

The menu is great and so is the beer selection. Sixty beers, including six on tap, represent the best brews of twelve different countries, and you'll be amazed at the great prices. The menu consists of three parts: Separating Colors (appetizers), Wash & Dry (entrees), and Fold 'Em Up (desserts). There are plenty of burgers, chicken, and heart-healthy items to choose from. Several television monitors feature sports programming, and a couple of computers offer Internet access for $1.00 for fifteen minutes.

Located close to Centennial Park at 106 29th Avenue North. Open seven days a week. (615) 322–WASH.

The newest museum to set up shopkeeping in Nashville is the *Sankofa-African Heritage Museum,* where a large permanent collection of art and artifacts from all parts of Africa is on display. Some of the amazing collection dates back to the mid-1440s. In addition to the art and artifacts, the museum offers special cultural musical programs and a variety of seminars. This is a well-kept, friendly museum where you're made to feel right at home. If you love African culture, make this place a must-see. Open daily, admission charged. 101 French Landing Road, (615) 726–4894.

For a truly amazing site, visit the **Upper Room Chapel and Museum.** The stars of this establishment are an 8-foot-by-17-foot wood carving of da Vinci's *The Last Supper* and an 8-foot-by-20-foot stained glass window with a Pentecost theme. Beautiful!

The museum features religious paintings and art objects dating back to the 1300s as well as religious artifacts from throughout the world. At Christmas time the museum displays its collection of Ukranian eggs and more than 100 nativity scenes. Open Monday through Friday; free. 1908 Grand Avenue. (615) 340–7207.

For the best fried chicken and country ham dinners in middle Tennessee, follow West End Avenue (it turns into Highway 100 farther out) to the **Loveless Motel and Cafe.** It's about 15 miles from downtown. Owner Donna McCabe has herself a neat piece of roadside Americana here, including a colorful neon sign. The food is served family style, with fresh biscuits and homemade preserves. While you're waiting for a table, be sure to read the clippings on the walls. This place has been visited by some very important people through the years, including Captain Kangaroo. It's located in a little house, so reservations are almost a must. Open Monday through Friday 8:00 A.M. to 2:00 P.M. and 5:00 to 9:00 P.M., and Saturday and Sunday 8:00 A.M. to 9:00 P.M. (615) 646–9700.

The Natchez Trace Texaco gas station next to the Loveless Cafe could really be called "Last Chance Gas & Food." It's located at the entrance to the Natchez Trace Parkway, where you won't find any food, gas, or lodging for your entire 450-mile trip to Natchez, Mississippi.

Curly's BBQ is inside the gas station. Here you'll find some of the most raved-about barbecued ribs and smoked pork, chicken, turkey, and beef brisket in Middle Tennessee. Curly is here by 6:30 each morning baking up some great breakfast biscuits. During lunch he has a nice selection of garden salads and baked potatoes. Open seven days a week until 9:00 P.M. (615) 673–6622.

If you're a beer can collector, the **Museum of Beverage Containers and Advertising** might very well be heaven for you. It's located about 16 miles north of Nashville in the small community of Millersville. Their collection of 30,000 soda and beer cans is claimed to be the largest in the world.

In addition the museum has more than 5,000 antique soda bottles on display and a great display of advertising pieces used by various bottlers over the years. The gift shop offers a fun experience itself! There are antique bottles, cans, memorabilia, and advertising signs for sale by the hundreds. Open Monday through Saturday 9:00 A.M. to 5:00 P.M. and Sunday 1:00 to 5:00 P.M. Admssion is charged; exit 98 on I–65, which is Highway 31. Go north 1.3 miles into Millersville, turn west on Cartwright Circle North, then right on Ridgecrest Drive. Follow signs. (615) 859–5236.

William Driver, a New England sea captain, is credited as the first person to ever call the American flag "Old Glory." He is buried in Nashville's historic *Nashville City Cemetery*. He died in Tahiti on September 3, 1821. His gravestone is in the shape of a tree stump wrapped in flowers, toadstools, and a frog and embellished with an anchor. No one seems to know why he's buried here. The cemetery is in the St. Cloud Hill area near Oak Street and Fourth Avenue South.

The downtown square of *Lebanon* is antiques heaven! Within a 2-block area there are more than a dozen antiques stores and antiques malls. Most are open daily. The largest, and probably the most packed with the biggest selection, is Cuz's Antiques, in the corner on the square. There's plenty of parking and there's always plenty of action in the downtown area.

The award-winning *Wilson County Fair,* voted the state's best county fair several times during the mid-1990s, is held each August and it truly is small-town Americana at its finest. Vice President Al Gore showed animals here as a child, and thousands of kids before and after him prepare for the fair all year long. The carnival is colorful and fun, the exhibits are great, and the entertainment is top-notch. (615) 443–2626.

The fair takes place at the James E. Ward Agricultural Center, where picturesque Fiddlers Grove is also located. The grove consists of twenty-three original and replicated log cabins moved to the fairgrounds, creating a compound of what a Wilson county community would have looked like in the 1800s.

There are such frontier staples as a jail, post office, blacksmith shop, and general store, and it's still growing, year by year. Here is a low-key, out-of-the-way community where the early life of Tennessee is preserved and presented. It's a lot of fun, and the workers here are well-versed in this particular era of the state's history. It's open during the fair and from 10:00 A.M. to 3:00 P.M., Wednesday through Friday from mid-March through mid-October. Free admission. (615) 443–2626.

If you like wildflowers, make sure you visit the *Wildflower Pilgrimage* each year in mid-April at the Cedars of Lebanon State Park, just outside Lebanon. The two-day event is structured to dazzle the experts and to create an interest in those just learning to appreciate one of nature's best gifts to us. Call Sandy Suddarth for more information. (615) 443–2769.

The country stars and the top bankers and businesspeople of the state might make their millions in Nashville, but when it comes to investing in their lifestyles and families, many come south to *Williamson County.* It consistently has the state's highest per capita income and the lowest unemployment rate.

- *More battles were fought in Tennessee than in any other state except Virginia.*

- *Tennessee was the last state to secede from the Union and the first state to be readmitted after the war.*

- *East Tennesseans were strongly pro-Union, while west and middle Tennesseans were primarily on the side of the Confederacy.*

- *The free booklet, "A Path Divided: Tennessee's Civil War Years" provides a thumbnail history of the war and a list of related events and attractions throughout the state. (888) 243–9769.*

Maps that show where many of the stars live are available at most bookstores. Dolly Parton, Gary Morris, The Judds, Tom T. Hall, and Waylon Jennings are among the inhabitants of the area. If you want to see them, though, you probably have a better chance hanging out at the local Kroger store than in front of their houses.

Franklin, the county seat, is 17 miles and "100 years" south of Nashville and is associated with old, restored homes and businesses, antique shopping, and the Civil War. The entire downtown section is on the National Register of Historic Places.

The *Carter House,* south of downtown on Columbia Avenue, was caught in the middle of the fight aptly known as the Battle of Franklin on November 30, 1864. Bullet holes are still evident in the main structure and various outbuildings. One of the outbuildings has 203 bullet holes in it, making it the most battle-damaged building from the Civil War still standing anywhere.

The property is one of the eleven historic sites in the state owned and operated by the Association for the Preservation of Tennessee Antiquities. Open daily; admission charged; (615) 791–1861.

The German woodworker and piano maker Albert Lotz built the beautiful mansion at 1111 Columbia Avenue, across from the Carter House, in 1858. The house stands on part of the original Franklin battlefield, and during the five-hour battle, the Lotz family took refuge with their neighbors in the cellar of the Carter House. Today the **Lotz House Museum** features the most comprehensive collection of Civil War and Old West artifacts in the mid-South. Open daily. Admission for adults is $5.00; children 12 and under, $1.50. (615) 791–6533.

About 5 miles away, the **Carnton Mansion** also played an important role in the Battle of Franklin. On the rear lines of the Confederate forces, the elegant estate witnessed a steady stream of dying and wounded during the battle. At one time the bodies of five slain Confederate generals were laid out on the back porch. Within view of that historic porch rests the only privately owned Confederate cemetery in the United States. Open daily; admission charged to the house; cemetery free; (615) 794–0903.

A few blocks east of the town square, where the Confederate monument (circa 1899) rests, is the **Hiram Masonic Lodge.** When the three-story building was built in 1823, it was said to be the tallest structure in Tennessee. It was constructed to house the first Masonic Lodge in the state, which was chartered in 1803, and later, in 1827, the first Protestant Episcopal Church in Tennessee was founded here.

Through the growing season, **Earl's Fruit Stand,** at 95 East Main Street, is your basic greengrocer. But something comes over "Mr. Earl" each October, and he turns his establishment into pumpkinland and puts on his orange cap. There are displays with thousands of pumpkins and gourds and everything else that is Halloween. You can buy them just about anywhere, but this is the *cool* place to buy pumpkins. And there are pony rides, a petting zoo, a hay maze, a spinning pumpkin ride, a spooky cemetery, and hot cider. There's even an area dedicated to celebrity pumpkins, faces of famous country singers and TV stars painted on appropriately shaped pumpkins. You should see the Dolly Parton pumpkin! (615) 794–5212.

The historic downtown area of Franklin is quickly becoming known as the newest "antiques capital of Tennessee." There are nearly three dozen antiques and craft stores within the downtown area, all within walking distance of the other. **Franklin Antique Mall** is the city's oldest and largest antiques mall. Used as a flour mill in the 1800s, the handmade brick structure was the county's icehouse at the turn of the century. Today it houses the goods of more than fifty different antiques dealers spread out over 12,000 square feet of space. At Second Avenue South and South Margin Street; open daily; (615) 790–8593.

South of Franklin on Highway 31 is **Columbia,** the center of commerce for Maury County. In addition to its reputation as the "Antebellum Homes Capital of Tennessee," Columbia claims James K. Polk, one of the three presidents from the state, as a resident. His ancestral home is open to the public at 301 West 7th Avenue. Built by his parents in 1816, this is the house where Polk began his legal and political career. There is plenty of one-of-a-kind memorabilia housed here, and the gift shop has more books written about Polk than you could have ever imagined. (931) 388–2354.

If you think you have stubborn friends, they are probably nothing compared to the critters that gather here each year during the first week of April! That's when the **Mule Day Festival** and parade takes place to celebrate the city's proud heritage as the mule-raising capital of the state.

The Plant That's Eatin' Tennessee

That's kudzu (pronounced cud-zoo) you see growing all over the roadsides throughout Tennessee. The large hairy-leafed, bright green invasive vine is also known as the mile-a-minute vine and the vine that ate the South. It grows as much as a foot a day or 60 feet a summer in good weather and can take up to a decade to kill. It is said that Southerners keep their windows shut at night to keep out the kudzu.

Kudzu was introduced to the United States in 1876 at the Centennial Exposition in Philadelphia by the Japanese. During the Great Depression of the 1930s, the Soil Conservation Service promoted kudzu for erosion control, and hundreds of men planted the plants on roadsides throughout the south. Farmers were paid by the government to plant fields of the vines in the 1940s.

It does control erosion, but it also runs rampant and kills virtually everything in its place and climbs anything it contacts, including telephone poles and trees. Where it grows, kudzu has the ability to outcompete and eliminate native plant species and upset the natural diversity of plant and animal communities.

The vine has been known to kill entire forests by preventing the trees from getting light. During warm weather, the plant, classified a weed by the government in 1970, bears 6- to 10-inch spikes of small purple fragrant flowers.

Don't be tempted to dig up any of the plants to take home with you, because they will soon become a nuisance, and you'll spend the rest of your life trying to get rid of it.

The parade features mules pulling just about everything down the highway, and the festival is loaded with arts and crafts booths, all kinds of food (no mule meat), a liar's contest, square dancing, and a mule show. (931) 381–9557.

South of Columbia on Mt. Pleasant Pike, the *Rattle & Snap Plantation* stands among 1,500 rolling acres. Currently a working plantation, the house represents a museum-quality restoration, with all furnishings being from the mid-nineteenth century. The antebellum structure, built in 1845, is reputed to be the finest example of Greek Revival architecture in the South today. Open year-round, daily. Admission charged. (931) 379–5861.

Rattle & Snap Plantation is one of the sixty-plus homes along the *Tennessee Antebellum Trail.* Within a 30-mile radius of Nashville lies the highest concentration of antebellum homes in the South today. Eight of the houses are open to the public. A splendid tour map, which lists and describes each house is available at area attractions or by calling (800) 381–1865.

On Highway 50W about 8 miles from downtown Columbia you'll find a good example of how industry and nature can live together. From 1937 to 1986, the Monsanto company had a plant here that produced elemental phosphorous. Through the years as the company finished up strip mining an area of the 5,345 acres, it planted trees and created lakes. Wildlife began moving in, and when the plant closed in 1986 the company worked with the Tennessee Wildlife Resources Agency to turn the entire area into a wildlife enhancement zone.

Today, *Monsanto Ponds* is open to the public. There are several nice observation areas where you can hide and observe the abundant species of wildlife and waterfowl living in what is now considered one of the state's best wetlands areas.

Turn off Highway 50 at the Monsanto sign, and travel approximately 3 miles to an information center where you can pick up maps of trails and observation points. Free; open daily during daylight hours. (931) 388–2155.

Out Highway 43 from Columbia is *Mount Pleasant,* a small community that calls itself the "Best Kept Secret in Middle Tennessee." Their other slogan, which might be a bit more appropriate for this sleepy little burg is: "Stop, Shop, Eat, and Tour."

The town witnessed a great deal of troop movement during the Civil War, and after discovery of high-grade phosphate in 1896 the village of 400 residents became a boom town of more than 2,000 when workers from twenty-five states and ten countries came to toil in the local phosphate mines. By the early 1900s there were more than a dozen companies operating here and it was known as the "phosphate capital of the world."

Today, the phosphate heritage and hundreds of other historical artifacts are preserved in the **Phosphate Museum,** downtown at 108 Public Square. Open weekdays and Saturday 9:30 A.M. to 5:00 P.M. Closed Wednesday.

You can enjoy a "Phosphate Soda" at **Lumpy's Malt Shop,** a 1950s-era soda fountain and restaurant also located downtown on the square. Glenn Lumpkins, a local pharmacist, ran Wright's Pharmacy until a major chain store came to town, bought him out, and hired him to work for them. He owned the building and the soda fountain that was installed in 1952, and he wanted to preserve it. He opened the malt shop and it has grown beyond his expectations. Lumpy acquired the town's first fire truck, from 1934. It is now the centerpiece of the eatery, and all tables, chairs, and stools have been authentically renovated.

One wall features high school memorabilia from the era, and the other walls are solid with his private collection of signs. A neon-lined "Time Passage Tunnel" to the back of the shop takes people from the 1950s era, to a themed 1940s party room.

The menu is full of malts, banana splits, and sundaes, plus burgers, salads, fried peanut butter and jelly sandwiches, and fried marshmallow and banana sandwiches. The Woolly Bully is a fried bologna sandwich. There are three types of barbecue: Up Yonder, Down Yonder, and Over Yonder, all cooked with different woods and seasonings. A special root beer is made for Lumpy, and it's called Root 66. It's slogan? "Get your lips on Root 66."

Open Monday through Thursday 5:30 A.M. to 8:00 P.M., Friday until 10:00 P.M., Saturday 6:00 A.M. to 10:00 P.M., and Sunday 11:00 A.M. to 3:00 P.M. (931) 379–9268.

One mile from downtown Murfreesboro is an obelisk marking the geographic center of the state. **"The Dimple of the Universe,"** as it is called locally, is on Old Lascassas Pike. Turn left off Greenland Drive opposite the football fields at Middle Tennessee State University.

In the early days Murfreesboro was a little village known as Cannonsburgh. Today **Cannonsburgh Pioneer Village** is a living museum depicting 125 years of Southern life amidst the hustle and bustle of the metropolitan area the city has become. Among its collections are a log house, blacksmith shop, general store, gristmill, one-room school-house, and a museum.

But the real star here is the **World's Largest Red Cedar Bucket,** manufactured locally by a bucket factory that toured the oddity as an advertising gimmick. It was built in 1887, is 6 feet tall, 24 feet around the top, and holds nearly 2,000 gallons of water. The museum here also holds what officials feel is the **World's Largest Spinning Wheel.** It stands 8 feet tall and was made by a local mortician.

Cannonsburgh is the site of the popular Uncle Dave Macon Days early every July. There's plenty of music, food, games, and activities for the kids. There are juried arts and crafts show and a special gospel music celebration on Sunday morning. Cannonsburgh is open May through October, Tuesday through Sunday, at 312 South Front Street. (615) 893–6565.

Farther out Highway 96, just past Lascassas, lies the small unincorporated village of Milton. With a population of about 200, the place has two businesses, the mandatory post office and **Manuel's Cajun Country Store.** The latter is the place to be.

Among the grocery items, which include Louisiana specialties such as syrup, coffee, and hot sauces, are red-checked, oilcloth-covered tables that come alive four days a week with the best Cajun food in the state. Abe and Dottie Manuel head up the family operation while the rest of the family cooks and serves the fried alligator, shrimp, crayfish, and other ethnic specialties. The Manuel relatives in Creole, Louisiana, are involved. They trap the 'gators the restaurant serves.

On Friday and Saturday nights, a Cajun band fills the streets of Milton with music as it plays from the front porch and people dance on Main Street. Meals are served from 11:00 A.M. to 2:00 P.M. Wednesday and Thursday and from 11:00 A.M. to 9:00 P.M. on Friday and Saturday. (615) 273–2312.

One of the most interesting factory tours in the state is located north of Murfreesboro, just off Highway 41. The **Nissan Motor Manufacturing Corporation** Truck/Auto Plant offers tours on Tuesday and Thursday. During the hour-long tram ride through the modern plant you'll see men and women working arm and arm with hundreds of robots to produce more than 1,000 vehicles a day.

The complex covers about 800 acres and employs more than 6,000 local workers. To be safe, it's best to call ahead and make a reservation for your tour. Admission is free, but of course they don't give samples. (615) 459–1444.

Mr. Miller ran Christiana's only grocery store for seventy-five years, and in that funky old building today is *Miller's Country Cafe.* It's a meat and three during the week, a bluegrass music and catfish eatery on Friday night, and a four-course, gourmet meal, fine dining reservations-only restaurant on Saturday night. It's also the tiny town's only restaurant.

Two meats and an array of veggies are available as a Blue Plate lunch Monday through Saturday from 11:00 A.M. to 2:00 P.M., and the dinners are served Friday and Saturday night from 6:00 to 9:00 P.M. There's a lot of old-time flavor in this old building. Oilcloth-covered tables, wood floors, and all kinds of antiques and memorabilia line the walls. Located about 8 miles from Murfreesboro and 7 miles south of I–24 off Highway 231. Head south and when you see the Christiana signs, turn left onto Highway 269. Cross the railroad tracks and make an immediate left and you're in the neighborhood. (615) 893–1878.

Life's a lot calmer around here since Billy Lynch decided not to run for another term as mayor of Eagleville, population 460. He now spends more time running his other businesses, which include *Lynch's Restaurant and Dairy Bar,* at the corner of Highway 41A and Highway 99. He used to run back and forth from city hall to the restaurant. Now you'll probably find him tending to his thirty-two-seat diner, which is usually packed with long-time customers who have come to love the food, service, and smiles at the restaurant.

Open 5:00 A.M. to 8:30 P.M. six days a week, Lynch's is best known for the "meat and three" plate lunches it serves up daily. You get a meat dish and three vegetables for $3.00. On Friday he buys up a mess of fresh catfish and offers a fish fry dinner for $5.95.

Dessert? With "Dairy Bar" as part of the name of the establishment, you can only imagine some of the delightful ice-cream dishes Billy and his crew serve up. And that's not to mention the fresh-baked pies available each day! Make sure you try the banana split. They are made the old-fashioned way and are the best in town.

Open daily except for Sunday, Thanksgiving, and Christmas. (615) 274–6427.

Follow Highway 31A/41A north out of Eagleville to where it intersects with Highway 96. That little burb is known as Triune, and it has two claims to fame. The weekly *Triune Flea Market,* right at that busy intersection, and the annual Tennessee Renaissance Festival, east of town on Highway 96 at Castle Gwynn.

The flea market is of the small-town, lets-dig-deep-for-a-bargain type of event. Cars pull up, open their trunks, throw out a few blankets full of stuff, and start selling. If it rains, you'll get wet and plenty muddy. As in any type of flea market, there's a lot of junk out there, but if you are patient, you'll probably find some good things. Prices seem a bit high on the true antiques and popular collectibles, but the dealers will usually come down, especially on Sunday afternoon. Open every Saturday and Sunday 7:00 A.M. to 5:00 P.M.

The sixteenth century is celebrated at the *Tennessee Renaissance Festival,* held every weekend in May each year at Castle Gywnn, a wonderfully eclectic twentieth-century castle. This is the time of King Henry VIII, and he's joined in the festivities by plenty of court jesters, street entertainers, musicians, Shakespearean actors, period games, combat chess, and full-armor jousts. Hundreds of craftsmen are open for business in the medieval marketplace, and there's a whole lot of great, unusual food and beverages. (615) 395–9950.

Southeastern Heartland

I f you happen to be in Manchester during the early part of October, be sure to visit the *Old Timer's Day* celebration. The city fathers shut down the streets around the square for a Saturday and fill it with fun things to do, including a bluegrass music concert, arts and crafts, kiddie rides and games, and a whole lot of food. (931) 728–7635.

Foothill Crafts in Manchester may be the ultimate quality crafts store. Run entirely by volunteer members of the Coffee County Crafts Association, the shop has an amazing array of hand-crafted items for sale. It's a hard process to get your crafts represented here, but that process assures that only the highest-quality items will be represented. Currently more than 400 different artisans are selling their items out of this old-time grocery store. Open daily year-round. (931) 728–9236.

On Highway 55, just before you reach Tullahoma, be on the lookout for the *Coca-Cola Bottling Company* plant. Next to it is the Company Store, a retail outlet open to the public. You'll be amazed at how many things are made with the Coke logo on them. It's a virtual plethora of Coke red and white merchandise, from clothes to antique reproductions to glasses. Open Monday through Saturday 10:00 A.M. to 6:00 P.M. and Sunday 1:00 to 4:30 P.M. (931) 454–1030.

In Tullahoma, at 2102 North Jackson Street, **Worth Inc.** operates the world's largest bat and ball manufacturing plant. The company makes more than seven million balls and more than a million bats each year. There's another company that makes more balls, and another that makes more bats, but none can top Worth for combined production.

Worth brand softballs include the Red Dot, Blue Dot, and Green Dot brands and the RIF (reduced injury factor) baseball. The patented RIF greatly reduces hit-by-baseball (and softball) injuries, and its sales are skyrocketing each year. In fact, Worth doesn't make a traditional youth baseball anymore.

Tours are given on Wednesday if they know you're coming. On your trek through the plant you'll get to talk with the women who hand sew all the baseballs and softballs. They'll show you how they do it, and they might give you a chance to work on one as well. You'll also walk through the stamping and boxing operation. (931) 455–0691.

The **Tullahoma Fine Arts Center** and the **Regional Museum of Art** share space in the city's oldest brick house at 401 Jackson Street. The fine arts center features work of local and regional artists, including crafts as well as the fine arts. All items on display may be purchased. The Regional Museum of Art features traveling exhibits and the museum's private collection. Open Monday through Friday; free; (931) 455–1234.

It wasn't soft drinks that George Dickel of **George Dickel Distillery** had in mind when he and his wife arrived in Tullahoma in the 1860s. He was searching for the right water to make whiskey. He found the towns-folk sipping a limestone water from nearby Cascade Spring; he investigated, liked what he tasted, bought some land, and in the early 1870s opened his distillery.

The facility closed in 1911 when the state went dry but was reopened by Schenley Distillers in 1958 when the county voted to allow the manufacture of alcoholic products. Most of Coffee County remains dry to this day. The whiskey is still made the old-fashioned way, and all through the free tour, people are reminded that this is not bourbon but Tennessee sour mash whiskey. The difference is in the charcoal-mellowing processing.

Miss Annie runs the George Dickel General Store, located across the wooden bridge, which spans Cascade Creek. Ask her how you can be recognized for your good taste, and she'll hand you an application blank for the George Dickel Tennessee Whiskey Water Conservation Society.

To get to the distillery, head north on Route 41A from Highway 55 for about 5 miles and then turn right on Marbury Road and follow the signs. Tours are weekdays only. Admission is free. (931) 857–3124.

Shelbyville, the Bedford County seat, is also the center of Tennessee's horse country. It plays host each year to the **Tennessee Walking Horse Celebration,** an event during which the World Grand Champion is named.

This special breed of horse, developed during 150 years of selective breeding, is promoted today as the "world's greatest show and pleasure horse." The horse has an unusual rhythmic gliding motion in which each hoof strikes the ground separately in an odd one-two-three-four beat.

The celebration takes place on what is known as the Celebration Grounds, where you'll also find the **Tennessee Walking Horse Museum** tucked away inside the Calsonic Arena. Established in 1993 the museum tells the story of this special breed, which is the only horse named for its state, through state-of-the-art displays and interactive exhibits. Open Monday through Friday 9:00 A.M. to 5:00 P.M. Admission for adults is $3.00; seniors and children 7 to 12, $2.00; ages 6 and under, free. The Celebration Grounds are located on Madison Avenue, which is Highway 41A, east of downtown Shelbyville. Follow signs to the museum once on the grounds. (931) 684–0314.

The breed emerged from the plantations around here during the later part of the nineteenth century but today can be found across the country. The area around Shelbyville is still known for its farms, and most of the owners are happy to show off their facility. Many have signs out welcoming you, but you might want to call the Breeders Association in advance. There may be a special event or training session at one of the farms that you'd find interesting. (800) 359–1574.

The Walking Horse & Eastern Railroad runs along one of the oldest branch lines in the state and connects Shelbyville to Wartrace. Long abandoned as a passenger line, some folks in the area decided it was time to put it back in service, which they did in 1997. The Volunteer makes one run a week, on Saturdays at 10:00 A.M. It's a one-hour trip over to Wartrace, and passengers have two hours to look around, shop, and have lunch. Then it's back to Shelbyville. The round-trip fare is $18 for adults, $10 for kids; three and under ride free.

The Civil War reenactors club of Wartrace has written a short play about the area, and on certain Saturdays, acts it out on the way to Wartrace. An old-fashioned Rebel train robbery takes place along the line as well. The train runs April through October and loads and unloads next to the Shelbyville Chamber of Commerce. Patty Conklin's dad is the engineer, and she handles the ticketing. Call her at (931) 695–5066.

Within a stone's throw of the railroad tracks in **Wartrace** is the historic **Walking Horse Hotel.** Opened as a railroad hotel in 1917, the facility has had many lives during the years. When John and Bea Garland came out of retirement "to buy" themselves a job, they completely restored and modernized the rooms and brought everything else up to code. The Strolling Jim Restaurant is on the first floor, several retail shops on the second, and six rooms on the third. A 3,500-square-foot outdoor deck patio seats an additional 250 people.

Open every day but Monday, the restaurant serves up a hearty southern breakfast, a full luncheon menu, and specializes in steaks and seafood for dinner. The town is dry, so they don't sell any alcohol, but you can bring your own. Tennessee Walking Horse memorabilia lines the walls and the hotel could almost be considered a museum of its own.

Strolling Jim, the first World Champion Tennessee Walking Horse, lived in the stables behind the hotel and is now buried out under an oak tree. People are allowed to visit the stables and the well-marked grave. (931) 389–7050.

While you're in Shelbyville stop by **Pope's Restaurant,** located on the square in a long line of beautiful Victorian buildings, for the best deep-fried chicken livers in the state. (931) 684–9901. Farther north on Highway 41A, business at **Carlton's General Store** in Rover is good. "Sure is—we sell something just about every day," claims owner Earl Carlton. "But the world is trying to crowd us out." (931) 294–5272.

Carlton, a character in his own right, has a small room next to his store where the locals come to solve all the world's problems. They start arriving about 5:30 A.M. and spend several hours just whittling and talking. "They whittle all the time and never make anything but a mess," complains Carlton, who is the seventh generation to live within a 2-mile area of the store.

Nobody seems to know exactly how Rover got its name, but the most accepted story is that a bunch of bickering regulars at a local drinking establishment decided to name their community. After hours of arguing over a name, one of them piped out, "Why don't we just call it Rover—we all fight like dogs anyway." So be it.

Along Route 269 in the northern corner of the county lies the quaint little village of **Bell Buckle.** The little downtown area, located along Railroad

Square facing the active railroad, is a trip back in time. A covered wooden sidewalk leads you from one store to another. All the benches, rocking chairs, flowers, and store displays have a tendency to slow down pedestrian traffic a bit, but it gives you more time to look in the window or watch a train go by.

Ten little shops ranging from antiques and craft stores to a great used bookstore make up the downtown lineup. Margaret Britton Vaughn (friends call her Maggi), the state's official poet laureate, runs the **Bell Buckle/Iris Press.** Take time to drop in and chat with her for a few minutes; she's a true southern lady. (931) 389–6878.

Featured prominently a few shops down is J. Gregry's **Bell Buckle Cafe and Music Parlour.** In addition to some great hickory-smoked barbecue and the world's greatest hand-squeezed lemonade, the cafe features live music four nights a week and is the site of a Saturday afternoon live broadcast on WLIJ Radio 1580 AM. You'll hear a lot of new and old country and bluegrass coming from the back room here. Thursdays are writer's nights, and there's at least a couple shows each night through Sunday. Food is served seven days a week. (931) 389–9693; www.bell-bucklecafe.com

Tucked up right next to the railroad is the **Louvin Brothers Museum,** with exhibits and memorabilia highlighting the Grand Ole Opry careers of The Louvin Brothers. Charlie and Berry Louvin are the proprietors and can usually be found tending the museum. Friendly Charlie loves to talk with strangers and loves to talk about his career. They've got a nice selection of old recordings of the brothers, and there are plenty of other gift items and photos you can buy, have Charlie sign, and take home with you. It's not every day you meet a Grand Ole Opry star! Hours vary, depending on whether Charlie has a gig that night. There's an ATM out on the porch.

For a bit of the true South, be here during the third weekend of June to help celebrate the **Moon Pie Festival.** That's when you'll get to join in the celebration of one of the area's finest traditions, Moon Pies and RC Cola. Yum yum.

The village is also the home of **Webb School,** a preparatory school that has produced ten Rhodes Scholars and the governors of three states. The Junior Room, the original wood-shingled one-room schoolhouse built in 1870, has been preserved as it was then, complete with potbellied stove and teaching paraphernalia. It's open for visitors daily and is free. The school hosts a well-respected art and craft festival the third weekend of each October. (931) 389–6003.

Been trout fishing lately? Here's your chance. The owners of the *Nut-cave Trout Farm* say the odds are in your favor that you'll catch something during your stay with them. In fact, you only pay for the rainbow trout you do catch. The Sells family provides the cane pole and the bait, or you can bring your own. "Most of them weigh in around a pound," Tom Sells told me. They charge $2.24 a pound for all you catch, and they'll pack it in ice for your trip home. They'll clean it for you at 10 cents a pound extra, or they'll filet it for an additional 50 cents a pound. "This is a fun place to bring the kids fishing," he added.

They raise their own trout here and the hatchery is open to the public. The fresh, cold water, which is perfect for trout, comes out of the mouth of Nutcave, and you can walk back about 15 feet into the mouth of the cave if you're careful. There are picnic tables around, and Tom says a lot of people come out with their own grill, catch a fish, and cook and eat it right there. Located 8 miles out of Shelbyville, 6 miles out of Tullahoma, off Highway 41A. Open daily, year-round, but closed for two weeks around Christmas. Free; (931) 857-3315.

The area west of Shelbyville on Highway 64 is loaded with horse stables and horse farms. A drive along this corridor into the city of Lewisburg definitely reminds you that you're smack dab in the middle of Tennessee Horse Country. If you see training sessions taking place, chances are the owners won't mind if you stop and watch, but, of course, it's always polite to ask first.

If you're hungry and happen to be in downtown Lewisburg, or if you're from Chicago and yearn for the food of the Windy City, stop by *DC's Corner Diner* on the square. Leon Brand moved down here from Chicago specifically to sell the famed Chicago Dog in these parts of Tennessee. It's an all-beef Vienna hot dog topped with mustard, relish, onion, tomatoes, and a kosher pickle. "That's our biggest draw, the people down here have learned to love them," Brand noted. He has other things on the menu, but 30 percent of it is imported from Chicago, including the French bread, sandwich buns, and Eli's Famous Cheesecake. There's an ice cream fountain up front, and he sells the quality Mayfield Ice Cream products.

The diner is '40s and '50s themed and he's open six days a week 10:00 A.M. to 10:00 P.M. (931) 270-5238.

If you'd like to learn a little history while you're in town, drive South on Highway 31A from downtown and you'll run into the Abner Houston home, across from the Lone Oak Cemetery. The log cabin was the site of the first court of Marshall County in October 1836. It was moved to this site in 1957.

Deep in dry Moore County you'll find another, possibly more famous, distillery known for its Tennessee sour mash whiskey. *Jack Daniel Distillery* put Lynchburg, a community of 360 residents, on the map.

Mister Jack (as he is locally known) founded his business in 1866 and received the first federal license ever issued for a distillery. It still holds that number-one distinction.

If you want to take a tour, make sure you wear comfortable shoes: There's a lot of walking and hill climbing. This is true history and Americana at its finest. They'll even let you taste the sour mash by dipping your fingers into the fermentation vat during the tour, but since this is a dry county, no samples are permitted.

One of the highlights of the tour is the visit to Daniel's office, left virtually the way it was when he died. Make sure you ask the guide to show you where Mister Jack lost his temper one day, eventually causing him to experience a slow, painful death.

January of 1995 was a historic time here in Moore County. For the first time since the Jack Daniel Distillery began making the world-famous sipping whiskey, it was able to sell a specially packaged sample of its product to those who visited Lynchburg. Located in a decades-long "dry" area of the state, voters approved the sale only of small novelty bottles of the whiskey. (931) 759–6180.

There's a great deal of charm in the nearby village of Lynchburg, where Daniel lived his entire life. Today, surrounding the 1855 redbrick courthouse, the square is chock full of gift shops, general stores, arts and crafts outlets, and stores selling Jack Daniel merchandise. Among the shops that are fun to visit is the Lynchburg Ladies Handiwork, on the north side of the square. The shop features handmade items, mostly needlework, by people in Moore County. The ladies working the shop spend their time quilting, sewing, and crocheting. (931) 759–7919. Used whiskey barrels, Jack Daniel memorabilia, and antique reproductions can be found at the *Lynchburg Hardware and General Store,* on the east side of the square.

The best-known place to eat in these parts is *Miss Mary Bobo's Boarding House* in the southwest corner of downtown. Miss Mary began serving meals in 1908 and served many of them to Mister Jack, who had lunch here quite often. Of course, both Mister Jack and Miss Mary are gone now, but the tradition lives on. Specializing in Southern traditional foods, meals are served family style.

Each meal is different and the usual offerings include your choice of two meats, six vegetables, bread, beverage, and a totally awesome dessert. Reservations are a must, since the popular eatery seats only sixty-five people. One seating is planned daily Monday through Saturday at 1:00 P.M., but during peak times, an 11:00 A.M. seating is added as well. Meals for adults are $10.25; children 10 and under, $5.00. For reservations call (931) 759-7394.

As you head west across the mountain from Monteagle on Highway 41A/64, you'll pass the beautiful *University of the South* in Sewanee. Founded in the late 1850s, the 10,000-acre mountaintop campus is known for its shady lawns and Gothic sandstone buildings patterned after Oxford University in England.

Farther down the mountain you'll enter the village of Cowan, where you'll find the *Cowan Railroad Museum* along the still-busy railroad tracks. The museum is housed in the large circa-1904 depot that once served as the busy passenger station.

People would come from all over the south to visit the Sewanee area and the Monteagle Assembly. They would disembark from the passenger train in Cowan and take the "Mountain Goat," a smaller train, up the mountain to their destinations. The mountain goat track, built in 1853, is no longer in use as a railroad track. It has been converted to a mountain bike trail.

Today the museum is full of railroad antiques and memorabilia of those early days. Outside there's a steam engine, a flat car, and a caboose. Run by volunteers, the facility is open from May through October on Thursday, Friday, and Saturday from 10:00 A.M. to 4:00 P.M., and on Sunday from 1:00 to 4:00 P.M. (931) 967-7365.

Hang on, we're really going off the beaten path on this one. The *Cumberland Tunnel* is the longest and steepest railroad tunnel in the United States. Built in 1852, it's 2,200 feet long, 21 feet in height to ceiling, and 15 feet wide. It's still used today and is listed on the National Register of Historic Places.

To get there is a somewhat tedious, albeit fun and adventuresome, trek. Across the track and the small park from the museum is Tennessee Avenue. Take it south to the first right possible and go over the tracks. Make an immediate left turn onto a gravel road located next to the track. The tunnel is located nearly 2 miles up that road. Go slow and if you have a low-rider, forget it. It's bumpy, uneven, and when it rains, a bit muddy in spots, but it's worth the trip once you're there.

The gravel road crosses about 25 feet above the track, just 50 feet from the tunnel entrance. Before you come up, get a train schedule and plan on watching a few trains go through, it's quite fun. Pack a lunch, and between trains take a hike into the raw mountains that surround you. The working railyard in Cowan has a pusher locomotive working twenty-four hours a day to help trains climb up to the tunnel and then help them through it.

Remember when you could buy a house from Sears & Roebuck? The company sold a great many for several years and a few are left, including the one at 518 West Cumberland Street (Highway 41) here in Cowan. The house was ordered from the catalog in the early 1900s and is now owned by Leland Farmer.

Do not pass through Winchester without first going to visit the **Old Jail Museum.** Built in 1897, the structure is now open only to those who REALLY want to be here. After having served as the county jail for more than seventy-five years, the museum now preserves the various elements of the jail, including the cell area and maximum security block. Six additional rooms have exhibits highlighting the county's history, from the frontier days through the Civil War to the present. The Old Jail Museum is located on Dinah Shore Boulevard at Bluff Street, a few blocks from the Winchester Courthouse. Open mid-March through mid-December, Tuesday through Saturday 10:00 A.M.

The Candy Bar B&B

*F*rank Mars, the founder of Mars Candy Company, may have made his millions elsewhere, but he came to the rolling hills of Tennessee in 1922 to build his dream mansion and farm. Milky Way Farm is nestled among one of the most stately stands of grand Magnolias in the South, and the Tudor mansion has twenty-one bedrooms and fifteen baths.

During its heyday, the Milky Way Farm consisted of 2,800 acres, 38 barns, numerous houses, the grand mansion, and its own railroad. The farm pro-duced prizewinning cattle and horses, including a Kentucky Derby winner. The mansion is listed on the National Register of Historic Places.

Today, the Milky Way Farms B&B offers a wide range of accommodations, from a single room with shared bath to a suite with private bath. Prices range from $79 to $185 per room, per night. House tours are available with reservations for $6.00 per person, with a four-person minimum.

The facility is located on Highway 31, 8 miles north of Pulaski (931) 363–9769.

to 4:00 P.M. Admission for adults is $1.00; children, 50 cents; (931) 967–0524.

As you head west through Belvidere on Highway 64, you'll pass the **Belvidere Market** on your right. It's a great pit stop for you. There are plenty of local crafts here, including some very creative birdhouses, as well as local food products, gift items, and sandwiches.

In 1987 a group of Mennonite families migrated to mid-south Tennessee in search of farmland and a desire to start a Mennonite church in an area that had none. Among

Falls Mill, Belvidere

those in the group was the Miller family, who saw the demand for homemade breads and pastries. **The Swiss Pantry** had its beginning in the kitchen of Mrs. Miller, who sold her products to friends and neighbors. In 1989 Mrs. Miller was joined by her three sisters, and they moved the business into the present building, located along Highway 64 just west of Belvidere.

Not only will you find ten different types of fresh-baked breads, but rolls, cookies, pastries, homemade salad dressings and relishes, a large selection of fresh herbs and spices, more than thirty different cheeses, smoked bacon and sausages, nuts, snacks, dried fruits, homemade candies, and a selection of baking and cooking supplies. Outside, a small garden center has been established. Open Tuesday through Friday 7:00 A.M. to 5:30 P.M. and Saturday 8:00 A.M. to 4:00 P.M. (931) 962–0567.

When you leave The Swiss Pantry, continue west on Route 64 and head into Davy Crockett country. You'll be going by a roadside marker designating "Kentuck," the homestead that he left in 1812 to go off to the Creek War. He and his first wife, Polly, and their children settled near here when he came back from the war. She died in 1815 and is buried in an old cemetery overlooking nearby Bean's Creek.

If you want any further information on Davy Crockett's ties with this part of Tennessee, stop by **Falls Mill** near Belvidere and talk with owner

Janie Lovett. In addition to her duties at the mill she owns with her husband, John, she's active in the local historical association and seems to know everyone in the area.

The Lovetts bought the mill in 1984 and have been busy restoring it since. Built in 1873, the mill has operated as a cotton-spinning and wool-carding factory, a cotton gin, a woodworking shop, and a grist and flour mill through the years. Since 1970 it has also served as a sort of museum. But it wasn't until the Lovetts bought it that it started realizing its true potential.

Make sure you take a walk down to the river behind the mill to get a good view of the falls and the 32-foot overshot waterwheel, which is the largest still in operation in the country.

Grain is still ground and is available at the mill store, along with other local items. There's a weaving exhibit upstairs in the mill, and outside, the reconstruction of an 1836 log stagecoach inn that will eventually serve as a bed and breakfast continues.

Currently an 1895 log cabin has been moved here and reassembled and serves as a bed and breakfast for up to five persons. Rates are $75 per night for two people, $5 for each additional body. The mill and picnic grounds are open daily. Admission is charged. (931) 469–7161.

Tim the twig guy lives way off the beaten path in northern Lincoln County. In a little workshop built over the creek on his forty-acre farm, Tim O'Dea makes his living as one of the few traditional willow twig furniture builders in the country. He calls his company *Creekhouse Willow.* He was a construction worker in Miami, Florida, and decided to leave the stresses of big city life behind and set up shop in the hills of Tennessee. Since 1989 Tim and his wife, Rebecca, have been living and communing with nature on their Sunnybrook Farm near the tiny community of Mimosa (pronounced My-mosa).

His specialty items are chairs, rockers, and loveseats, but he'll build anything on a custom order. Everything Tim makes is different and has its own personality. "I like to leave the natural aspect, like the twists and knots on each twig as I make something, and as a result everything is unique. I don't think I've ever made anything that looks exactly the same as anything else I've made," he said. A big part of his business comes from arts and crafts shows he sells, from Michigan to Miami, including the five juried shows he sets up for in Tennessee. Take Mimosa Road off Highway 231, about a half mile south of Belleville. Follow that gravel road for 2 miles, and turn left on Paint Hollow Road.

Sunnybrook Farm is the first house on the left. Give Tim a call before coming out; chances are good that he may be away at a show or out in his workshop. (931) 433–1105.

Farther south on Highway 231 is Fayetteville, the seat of Lincoln County. The downtown area around the county courthouse is probably one of the busiest in the state. There's nary a building vacancy on the square, and it can be hard to find a parking spot at times. Among the most popular of all the bustling shops is *Marbles Mercantile,* which is located in an old hardware store building at the corner of Main and Market Streets. Inside you'll find the shelves lined with Tennessee salt-glazed pottery, yard art, craft items, and the largest selection of glass marbles in the state.

There are nearly two dozen tubs full of the colorful objects, and you can mix and match as many colors and designs as you wish for $3.00 a pound. The owner says she sells nearly five tons of marbles a year, "and 85 percent of those who buy them have no idea of what they are going to do with them." Open Tuesday through Saturday; (931) 433–3024.

Around the corner, 1 block off the square on Market Street, you can have lunch or dinner at Cahoots, located in an old firehouse and city jail. Sit out front or in back in one of the rugged limestone cells. Built in 1867, the building was the city's jailhouse until the 1970s. Menu items include burgers, chicken, a variety of sandwiches, and Mexican dishes, and for dessert try the French silk pie. Yum! Open Monday through Saturday 10:30 A.M. to 9:00 or 10:00 P.M.; (931) 433–1173.

Western Heartland

Three miles west of I–65 on Highway 64 in Giles County, look for an old barn housing *Mama's Cedar Chest,* the queen of junque shops in this part of the state. Emily Lanier is Mama and she has one huge collection. Mama's daughter Edith Edwards is usually at the barn helping out. You'll find old glass, plates, farm tools, posters, books, records, and just about everything else.

Located at 125 Green Valley Road (Highway 64), the shop is open year-round, mostly on weekends. "Whenever Mama wants to be here is when the shop is open," Lanier told me. There's a sign on the door with her home phone number, and there's a phone you can use next door at a shop, so call her and tell her you want in. She lives out back, and she'll come up and unlock the door. (931) 363–5869.

One-Stop Graveyard

The Old Graveyard Memorial Park in Pulaski is a city park, cemetery, and historic monument all rolled into one. It's a great example of how an old, neglected cemetery can once again be useful while preserving the respect due to those buried there. It's a well-lit area where one can stroll and truly absorb the area's history. The monuments have all been restored, with inscriptions dating back to 1753. Located at the corner of Cemetery Street and Highway 31. Call the mayor's office for more information.
(931) 363–3789.

The bell that was cast in 1858 and still hangs in the *Giles County Courthouse* on the public square in Pulaski still strikes on the hour, each hour, every day. The sound coming from the cupola is just one of the beautiful elements of this neoclassical building built in 1909. Outside, tall Corinthian columns mark the architecture. Inside, a balcony encircles the third floor and sixteen caryatids (female figures) hold up the arched vault of the rotunda, with its stained glass skylights. The courthouse is open Monday through Friday during business hours. (931) 363–5300.

Out in front of the courthouse, on the south side of the public square, is a statue of Sam Davis, the young Confederate scout who was captured and executed in Pulaski. He was captured behind enemy lines with damaging information in his possession, and instead of betraying the source of that information he chose to be hanged. The *Sam Davis Museum* now stands on the spot where the "Boy Hero of the Confederacy" was executed on November 27, 1863. The museum contains Civil War memorabilia as well as the leg irons worn by Davis. Located on Sam Davis Avenue, the hours are sporadic, so call the chamber of commerce first if you want to visit. (931) 363–3789.

The chamber of commerce publishes a driving tour guide map of Giles County's top twenty-six antiques, crafts, and collectible shops. Pick up a copy at the chamber's office, 100 South Second Street. (931) 363–3789.

While there are few, if any, physical reminders, there's one part of local history most residents would like to forget—the Ku Klux Klan was founded in Pulaski. Resentment against the move toward black equality fueled the creation of white supremacist groups throughout the South. The most enduring of those, the KKK, was founded in 1866 by six Confederate officers.

Historic *Lynnville,* population 408, has quite the history as a railroad town, and to help preserve that grand heritage a reproduction of the old circa-1877 depot was built in 1997 to house a local museum of railroad artifacts and vintage railroad equipment. The town's history as a railroad town is unique in that the city was originally located 1 mile away from where it is now.

After the Civil War the city fathers decided to move everything to make it more convenient to the railroad. Today, the entire town of fifty-nine buildings is listed on the National Register of Historic Places. Among the quaintness of the downtown business district of the village are several craft and antiques shops and Soda Pop Junction, an old-fashioned soda shop inside the Lynnville Pharmacy, built in 1860.

The museum is open May through October, Thursday through Sunday until 5:00 P.M. Lynnville is located on Highway 129, 7 miles from exit 27 off I–65. (931) 363–3789.

The **Green Valley General Store** is located 8 miles west of Pulaski on Highway 64, and if you're looking for some great fried pies, this is the place! Every day they have an amazing selection of peach, apple, chocolate, and apricot fried pies. In season, they add cherry (my favorite) to the line-up. Open by 7:30 A.M. every day, the store features freshly prepared sausage biscuit sandwiches and country ham croissants. Throughout the day, until closing time of 6:00 P.M., they'll make deli sandwiches for you. The shop also has a fun selection of junk and antiques, and there are gas pumps out front if you need refueling. (931) 363–6562.

Although his legacy is divided among several areas in the state, David (a.k.a. Davy) Crockett only helped in the organization of one of the counties in which he lived, Lawrence County. He was working as a justice of the peace in the area in 1817 when it was ceded by the Chickasaw Indians to the United States. He helped get things organized and was instrumental in getting Lawrenceburg named as the county seat of government.

In 1922, during the dedication of a large monument that still stands on the south side of the square in Lawrenceburg, officials gave Crockett the title of *"Father of Lawrence County."*

Davy Crockett was truly a Tennessean. He was born in the eastern part of the state, ran a gristmill, was elected to Congress in 1821 from Lawrenceburg, and went off to fight in the Alamo from the west. Over his lifetime, Crockett was a pioneer, soldier, politician, and industrialist. He came here in 1817 and served as the justice of the peace.

While serving in that role, Crockett established a diversified water-powered industry consisting of a powdermill, a gristmill, and a distillery. His entire complex and his financial security were washed away in a flood in 1821, causing him to move further west a few years later.

Today, on the site along the river where Crockett lived and worked, Tennessee has created **David Crockett State Park.** The 1,100-acre park has an interpretive center, which is staffed during the summer months and has exhibits depicting Crockett's life here and a replica of the gristmill he once owned. Other facilities in the park include a swimming pool, 100 campsites, and the David Crockett Restaurant, one of the best eateries in this part of the state. Located on Highway 64, just west of Lawrenceburg. (931) 762–9408.

During the second full weekend during August, the park hosts David Crockett Days, a fun and education festival featuring a bevy of frontier-type activities, from tomahawk throwing to long rifle gun making. There's a Crockett film festival, snake shows, and bluegrass music concerts. An arts and crafts festival takes place the first weekend in September each year, featuring a wide variety of exhibitors. Additional unusual events run throughout the year. Call Mike Robertson for more details; (931) 762–9408.

By the way, the county was named in honor of Captain James Lawrence, who commanded a ship in the War of 1812. Mortally wounded, it was he who shouted out the famous command "Don't Give Up the Ship."

At the crossroads of Highways 43 and 240 in Summertown, Ray and Pat Strickland's **Duck River Orchards** is a must if you enjoy good eating! Wow! Of course the store sells freshly picked apples, peaches, plums, and apricots from the Strickland's three orchards, but the baked products are what put this place on the map. Each morning the friendly bakers come in and prepare a wide variety of donuts, muffins, and seven different varieties of breads. If you like pizza, try the tomato bread, and if you'd prefer an herbal rush, try the garden bread. The glazed cider donuts are a taste treat like none other.

Freshly made fudge (thirty-seven varieties), cider ICEES, freshly squeezed cider, and a variety of gift items round out the offerings. Along one wall the locals have posted their favorite recipes. Feel free to bring a pad and pencil and copy a few for your own use. If you want to meet the locals, get here in the morning when just about everyone in the county stops by for coffee and donuts. Open year-round Monday through Saturday 10:00 A.M. to 5:00 P.M. and Sunday 1:00 to 5:00 P.M.; (931) 964–4040 or (800) 964–4043.

Farther down Highway 43 in Ethridge, you'll find the town's unofficial welcome center run by local celebrity Sarah Evetts. She runs the info center/flea market/gift shop at 4001 Highway 43. She also operates her own television station, known as **Granny's Network.** Stop by, talk to her, and she may invite you to go into her studio and appear on her privately owned ten-watt station. If she does she'll make a videotape for you to take home as a souvenir. Even if you don't go on the air with her, you'll enjoy talking with her about the area. She's quite a character. (931) 829–2433.

The pace in the *Ethridge* area is definitely life in the slow lane. More than 200 Amish families call this community their home. The Amish, known as the Plain Folk, have a reputation for being productive farmers and expert craftsmen. Many families sell their wares from their front porches, but the best place to start your shopping is the *Amish Country Galleries,* a five-room antiques store/gallery featuring the works of nearly 200 local craftsmen.

Among the locally produced items you'll find here is the hickory bent rocking chair, a wonderfully comfortable rocker made and used by the Amish in their homes. There is also a great selection of Amish baskets. Located 5 miles north of Lawrenceburg on Highway 43, the shop is open Monday through Saturday 9:00 A.M. to 6:00 P.M. April through New Year's Day.

Out on Highway 64, 10 miles west of Lawrenceburg, Mary Alley runs a funky little antiques shop on her family's cattle farm, know as Clover Leaf Farms. On the south side of the highway, *Clover Leaf Antiques* is housed in a rustic little building bedecked with all sorts of signs and memorabilia. Inside you'll find antiques and collectibles, featuring a nice selection of petroleum collectibles including gas pumps and advertising signage. Out back you'll see the family's 100-acre farm, which is full of registered Santa Gertrudis cattle. Clover Leaf Antiques is open Monday through Saturday, but since she's a one-woman operation, she may lock up for a while when she runs into town to the grocery store. It's wise to call first. (931) 762–5658.

Up in the corner of Wayne County, along the Tennessee River, is *Clifton,* the site where the Tennessee River Boat Races, sponsored by the Tennessee Drag Boat Association, takes place on the river here in Clifton in mid-August.

On Route 128 is the longtime home of the great American novelist Thomas Stribling (1881–1965). He was born in Clifton and wrote many of his novels while residing in this house. One of his novels, *The Store,* won a Pulitzer prize in 1933. The *Stribling House Museum* now has many items from Stribling's life and career. 300 East Water Street; (931) 676–3678.

The Natchez Trace is truly a road trip back in time. The 450-mile road has been a major highway between Nashville and Natchez, Mississippi, since the late 1700s. It is preserved today as a scenic two-lane parkway with few intersections, no commercial activities of any kind, and numerous pull-offs at historic stands (resting areas usually placed one day's travel from the other). The parkway ends on Highway 100, across from the Loveless Motel and Cafe, in Davidson County.

One of the early travelers on the trace was Meriwether Lewis, the famed leader of the Lewis and Clark expedition. In 1809 he met a violent and mysterious death at Grinder's Stand. His grave is marked by a broken column, symbolic of his broken career. The monument is located near the intersection with Tennessee Highway 20 here in Lewis County, east of Hohenwald.

The trace is overlooked by those in a hurry because the 50 mph speed limit is monitored quite closely. Make sure you have a lot of gas before you set out. For a map and other details, call (931) 796–2921.

Just east of the Natchez Trace Parkway on Highway 412 is the little village of Gordonsburg, founded in 1806 by early white settlers traveling the original Natchez Trace. The community became the seat of the county's first government in 1843, and in the early 1900s it was a bustling village of 1,600 inhabitants, thanks to the phosphate mines in the area. The mines closed in 1937, and most of the population has since moved on.

Today, parts of that original village are preserved on the grounds of the *Historic Blackburn House and Folk Museum,* on Highway 412, 2 miles east of the Natchez Trace Parkway. Ambrose Blackburn cleared the land in 1806 and built his homestead, one of the few original trace-side farms still extant. Open to the public on weekends, the attraction contains the first Lewis County Post Office, and the circa-1806 corncrib in which the first Lewis County jury deliberated; both are listed on the National Register of Historic Places. (931) 964–3478.

Further west on Highway 412, on your left side heading toward Hohen-wald, is the two-story stone block building that once served as the phosphate mine company's commissary, post office, and boarding-house. Across the highway is *Wishing Well Collectibles,* which offers a fun and funky assortment of Tennessee-made goods, birdhouses, yard art, and antiques. Just a short hop west on Highway 412 leads you to the *Gordonsburg Farm Market.* Open seven days a week, the market carries fresh fruits and vegetables and some of the area's best home-canned goods, including twenty-two varieties of jams and jellies. They also have a nice selection of country crafts and concrete statuary.

The village of *Hohenwald* is a junker's paradise. The downtown streets are lined with junk and secondhand clothing shops, and people come from miles away to do their bargain hunting. Used clothing is brought in from the Midwest and Northeast in bales and dumped on the floors of the shops. The bales are broken open each Wednesday, Saturday, and Sunday, the days to be there for the best selection. If you're knowledgeable about brands and clothing quality, some real big bargains await you here. There are tales about people finding money and even diamond rings in the old clothes.

One of the most popular "dig stores" is *A. W. Salvage* at 336 East Main Street. There, in addition to piles of used clothing, you'll find a selection of discounted gift items, tools, and collectibles. Bales are opened at 8:00 A.M. on Wednesday and Saturday and 1:00 P.M. on Sunday. The store is open daily. (931) 796–3026.

German immigrants created Hohenwald (which means "high forest") in 1878 as they developed a lumber industry in the area. With the help of the railroad, an organized colony of Swiss immigrants settled in 1894 and built New Switzerland, just south of Hohenwald, and the two towns later merged. A great deal of the German architecture is still evident throughout the community.

The *Lewis County Museum of Natural and Local History,* located at 108 East Main Street, houses one of the largest collections of exotic animal mounts in the United States, including one example of each species of North American sheep. There are also skins of lions, Bengal tigers, and tundra grizzlies. The museum serves as the local history museum and has several displays on the county's past. Open Monday through Saturday 10:00 A.M to 4:00 P.M. and Sunday 1:00 to 4:00 P.M. Admission for adults is $2.00; children, 50 cents. (931) 796–1550.

Carol Buckley and her elephant, Tara, traveled and performed with circuses for years, and then Carol decided Tara would be a lot happier away from show business and in an environment more natural and more fitting for elephants. She moved the two of them to Hickman County, where she is in the process of setting up the *Elephant Sanctuary,* the country's first official elephant retirement home. "It's for the old, sick, and needy," she said, "There are many elephants out there that need a place like this. I have a strong feeling that we're going to be the first of many such homes." Through donations, special events, and a lot of help from concerned friends, Carol has been able to raise the money to build the necessary facilities. They are not open to the public on a regular basis, but if you'd like to meet Tara, Carol, and any other residents who may be living here, give her a call and she'll set up a time for you to come out and take a look. School groups are welcome, she adds. (800) 98–TRUNK.

There's not a single traffic light in the entire 613 square miles of Hickman County. "We used to have one, but some kid kept shooting it out, and they finally took it down," said one county resident. While many of the communities in the state have groups who sit around outside near the courthouse and spit and whittle their days away, you'll find the old-timers in Centerville, the county seat in this county, playing checkers while they spit.

Nicknamed the Keg County, there's still a lot of moonshine made in these hills. If you're interested in sampling some, just put out the word. It has a way of finding you.

And speaking of tasty things, make sure you stop by *Breece's Cafe*, on the square in Centerville. In business since the 1940s, it offers country cooking at its finest. A different plate lunch is offered each weekday, and they always have a selection of home-baked pies on hand. Ask for the blackberry; it's especially good. Open Monday through Saturday 5:00 A.M. to 8:00 P.M. and Sunday 6:00 A.M. to 8:00 P.M. (931) 729–3481.

Across the square, Joe and Marjorie Breece own and operate *Breece's Variety Store*, an old-time five and dime, complete with worn wood floors and overstocked shelves. "We have learned we can't sell it if we don't have it," said Joe Breece. "We have a license to sell and that's what we try to do here."

The building has been a lot of things through the years, including a feed store and a grocery store. Breece opened his business in 1965 and is proud of the old place. He has a guest book that only out-of-state visitors can sign, and it is filled with not only out-of-state guests, but out-of-country folks as well. Even if you don't need anything but a few fun stories, stop by and talk with Joe. He's lived here all his life, and seems to know everyone and everything about the county.

Open every day but Sunday 9:00 A.M. to 5:00 P.M. On Saturday, they may open later or close earlier, depending on what else they want to do. (931) 729–2647.

Head out Highway 100 toward Nashville, and as soon as you cross the Duck River, look to your right and you'll find the hottest spot in town for a catfish dinner. *The Fish Camp Restaurant*, located next to two ponds, features Tennessee River catfish, and people come from all over to sample it. In addition to the fish, they have a full menu, including some great barbecue they smoke right on-site. No alcohol served or allowed due to city regulations. Open seven days a week for lunch and dinner. (931) 729–4401.

The strangest name of any community in the state is probably located here in Hickman County. Out on Highway 50 south of Centerville is the small community of **Who'd A Thought It.** Story goes that a schoolhouse was being built out in the middle of nowhere, and a man pulls up in his buggy and asks what they were building. They told him, and he was last seen shaking his head and mumbling "Who'd a thought it" as he pulled away.

Other interesting names in the county are Defeated Creek, Little Lot, Only, Pretty Creek, Ugly Creek, Spot, and Grinders Switch. The Chamber of Commerce in Centerville has a book for sale that explains how more than sixty-four communities got their names and where to find each. At 117 North Central Avenue; (931) 729–5774.

Up in Nunnelly, behind the Church of Christ where Highways 48 and 230 split, you'll find a monument marking the birthplace of Beth Slater Whitson, the writer of poems, songs, and short stories. Her best-known song lyrics were "Let Me Call You Sweetheart" and "Meet Me Tonight in Dreamland." She lived here from her birth in 1879 to 1913, when she moved to Nashville. She died there in 1930.

There's a nifty piece of the 1950s alive and well just 3 miles out of Centerville on Highway 100. The **Pink Cadillac Drive-In Theater** is one of the few existing drive-in movie theaters still operating in the state. The ticket office is lined with pink neon, rock and roll scenes are painted on the front fence, and the smell of fresh popcorn permeates the air. Open during the summer months, Friday, Saturday, and Sunday nights at dark. (931) 729–2386.

The coal miner's daughter not only lives in Hurricane Mills, she owns it. When country music's most-awarded female vocalist, Loretta Lynn, and her husband, Mooney, were house shopping back in 1967, she was searching for a big old "haunted looking" place. When she saw this century-old mansion, she knew this was her dream. She wanted it immediately, not knowing the entire town and old mill came with it. The **Loretta Lynn Ranch,** on Route 13 in Hurricane Mills, is her home as well as her museum and special place to welcome fans.

In 1975 a campground was developed, and since then numerous other attractions have been added to the ranch, including Loretta's personal museum, a replica of the coal mine her father worked in, a replica of her "Butcher Holler House," a Western store, and a gift shop.

Tours of the first floor of her antebellum plantation mansion are given daily. Make sure you ask the guide about the haunted aspects of the building. There is no charge to enter the ranch, but there is for the tours, museum, and other activities, including miniature golf and canoeing. There are dances every Saturday night during the summer, and Loretta schedules a few concerts during that time also. When she's home she enjoys walking around meeting people and signing autographs. Located 7 miles north of I–40; open April through October. (931) 296–7700.

A few miles north on Route 13, Hunter Pilkinton lives out his fantasy in his **World O'Tools.** "Everybody needs a world of something," said the lifelong collector. "Mine happens to be tools." Hunter's world contains more than 25,000 tools of all sorts and a large library of books and pamphlets about those tools. The museum is the result of a hobby that got out of control. A large building on the property contains his treasures.

The retired, personable Hunter has a story for each one of the items. It's best if you call first. "I may be out hunting for more tools and miss you." Located at 2431 Highway 13 South, approximately 2 miles south of the courthouse in Waverly and 5 miles north of the Loretta Lynn Ranch. (931) 296–3218.

Along the Tennessee River at Highway 70 is the Johnsonville Tennessee Valley Authority (TVA) facility. Built in 1950 it was the TVA's first major coal-fired power plant. Tours are given "when someone shows up who wants one." The length of tour and how long you might have to wait for one to start can vary depending on the workload of the staff at that particular time. It's most likely they'll find time for you Monday through Friday during the morning or on Saturday morning, up until noon.

One of the things to look for during the tour is the coal-unloading facilities. If you're lucky enough to be there on the day the coal is being unloaded from a barge, you'll see a huge crane in operation that is capable of unloading coal at a net rate of 700 tons an hour. The coal then goes by conveyer to the crusher building, which is a sight in itself. After you leave here, you'll have a real appreciation for electricity and the work that goes into producing it. (931) 535–8212.

Charlotte, the seat of Dickson County, looks much as it did in the mid-1800s. The circa-1834 courthouse is considered the oldest such building still in use in the state. Pre–Civil War buildings line the downtown square, and the old-timers still gather at the drugstore on the square to solve the world's problems.

But it could have been so different! The now quaint and quiet town was two votes short of becoming the capital of Tennessee. Only Nashville received more votes.

North of Charlotte, just off Highway 48, you'll find Norman Bowlby's collection of birds and goats. At any one time he has nearly one hundred birds, including four different species of peacocks, parakeets, turkeys, geese, several species of ducks and chickens, potbellied pigs, and llamas. You'll also find a few turkens—a half-chicken, half-turkey creation—walking around. "It's a hobby; I love exotic things," Bowlby said.

Five acres (including a small pond) of his 100-acre farm are dedicated to his birds and the goats. "The goats are a great clean-up crew," he noted. He loves company and is eager to show the birds to visitors. He's in the feeder-pig business and usually has a lot of baby pigs that he'll also be glad to show you. Call him first and let him know you're coming.

To find **Bowlby's nature park,** turn west on Harper Lane off Highway 48 just south of the BP service station. Then take a left on Old Highway 48 and go less than a half-mile to Daniel Lane. Take a right and Bowlby Lane is on your right a half-mile down the road. The animals are located in pens at the front of the property. (615) 789–5536.

When you leave the birds, go back out to Highway 48, take a left, and follow it to Dry Hollow Road a couple miles up the road from the Bowlby spread. Take another left and you'll enter the historic town of **Cumberland Furnace,** where an iron plantation village and iron furnaces thrived for nearly 150 years.

Today the area has more than thirty extant buildings related to the iron industry, and in 1988 the village was placed on the National Register as a Historic District. One of the owners of the iron business, Montgomery Bell, who bought the business in 1804, was the chief supplier of cannon shot to General Andrew Jackson's southern army in the War of 1812.

In 1891 the Louisville and Nashville Railroad built a branch line through the county with a spur to the village to serve the furnaces. The depot for that spur still stands today and is owned by the Travis family. The original circa-1891 building was destroyed by fire in 1919 when a load of hot slag fell on it. The one standing today was built in 1920.

Next to the depot is the big red commissary building. Built in 1870, it was moved to the present location in 1906 and served as a company store until the mid-1920s. For more information and for a detailed brochure of the history and a driving tour of the area, call George Jackson, president of the historic village association. (615) 446–1655.

Northern Heartland

The 170,000-acre peninsula between Kentucky Lake and Lake Barkley is owned and operated by the Tennessee Valley Authority and is aptly called the **Land Between the Lakes,** or LBL, as locals refer to it. About a third of it lies in Tennessee and the rest in Kentucky.

The area is an awesome display of nature. The Trace, the main north-south road, is 60 miles long, with southern entry just west of Dover off Route 79. There's plenty to do here, and according to the rangers, most of the area is underutilized.

In addition to all the hiking trails and water activities, there are more than 100 miles of paved roads for biking. The **Homeplace** is a nineteenth-century living-history museum with sixteen restored structures that were moved from other LBL locations and rebuilt. Costumed personnel work the farm, and most will take time from their chores to talk history with you.

Homeplace employees eat here, with all food prepared over the open fires and in the kitchens of the restored buildings. While walking through the kitchens, talk with the cooks. They have some great stories to tell about their past cooking experiences.

There is a fee for many of the attractions and there are several special events during the year that the LBL newsletter covers in detail. Call (phone number at the end of the next paragraph) for a free copy.

One of the unique events held here each year is the Habitat Helpers Weekend, which usually takes place in early May. The program was named one of the American Horticultural Society's Top 75 Events in 1997 and is based on how individuals can improve backyard habitats. Bird feeders, bat boxes, and wildlife gardens are explained, as are butterfly gardens and ways to attract the great mosquito conqueror, the Purple Martin. Takes place at the Nature Station. (800) LBL–7077.

Dover's Town and Country Restaurant, specializing in southern cooking, is a favorite among the locals for a good meal. You can order from the menu or partake of their breakfast, lunch, or dinner buffet. A special seafood buffet is offered on Friday and Saturday nights. Reservations are suggested for Saturday, especially during the summer. Open seven days a week from 5:00 A.M. to 9:00 P.M.; (931) 232–6930.

Although it has to share honors with Kentucky, Montgomery County is the home of the famed 101st Airborne Division—Air Assault of the

U.S. Army. ***The Fort Campbell Military Reservation*** covers more than 100,000 acres on the state line and is the county's largest employer.

The base is open, which means visitors are welcome as long as they pick up a pass at Gate 4 on Highway 41A. Located near the gate is the visitors center and the Don F. Pratt Memorial Museum. Named after Brigadier General Don Pratt, who was killed while leading the 101st Airborne's legendary glider assault into Normandy, the museum traces the history of the division from World War I through the present. Exhibits also depict the history of Fort Campbell and the land it occupies.

Probably the most interesting exhibit in the place is the replica of the fragile-looking glider that the members of the 101st Division used in France during the D-Day invasion of 1944. More than 14,000 of the canvas-covered cargo gliders were built during the war, with such unlikely businesses as the Steinway Piano and Heinz Pickle companies contributing to the effort.

Across the street from the large indoor portion of the museum is a lot with a large collection of tanks, artillery field pieces, and airplanes. Open every day 9:30 A.M. to 4:30 P.M.; admission free; (502) 798–3215.

Clarksville is the state's fifth-largest city, with a population of about 60,000, but it probably has the largest selection of architectural marvels of any one city in the state. "Anyone interested in architecture will have a field day in Clarksville," maintains the curator of the ***Clarksville-Montgomery County Historical Society.***

Any tour through the city should start at the historical society's headquarters at the corner of Commerce and Second Streets. Originally constructed as a U.S. Post Office and Customs House in 1898, its eclectic architecture consists of Italianate ornamentation, Far East–influenced slate roof, Romanesque arches, and Gothic copper eagles perched at each of the four corners.

Attached to the post office, the museum has a new 53,000-square-foot cultural center complete with a 200-seat auditorium, several different art galleries, classrooms, exhibit halls, and the state's best artisan gift shops. If you can't find something here, you're too picky!

Exhibits include one on the local tobacco industry and a salute to the local firefighters. This is one of the finest local museums in the state. Area tour maps can be picked up here. Open Tuesday through Sunday with the first Sunday of every month being "Free Sunday," when admission is free from 1:00 to 4:00 P.M.; admission is charged; (931) 648–5780.

There are two self-guided tours of the city and county—a 2-mile (twenty-five site) walking tour of the downtown architectural area and a 14-mile (fifty site) driving tour. One of the highlights of the walking tour is the Madison Street Methodist Church. Built in 1829 by a Jewish architect, the Star of David appears in the construction in at least two locations. Presumably they weren't discovered until after the architect got paid.

Clarksville has a proud river heritage, and to celebrate the relationship between the city and the mighty Cumberland River, the city is in the process of building the *Cumberland RiverWalk* along the banks of the river. Eventually it will meander along the downtown area of the river and will have several amphitheaters and a pedestrian bridge connecting it with the historic downtown area. Now, the completed section of lighted paths offers a good vantage point of the river.

Along the path near McGregor Park, the River Master's House serves as an interpretation center, offering visitors a historical, cultural, and commercial perspective of the river's longrunning importance to the region.

The entrance to the RiverWalk is defined by the International Avenue of the Flags, an area designed to honor the city's cultural diversity. It's quite a colorful site, especially on a windy day. The flags line Riverside Drive. Wilma Rudolph, the Olympic star, is a Clarksville native. A bronze statue of her was hand crafted and is now on display at the Clarksville-Montgomery County Museum. It will remain there until the city walk is completed, and then the life-sized statue will be moved to its permanent location along the river, where it will be a lasting tribute to the three-time gold medal champion.

Annually judged as one of the Top 20 March Events in the Southeast, the Old-Time Fiddlers' Championships is a unique visit for some great, authentic old-time music. It takes place at the Clarksville High School and with a large cash purse for the winners, attracts some great nationally known entertainers. One thing nice about this contest is that it takes place before the myriad outdoor music festivals are held during the summer throughout the state. It's like a warmup to get you excited about great Tennessee music. Categories include: Dancing 30 and Under, Harmonica, Dobro, Bluegrass Banjo, Mandolin, and Beginner Fiddler. (931) 647–2331.

Located in the Sango Community east of Clarksville on Highway 41A South is *Sango Mills,* a working farm and a wonderful attraction if you're into local production farms. Here you'll find apples, cider, breads, apple cider donuts, vegetables in season, and a whole lot of other fun and tasty stuff.

Sorghum cane (a natural sweetener similar to molasses) is grown on the farm and is harvested in the fall. Visitors are welcome to go out and watch the sorghum cooking process, or to watch fresh McAdoo Creek Corn Meal being ground. A dining area features white beans and cornbread, and the fried apple pies are the best in the area! Located at 154 Towes Lane; (931) 358–2637.

Just outside Clarksville is **Historic Collinsville,** an authentically restored nineteenth-century log pioneer settlement that's a lot of fun to visit. It's a great glimpse into what it was like living in this area of the state 200 years ago. The buildings have all been saved and moved to the village and lovingly restored by JoAnn and Glenn Weakley. There are now ten buildings, including a dog-trot house and several outbuildings. Annual events range from a quilt show to a Civil War encampment. Located off Highway 48/13 on Weakley Road. Admission charged. Open mid-May through mid-October, Thursday through Saturday 1:00 to 5:00 P.M. (931) 648–9141.

Montgomery County's answer to California's Napa Valley can be found at the **Beachaven Vineyards & Winery,** a few miles off I–24's exit 4. Co-owner Ed Cooke thinks his winery can offer as good a tasting tour as do his counterparts in California. "We offer the same thing, but we add southern hospitality," he said.

Beachaven's tasting concept is a great plus for those needing a little education before buying a wine. Ed or one of the employees will be glad to give you a taste of all their varieties. Tours are given year-round for those who would like to see how the fruit of the vine becomes so divine. And these wines are really divine. Wine judges across the country think so, too. Look at all those ribbons awarded to the various products of Ed and his family lining the walls. Their champagne is of "world renown," having been written up in the major wine books.

The most exciting (and aromatic) time to visit is in the fall while the crushing is taking place, but there is always something going on. During the summer special concerts are presented in the vineyard's picnic area. They can't sell by the glass, but they would be glad to sell you a chilled bottle to enjoy with your cheese during a concert. (931) 645–8867.

The **Dunbar Cave State Natural Area** is 110 scenic acres of true history and legend. The activities on this site range from when the local Indians inhabited the cave entrance 10,000 years ago to when country music legend and Grand Ole Opry star Roy Acuff owned the property and held weekly country music shows in the cave entrance.

A stately old bathhouse now serves as a visitors center and museum. If you want to take a cave tour, you have to call ahead and see when the group tours are being held. Even if you don't take the tour, the museum and the nature trails make this a fun place to visit. Fishing is permitted on the lake. Located on Dunbar Cave Road just off Highway 79, 4 miles from I–24 (exit 4). (931) 648–5526.

While new 1950s-style eateries currently are being built across the country, **Stratton's Restaurant and Soda Shop,** in Ashland City, continues quietly to serve up ice cream and hamburgers as it has since 1954. The interior of this neat little place is truly a blast from the past.

"Everything you see in here is authentic, I guarantee it," said Steve Stratton, the founder's son and the current owner. From a 1954 Seeburg jukebox to original Coca-Cola posters on the wall, Stratton takes great pride in preserving the past in his popular establishment.

Built by his father in 1954 as the Dairy Dip, Steve has been running it since 1972. Originally a carryout that sat twelve people inside, Steve remodeled in 1985, expanding the eat-in capacity to fifty, now after another expansion it's up to seventy-five.

Traditional platters are served with house-made coleslaw or hush puppies. Besides the tasty burgers, menu items also include grilled chicken sandwiches, chopped steak, and charbroiled chicken breast.

But save room for dessert! Twenty-ounce malts are made with Carnation powdered malt, and other tasty concoctions can be made from soft-serve or hand-dipped ice cream. They also make their own pies and cobblers.

You'll find Steve here every day except Sunday. Make sure you say hi to him; he'll be happy to share some of the history of the place with you. Located at 201 South Main Street; open 361 days a year; (615) 792–9177.

There have been ghosts and there have been legends, but the **Bell Witch of Adams** is probably the most documented story of the supernatural in all of American history. This witch is unique because of the large number of people who have had direct experience with it.

John Bell was a well-respected and influential member of the Adams community. He and his family lived on a thousand-acre plantation along the Red River. The trouble started in 1817 when bumping and scratching sounds were first noticed in the house, but the Bells passed them off as being caused by the wind. The big problems started in 1818, when continuous gnawing sounds were heard on each member of the family's bedposts each night. When someone would get up to investigate, it would stop. The sound would go from room to room until everyone was awake. Then it would stop until the candles were blown out and everyone went back to bed, when it would start all over again.

Things grew from there. People came to town to witness the occurrences and weren't disappointed. General Andrew Jackson came up to Adams from his Nashville home to investigate the matter but turned around when the wheels on his carriage mysteriously locked.

This has gone on through the decades. A few years ago, several reporters came to Adams with plans to stay in the Bell cave, where many of the experiences have occurred. They lasted a few hours before fleeing.

Today the **Bell Witch Cave** is open to those who think they are brave enough to possibly face the witch herself. Many have. Located off Highway 41 on Keysburg Road, the cave is open daily May through October but is closed during rainy periods due to possible flooding. Admission is $5.00 per person. (615) 696–3055.

All the Bell buildings are gone now, except for a small, log slave building. It has been moved to the grounds of the old elementary schoolhouse and is open for viewing. You can't miss the graves of the Bell family at the Bellwood cemetery. There's a magnificent tower marking the graves and a stone fence keeping the Bell Witch out.

If you'd like to meet some of the locals who can tell you some great Bell Witch stories while you enjoy some great country music, attend the **Bell Witch Opry,** held each Saturday night at 7:30 P.M. at the Old Bell School in Adams. For more than twenty years, the opry has featured local pickers and singers who want to entertain and have fun without the pressures of trying to make it big in nearby Nashville. If you want to appear on the stage, give Claude Warren a call at (502) 726–7847. If you want to join in on the local fun, drop by, or if you're coming from a distance, you might give Claude a call to see if the show is on for sure.

The **Tennessee-Kentucky Threshermen's Association** holds its annual wheat threshing and steam engine show on the grounds of the Old Bell School during the last part of July. Antique threshers, tractors, and hundreds of other steam engines are in action during the event. (502) 726–7847.

If you've ever wondered where those wild horses and burros that are rounded up from the western wilds go, you need not wonder anymore. Many of them come to Cross Plains and are adopted out of the *Southeastern Wild Horse and Burro Adoption Holding Center.* On any given day, the pens are full of animals from Nevada, Arizona, New Mexico, and California waiting for new homes.

The adoption program is a partial solution to the problems of overpopulation among wild horse and burro herds that roam public rangelands in ten western states. When this facility opened in 1979, it was the East's first way station for these animals. Due to budget cuts, it is now the last center in the East. The center is run by Randall and Paula Carr on their 1,000-acre farm and is funded by the federal government.

Each year during the last weekend in June, the center holds the *Tennessee Wild Horse & Burro Days* celebration and invites those who have adopted to bring back the animals and compete in the Middle Tennessee Mustang Association Horse Show. The adoption center is off Highway 25 just outside the village of Cross Plains. There's no charge unless you take a horse or burro home with you. In that case it'll cost you up to $125. Open one day a month for adoption. Call for the number of animals they have on hand and when adoption day is scheduled. (615) 654–7500.

Pharmacist Dan Green is now caretaker of a bit of history in Cross Plains. He and his wife, Debbie, are the owners of *Thomas Drugs* and its historic black and chrome antique soda fountain. While Green tends to the business of pharmacy, his soda jerk mixes up his own concoctions, from milkshakes to vanilla Cokes to ice-cream sundaes. Lunch is served Monday through Friday from 11:00 A.M. to 3:00 P.M. and includes an array of fresh sandwiches and soups.

In addition to the "regular" drugstore stuff, the store features antique reproduction toys and books, and local crafts including quilts and coverlets. Located at the corner of Main and Cedar Streets at the 4-way stop sign. Open Monday through Saturday; free; (615) 654–3877.

A few miles toward the interstate from "downtown" Cross Plains on Highway 25, turn north on Cedar Grove Road. Two miles down you'll find *Robin's Nest Orchards.* Open daily July through Christmas, Charles Robinson and his family feature peaches and apples as well as an unusually large and unique selection of gourmet food, including a lot of Tennessee jams and jellies. "We carry anything of quality that the grocery stores don't carry," Charles says.

The bakery features fried pies and other baked goods and sandwiches, as well as the best cider doughnuts you'll find anywhere! In September you can pick your own apples. Open 9:00 A.M. to 6:00 P.M. Monday through Saturday; 1:00 to 6:00 P.M. on Sunday; (615) 654–3797.

Head back toward I–65, and you'll find the large Red River Antique Mall at the interchange with Highway 25. Open daily.

Three miles east of I–65 at 3352 Highway 25 is the new, old-looking **Turner Station Country Store.** Built to look like an old country store, the store features some antiques, but mostly colorful and collectible advertising memorabilia. Proprietors Larry and Bev Turner, who live out behind the store, are open "around 10:00 A.M." and close "around 4:00 P.M. or later," Bev said. (615) 325–4610.

Three miles farther east on Highway 25, in the original downtown area of Cottontown, is **The Ole Store,** owned by Bill Summers, who has lived around here all his life. His store really is as old as it looks, and was a grocery store many years ago. He's got as many great stories and historical perspectives about the area as he has old appliances and collectable figurines. Open daily 9:00 A.M. to 5:00 P.M. (615) 452–7419.

In **White House,** on Highway 76, 1 mile east of I–65 at exit 108, next to the firehouse, is one of the most unique library and museum buildings you'll find anywhere in the state. It's a reproduction of the original White House Inn, which gave the area its name. The inn was a major stopover between Nashville and Louisville during the horse and buggy days.

The community library is on the first floor, the museum is on the second, and the chamber of commerce is out back in the bachelor's quarters. For a small community, they've done a splendid job in presenting a local history museum. Make sure you take a look at the firehouse next door and don't miss the fun statue of a Dalmatian dog out front. Nice touch! Open daily except Sunday; (615) 672–0239.

The downtown commercial area of Gallatin is quite the historic area. With more than twenty-five restored buildings, many of which pre-date the Civil War, the area has been listed on the National Register of Historic Places. Occupying some of those buildings are antiques shops and restaurants.

A block off the main square area, you'll find the **Sumner County Museum,** located behind the historic Trousdale Place. The museum, at 183 West Main Street, is the keeper of nearly a quarter million artifacts that tell the history of the county. Included in that collection are 475-million-year-old fossils and several displays featuring Native American and African American life in the area. Open seasonally and by appointment; (615) 451–3738.

Trousdale Place was the home to Tennessee Governor William Trousdale, who served the state from 1849 to 1851. The home has been restored and contains period antiques as well as a small Confederate library. Open Wednesday through Saturday 9:00 A.M. to 4:30 P.M. and Sunday 1:00 to 5:00 P.M. Admission is charged. (615) 452–5648.

In Castalian Springs, what may be the largest log structure ever erected in Tennessee still stands. **Wynnewood** was built in 1828 as a stagecoach inn and mineral springs resort, and by 1840 a row of cottages adjoining the inn had been built, as well as a horse racetrack.

The main house is 142 feet long with a dogtrot through the middle. Some of the logs, mostly oak and walnut, are 32 feet long. All the rooms have outside doors and are entered from a gallery that extends 110 feet across the back of the building. A stairway in the dogtrot goes to the second-story rooms.

Owned by the state, Wynnewood is located 45 miles northeast of Nashville, 8 miles east of Gallatin on Highway 25. It's open daily April through November. Admission is charged. (615) 452–5463.

About one hundred yards east of the entrance to Wynnewood is a stone monument marking the location of a giant, 9-foot-diameter sycamore tree in which Thomas Sharp Spencer lived during the winter of 1778–79. Spencer, the first white settler in middle Tennessee, called the tree home while he was building a cabin nearby.

Also located along Highway 25, about 5 miles from Gallatin, is **Cragfront,** one of the finest examples of Federal architecture in the state. Built between 1798 and 1802 by General James Winchester of Revolutionary War fame, the house has been restored and is open to the public. Open daily mid-April through October except for Monday. Admission is charged. (615) 452–7070.

PLACES TO STAY IN
THE HEARTLAND

CLARKSVILLE
Hachland Hill Inn B&B
1601 Madison Street
Rooms in 200-year-old
log guest houses
Furnished with antiques
(931) 647-4084

DICKSON
The Inn on Main Street B&B
112 South Main Street
Fireplace, cable TV,
children/pets accepted
(615) 441-6879

FRANKLIN
Lyric Springs
Country Inn B&B
7306 South Harpeth Road
Spa, gourmet meals,
fishing, hiking
(615) 329-3385

LAWRENCEBURG
Davy Crockett State Park
Camping, Highway 64
Swimming, restaurant, boat
rentals, fishing
(423) 762-9408

MANCHESTER
Tim's Ford State Park
Off Highway 50
Cabins and camp sites
Water skiing, boat rentals,
swimming, hiking
(931) 967-4457

MURFREESBORO
Rock Haven Nudist
Campground & Cabins
462 Rock Haven Road
Electricity, swimming,
grocery
(615) 896-3553

NASHVILLE
Opryland KOA
2626 Music Valley Drive
460 sites, 25 cabins
Free country music shows
(615) 889-0282

Union Station Hotel
1001 Broadway
Vintage Nashville
train station
Gold leaf mirrors,
Tiffany windows
(615) 726-1001

Westin Hermitage Hotel
At Sixth Avenue
and Unions Street
Beaux Arts design
(615) 244-3121

WARTRACE
Ledford Mill B&B
Rural setting next
to waterfall
Inside 1884 gristmill,
on historic registers
(931) 455-2546

Walking Horse Hotel
Downtown
Retail shops, restaurant,
and stables on premises
(931) 389-7050

PLACES TO EAT IN
THE HEARTLAND

ASHLAND CITY
Stratton's Restaurant
and Soda Shop
201 South Main Street
Hamburgers, hush puppies,
malts, and pies
Monday through Thursday
10:30 A.M. to 10:00 P.M., Friday and Saturday 10:30
A.M. to 11:00 P.M.
(615) 792-9177

ADAMS
Thomas Drugs
On corner of Main
and Cedar Streets
Soda fountain serving
lunch; vanilla cokes
Lunch Monday through
Friday 11:00 A.M. to 3:00 P.M.
(615) 654-3877

BELL BUCKLE
Bell Buckle Cafe
and Music Parlour
Hickory-smoked barbecue,
hand-squeezed lemonade
Food served seven days
a week
(931) 389-9693

CENTERVILLE
Breece's Cafe
On the square
Country cooking,
homemade pies
Monday through Saturday
5:00 A.M. to 8:00 P.M.,
Sunday 6:00 A.M. to 8:00 P.M.
(931) 729-3481

CHRISTIANA
Miller's Country Cafe
Meat and vegetables,
bluegrass music Friday
Blue Plate lunch Monday
through Friday 11:00 A.M.
to 2:00 P.M., dinner Friday
and Saturday 6:00
to 9:00 P.M.
(615) 893–1878

CLARKSVILLE
Buffalo Brady's
Wooden Nickel Pub
1009 South Riverside Drive
Family atmosphere,
selection of video games
Deli sandwiches,
 salads, pizza
Open daily for lunch
and dinner
(931) 552–1401

DICKSON
East Hills Restaurant
702 East College Street
Country cooking; chicken,
steak, country ham
Known for its coconut
homemade pies
Open daily for breakfast,
lunch and dinner
(615) 446–6922

DOVER
Dover's Town and Country
Restaurant
Highway 79
Southern cooking
favored by locals
Open seven days a week
from 5:00 A.M. to 9:00 P.M.
(931) 232–6930

EAGLEVILLE
Lynch's Restaurant and
Dairy Bar
At corner of Highway 41A
and Highway 99
Meat dish and three
vegetables for $3.00,
banana splits
Open daily 5:30 A.M.
to 8:30 P.M. except Sunday
(615) 274–6427

FAYETTEVILLE
Cahoots
Market Street
In old firehouse and city
jail; eat in a limestone cell
Monday through Saturday
10:30 A.M. to 9:00
or 10:00 P.M.
(931) 433–1173

FRANKLIN
Dotson's Restaurant
99 East Main Street
Popular local eatery;
family owned;
southern cooking;
bountiful breakfasts
Open daily for breakfast,
lunch and dinner
(615) 794–2805

LEBANON
Off the Square Cafe
109 South Cumberland
Inside Tennessee
Treasures Antique Shop
Luncheon specials, from
sandwiches to soups
(615) 444–6217

LEWISBURG
DC's Corner Diner
Located on the square
Chicago Dogs and other
food imported from Chicago
Open six days a week from
10:00 A.M. to 10:00 P.M.
(931) 270–5238

LYNCHBURG
Iron Kettle Restaurant
On the Square
Plate lunches daily,
home cooking
Monday through Saturday,
6:00 A.M. to 6:00 P.M.
(931) 759–4274

Miss Mary Bobo's
Boarding House
Southern traditional foods
served family style
One seating Monday
through Saturday at 1:00 P.M.
For reservations, a must,
call (931) 759–7394

MILTON
Manuel's Cajun
Country Store
Fried alligator; Cajun band
Friday and Saturday nights
Wednesday and Thursday
11:00 A.M. to 2:00 P.M.,
Friday and Saturday
11:00 A.M. to 9:00 P.M.
(615) 273–2312

MOUNT PLEASANT
Lumpy's Malt Shop
Malts, barbecue, fried
marshmallow and
banana sandwiches
Open Monday through
Thursday 5:30 A.M. to 8:00
P.M., Friday to 10:00 P.M.,
Saturday 6:00 A.M. to
10:00 P.M., Sunday
11:00 A.M. to 3:00 P.M.
(931) 379–9268

NASHVILLE

Alpine Bagels & Brews
422 21st Avenue South
Great bagels, toppings,
and bagelwiches
Monday through Friday
7:00 A.M. to 6:00 P.M.,
Saturday 8:00 A.M. to
4:00 P.M., Sunday 8:00 A.M.
to 3:00 P.M.
(615) 327–0055

The Bluebird Cafe
4104 Hillsboro Pike
Country superstar hangout
Hours vary
(615) 383–1461

Bongo Java Coffeehouse
2007 Belmont Boulevard
Great nontraditional food,
home of the NunBun
Open daily for
all three meals
(615) 385–5282

Boscos Nashville
Brewing Co.
1805 21st Avenue South
Brew pub known for
its pizza, sandwiches
Open daily for lunch
and dinner
(615) 385–0050

Cheeseburger Charley's
400 21st Avenue South
Healthy fast food
Veggie, turkey,
black bean burgers
Open daily, 10:30 A.M.
to 9:00 P.M.
(615) 327–0220

Curly's BBQ
Highway 100
At Natchez Trace
Texaco gas station
Open daily 6:30 A.M.
to 9:00 P.M.
(615) 673–6622

Farmer's Market
Eight Avenue North,
adjacent to
Bicentennial Mall
There are two restaurants
inside as well as the market
Open 5:00 A.M. to 9:00 P.M.
during summer. Shorter
hours in winter
(615) 880–2001

Fido
1821 21st Avenue South
Veggie paella, homemade
ratatouille, veggie lasagna
Monday through Friday
7:00 A.M. to 11:00 P.M.,
Saturday and Sunday
8:00 A.M. to 11:00 P.M.
(615) 385–7959

Harvy Washbanger
106 29th Avenue North
Eat, drink, and
do laundry here
Open seven days a week
(615) 322–WASH

Loveless Motel and Cafe
Highway 100
Fried chicken, country
ham, fresh biscuits
Monday through Friday
8:00 A.M. to 2:00 P.M. and
5:00 to 9:00 P.M., Saturday
and Sunday 8:00 A.M.
to 9:00 P.M.
(615) 646–9700

NASCAR Cafe
305 Broadway
NASCAR-themed,
memorabilia
All-American menu,
burgers, steaks
Open daily at 11:00 A.M.
for lunch and dinner
(615) 313–RACE

Nashville Palace
Music Valley Drive, across
from Opryland Hotel
Live music nightly
with delicious menu
Open daily 3:00 P.M. to 3:00
A.M. Food Service: 5:00 P.M.
to 11:00 P.M.
(615) 885–1540

Seanachie Irish Pub
& Restaurant
327 Broadway
Cobblestone floors,
gas lanterns
Contemporary Irish food,
fresh sea food
Open daily for lunch
and dinner
(615) 726–2006

NORMANDY

Cortner Mill Restaurant
1100 Cortner Mill
In historic mill,
part of Paris Patch Farm
Steak, ham, chicken, quail,
ribs, trout, beefalo
Open daily,
reservations needed
(931) 857–3017

SHELBYVILLE

Pope's Restaurant
Located on the Square
Deep-fried chicken livers
(931) 684–9901

The Western Plains

History on the Plains

Nathan Bedford Forrest, the notorious hard-riding Confederate cavalry officer known for his unexpected and often offbeat tactics, pulled off one of the Civil War's most interesting victories along the Tennessee River here in the fall of 1864. It was probably the first time in military history that a calvary force attacked and defeated a naval force. High atop Pilot Knob, the highest point in this part of the state, Forrest secretly assembled his troops. He had his eye on the Union army's massive supply depot, directly across the river.

At the time the depot had more than thirty vessels, most fully loaded and waiting to head out to Union forces. Stacks of supplies lined the wharf. Forrest attacked and caught the Yanks off guard. Within minutes all thirty vessels and the various warehouse buildings were on fire, and within two hours everything was destroyed. By nightfall Forrest's troops had vanished into the dense woods.

The land surrounding Pilot Knob is now known as the **Nathan Bedford Forrest State Park.** Atop the hill is a monument to Forrest. Also at the top is the **Tennessee River Folklife Center,** "designed to explore the relationship between the river and the people who use it."

Most of the exhibits incorporate segments of oral histories taken from the locals who "lived the life." Separate accounts recall the early industries and the music, religion, and community events of the area.

The most colorful audio presentation highlights the days when folks would gather at the river to welcome the big showboats to their landing. The biggest exhibit is **"Old Betsy,"** an entire workboat from the early musseling industry along the river. The most visual representation of early river life is from the Brownie camera of Maggie Sayre. She lived on

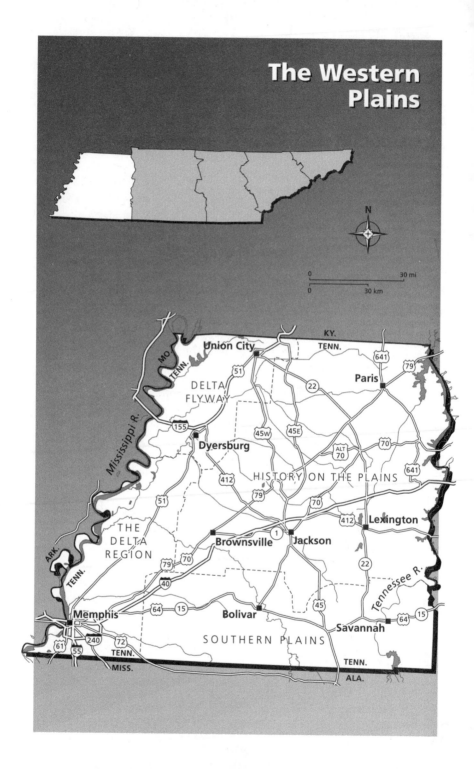

The Western Plains

Union City

Paris

51

641

79

MO.
TENN.

KY.
TENN.

DELTA
FLYWAY

22

155

45W

45E

70

Dyersburg

ALT
70

412

HISTORY ON THE PLAINS

641

79

70

51

THE
DELTA
REGION

412

Lexington

ARK.
TENN.

79

70

1

Brownsville

Jackson

22

Tennessee R.

40

Memphis

64

15

Bolivar

45

Savannah

64

15

61

240

72

55

TENN.

SOUTHERN PLAINS

TENN.

MISS.

ALA.

Mississippi R.

N

0   30 mi
0   30 km

**TIM'S TOP TEN PICKS
WESTERN PLAINS**

*Tennessee River
Folklife Center*

World's Largest Fish Fry

*Tennessee Strawberry
Festival*

*Buford Pusser Home
& Museum*

*Memphis Music Hall of
Fame, Museum & Archive*

*Danny Thomas Grave
& Gardens*

*Mindfield Outdoor
Sculpture*

*Tina Turner Resource
Center & Exhibit*

Dixie Gun Works

Flippins Hillbilly Barn

a houseboat for more than fifty years and photographed everyday life around her.

Most rural areas throughout the South have their own version of the liar's bench and the spit and whittle club. The view from the porch or from under the tree may be different from town to town, but the plot is the same. A story is told, then retold, then exaggerated to the point where it becomes a modern-day myth. A typical riverfront liar's bench has been reconstructed here at the center, with a breathtaking view of the Tennessee River far below. Walk up, push a button, and sit down and relax. The series of taped stories (from original spit and whittlers) will keep you in stitches.

The center is open Wednesday through Sunday 8:00 A.M. to 4:30 P.M. Admission free; (901) 584–6356. As you enter the park, the visitors center is to your right. Inside are several exhibits, including artwork and tanks containing local fish. Check here to see if the folklife center is open, if not, ask them and they will probably send someone up with you. The historical park area offers camping, hiking trails, and picnic areas. Both areas are located at the end of Highway 191, about 10 miles out of Camden.

Tennessee ranks twelfth in the nation in sorghum production, and Benton County is one of the largest producers in the state. Madison and Donice Furr run the **Tennessee Sorghum Company,** one of the largest operations in the county.

Sorghum is used mainly as a sweetener and is rich in vitamins. It's used in gingerbread and is poured over hot biscuits and butter. "It's very good and very healthy for you," claims Donice. "We sell a lot of it to health food stores."

The Furrs grow about thirty acres of sorghum cane and produce their own syrup. They also buy from other Benton County sorghum producers and market the product under the Tennessee Sorghum Company moniker. Locally produced honey is also available.

The most aromatic time to visit the Furrs's operation is in the fall when the sorghum cane is being stripped of its juices and cooked down to the right consistency. The cooking is done down at the Furrs's farm, and the marketing and packaging takes place at their warehouse in Camden.

Donice welcomes visitors to the farm and promises to let them stick a finger in the cooking sorghum for a once-in-a-lifetime taste treat. The farm is located off Highway 192 about 5 miles north of Holladay. Call her and see if anything is going on the day you want to go out, and she'll give you specific directions. (901) 584–3322.

Talented country music star **Patsy Cline** was killed on March 5, 1963, when her airplane crashed just outside Camden, Tennessee. Today, there's a small monument marking the spot, way off the main road, down a gravel path. The monument was set up to honor Cline and those killed with her: Cowboy Copas, Hawkshaw Hawkins, and Randy Hughes. Next to the monument is a mail box where fans can drop off fan letters. There's also a gazebo with newspaper articles describing the careers of the stars and the monument itself.

Located deep in the woods 12 miles north of I–40, off Highway 641. Just north of Highway 70, turn west on Mt. Carmel Road at Shell gas station, go 3 miles, turn right onto gravel road. Be careful and don't go too far— there's a big dropoff at the end of the path.

There's no place better than an organized wildlife refuge to observe that area's wildlife population, and the **Tennessee Wildlife Refuge** is no exception. Nature trails, paved roads, and observation points are plentiful in this 80-mile-long area along the Tennessee River. The area is an important resting and feeding place for migrating waterfowl each winter.

Beginning about mid-October, up to 100,000 Canada geese and 250,000 ducks start their annual fall trek to the refuge where they will spend the winter. The major attraction here for the animals is the farming program, which provides them with a great deal of food all winter long.

In addition to the waterfowl, the refuge is home for more than 200 species of birds, a fact that brings in serious bird-watchers from all over the country. Maps, brochures, and specific wildlife information is available. Open daily, year-round; (901) 642–2091.

In nearby Paris the *"World's Largest Fish Fry"* is held at the end of each April. Since the early 1950s the city has hosted the event at the fairgrounds and has achieved a (well-deserved) reputation for the quality of its catfish dinners and the traditional Tennessee way of preparing them.

Each year more than 10,000 pounds of fish are cooked in black pots containing more than 250 gallons of vegetable oil. The four-day event also includes a rodeo, a carnival, a three-hour parade, and a fishing rodeo.

For a good bologna or ham and cheese sandwich, or for a bucket of

ALSO WORTH SEEING IN THE WESTERN PLAINS

minnows, crickets, worms, or chicken livers, stop by *Culpepper's Store.* Owners Trenton and Rita Ward can usually be found there as can Baby, their poodle. "We call ourselves a country place inside the city limits," Rita said. The small store specializes in bait and fishing supplies, as well as food and drink for the fishermen. Rita, who was born in Germany, is a favorite among the returning servicemen at nearby Fort Campbell. "As soon as they get back from Germany, they come in and want to show me how much German they learned while they were over there. It's also fun for me to hear about their impressions of my country."

Look for the American flags flying just inside the city limits on Route 69A. Even if you don't need any bait, stop by; Rita and Trenton will tell you about the area and some of the people who live around here. Open every day; (901) 642–8230.

Here it is, a sugar heaven if ever I tasted one! With more than 100 varieties of freshly made candies, *Sally Lane's Candy Farm* is a stop I make every time I'm in the Paris area. Founded in 1958, the store has customers who regularly drive up to a couple of hours to get here. In addition people in forty-eight states use mail order to receive their treats, which range from hand-dipped chocolates to hard candies to the famous Kentucky Lake Frog, a chocolate, caramel, and pecan concoction. Make sure you try the divinity; it's made from scratch and is totally awesome, as are most of the goodies. It's the store's pink and green mints, though, that put them on the map. "We literally make tons of mints each year," said candy makers and store owners Jerry and Jean Peterson.

Look for the blue-and-white neon sign along Highway 79 near the Highway 218S intersection, and you'll find Sally's located in a cute little pink house. They close down on Christmas Day and stay closed for most of January as they prepare their Valentine's Day treats. Otherwise they are open every Tuesday through Sunday. (901) 642–5801.

Chucalissa Archaeological Museum, Memphis, (901) 785–3160

Memphis Botanic Garden, Memphis, (901) 685–1566

Memphis in May International Festival, month-long on weekends, Memphis, (901) 525–4611

West Tennessee Strawberry Festival, first week of May, Humboldt, (901) 784–1842

Tennessee River Bluegrass Festival, early July, Savannah, (901) 925–5595

Saltillo River Days, mid-October, Saltillo, (901)687–3697

Teapot Festival, mid-May, Trenton, (901) 855–2013

Britton Lane Battlefield, Jackson, (901) 935–2209

Tennessee Iris Festival, late April, Dresden, (901) 364–3787

International Washer Pitchin' Contest, late August, Yorkville, (901) 643–8110

And what would Paris be without the Eiffel Tower? There's a 65-foot scale model version of the famous structure standing at the entrance of Memorial Park on Volunteer Drive, east of downtown between Highways 69A and 79. Each year in mid-September *Eiffel Tower Days* are celebrated in Memorial Park with an arts and crafts show, classic car show, family activities, live entertainment, and a barbecue cook-off. Great fun, and probably the only celebration of its kind, outside the "real" Paris.

The E.W. Grove–Henry County High School was the first privately funded, public high school in the state. Know locally as the school "that came out of a bottle," the building was funded from the proceeds of "Grove's Tasteless Chill Tonic." Today the tower building houses the Henry County Board of Education and is located on Grove Boulevard, at the highest elevation in West Tennessee. Turn off Veterans Drive onto Dunlap Road, just north of Highway 79. Turn right onto Grove Boulevard and go to top of hill.

If you'd like to get a closer look at some of the historic structures in West Tennessee's oldest incorporated community, an audiotaped walking tour is available. Cassette players, tapes, and maps can be had at the Chamber of Commerce, W.G. Rhea Library, and the Paris–Henry County Heritage Center at no charge. The chamber is located at 2508 East Wood Street. (901) 642–3431; www.paris-net.com

Gordon Browning's first driver's license is on display at the *Gordon Browning Museum* in the old post office building in downtown McKenzie. What makes that license so special is that it is *Tennessee's First Driver's License.*

Browning got it because he happened to be governor of the state in 1938, when licenses were first required. In all, Browning served three terms as governor. He was also a U.S. congressman, a chancery court judge, and he served in both world wars; by the looks of the quantity of the memorabilia on display, he never threw anything away. A flag that he brought back from World War I is on display, as are various other patriotic mementos.

The museum is a great small-town collection dedicated to the life of the county's favorite son. It gives a good perspective on the values that he and the curator of the museum deemed important.

Patricia Clark is the curator for the county historical society and can tell you everything you need to know about this man. The museum is open Monday, Tuesday, Thursday, and Friday 9:00 A.M. to 5:00 P.M. Admission is free. The museum is at 640 North Main Street; (901) 352–3510.

Actress Dixie Carter was born and raised in McLemoresville, population 311. Even though she left town and became a successful star, she comes back home each year for several weeks to enjoy Tennessee and her family and friends. Her house is just off the little business section, and just about anyone around can point it out to you. **The Carroll County Museum** is located behind the fire station just off Highway 70A. Run by a spirited group of volunteers, the museum highlights the history of the community, as well as the entire county. The facility is dedicated to the late Billy O. Williams, who was the county's poet laureate and an associate poet laureate of the state. An exhibit honors his literary contributions and displays some of his printed, as well as unpublished, poetry, according to his sister, Rachel McKinney, who helps run the museum. Open Friday and Saturday afternoons by chance or appointment. If you get there and no one is around, call the phone number posted on the door, and someone will come over and let you in. (901) 986–4563.

When bare-knuckled pugilism was popular and legal in America during the first half of the nineteenth century, one area of Gibson County was well known for its unique version of prize fighting sans gloves.

Skullbone and the surrounding *"Kingdom of Skullbonia"* hosted a type of fighting that became known as skullboning. All bare-knuckled punches had to be delivered to the head. Hits below the collar were not permitted and considered fouls.

To "play," fighters would stand opposite each other and take turns trading blows. Each round lasted until one would fall to the ground. The match lasted until one was satisfied that he had had enough.

After bare-knuckled fighting became illegal in America and communities went "underground" for the excitement, matches in Skullbone continued to be held in the open. When adoption of standard rules for prizefighting occurred in 1866, nongloved activities died out just about everywhere except Skullbone, where it continued well into the twentieth century.

Today just about all that remains of Skullbone is the general store, built in 1848. It has been owned since 1964 by Landon and Ruby Hampton and is known locally as **Hampton's General Store,** widely as the Skullbone Store.

The busy little store serves what is left of the "kingdom." Yellowed newspaper clippings of the area's heyday hang on the wall. Outside, the building is quite a landmark. With a map of the Kingdom of Skullbonia painted on one side and various soft drink signs and paintings on the front, a stranger can't drive by without stopping to investigate.

Across the street a stacked row of directional road and mileage signs point the way to worldly centers such as Singapore, 9,981 miles; Anchorage, 3,320 miles; and Shades Bridge, 1 mile.

In addition to the regular fares of a country store, the Hamptons sell souvenir T-shirts. Skullbone isn't on most maps, but the Hamptons are trying to get Tennessee's governor to put it on the official state map. It's located on Highway 105 about 3 miles from Bradford. Open every day; (901) 742–3179.

It's amazing that just 3 miles away from the skullbone capital of the world one can find the **Doodle Soup Capital** of that same world.

What is Doodle Soup? It's a cold-weather dish, not good during summer because of its spicy nature. It's actually more of a sauce or gravy than it is a real soup. One of the most popular methods of eating it is by pouring it over a plateful of cracker crumbs or homemade biscuits, and letting it soak in for a while before eating.

Here is one of the "official" recipes. Be forewarned: There has been a battle going on for years as to which of the myriad recipes floating around should be considered official.

Take a large broiler chicken. Melt butter and run it all over the chicken. Put in broiler pan, split side down; salt to taste. Put in oven at 375 degrees; let cook until brown and tender. Take chicken out of the drippings that were cooked out in the pan. Add eleven cups of water, one cup vinegar, plenty of hot peppers, three tablespoons of cornstarch so it won't be just like water and will stay on biscuits good. Let cook until it gets as hot as you want. Taste it along.

Although it's a local tradition, most locals haven't eaten it, saying it sounds too greasy.

In **Trenton** at the municipal building you'll find the **world's largest collection of eighteenth- and nineteenth-century night-light teapots** (veilleuses-théières). A New York doctor, originally from Trenton, was going to give his multimillion-dollar collection of 525 pieces to the Metropolitan Museum of Art in New York City, but his brother convinced him to give them to his hometown instead.

Originally displayed in the trophy cases at the local high school, the unique collection found a permanent home when a new city building was built. The teapots now line the walls of the city's chambers. If you get there during regular business hours, you're welcome to walk around and study this one-of-a-kind collection. If you happen to get there late, a sign on the front door directs you to police headquarters, where a friendly policeman will hand over the key to city hall on the promise that you'll lock up and return the key before you leave town. Admission free; (901) 855–2013.

Up Highway 45W from Trenton is Rutherford, where a former home of Davy Crockett is open to the public. David (as residents prefer him to be called) moved to the area in 1823. His original cabin, built 5 miles east of town along the Obion River, was dismantled and stored with the intent of rebuilding it at a later

Signpost, Skullbone

date near where his mother is buried. But before it could be rebuilt, some of the logs were used in fires by campers.

Some of the logs were saved, though, and are now a part of the reproduction of that original cabin. On display are tools, furniture, and utensils from the period as are letters that Crockett wrote home during his years in Congress. The grave of Rebecca Hawkins Crockett, Davy's mother, is next to the log home.

The cabin is open from the end of May through Labor Day weekend. It's located on the city's grammar school property on Highway 45W. Open daily; admission is charged. (901) 665–7166.

Farther up Highway 45W you'll find an amazing colony of **White Squirrels,** one of only a few such colonies in the world. As you enter **Kenton,** a town of about 1,500 residents, you'll be greeted by a big sign proclaiming, KENTON: HOME OF THE WHITE SQUIRRELS. Although the exact number is hard to pinpoint, as most white squirrels look alike, the city's official stance is that about 200 of the critters live here. The squirrels are fed by just about everybody, and there's a $50 fine if you kill one.

A wildlife biologist explains that the animals are actually "albino gray squirrels who have survived for so long because the people have taken such good care of them." They have inbred for so long that the normally recessive albino trait has become predominant.

Exactly how the first such squirrels came to the area about 120 years ago is the subject of a great many speculations. The most common theory is that during the early 1870s a band of Gypsies spent the night on a local farm. The next morning, in appreciation of the farmer's kindness, the leader of the Gypsies presented two white squirrels to the farmer. Thus it began.

The best time to see the flock (bevy? herd?) of white squirrels is in the morning and evening when they are most apt to be scurrying from tree to tree. Stop by the city hall, which also informally serves as a white squirrel visitors information bureau.

Across the county from Kenton is Humboldt, home of the **West Tennessee Strawberry Festival** each May. It features a big parade, which is promoted as the longest non-motorized parade in the nation, a street dance, a checkers tournament, a strawberry recipe contest, and a carnival with all sorts of family and kiddie amusement rides, plus any kind of strawberry-flavored food you can think of.

A museum for a strawberry festival? Yep, this may be the only one of its kind. The West Tennessee Historical/Strawberry Festival Museum is located on the first floor of the 1912 restored neoclassical building, which once served as city hall. The museum salutes local Humboldt history as well as the history of the popular festival, from its beginning in 1934 to its latest event.

The **West Tennessee Regional Arts Center** is located on the upper floors, over the strawberry exhibits. It represents works of regional artists throughout Tennessee as well as surrounding states, including Red Grooms, Paul Harmon, Carroll Cloar, and Gilbert Gaul. The valuable collection was owned by a local doctor who donated it in honor of his parents and for the aesthetic education of students of all ages.

The museum and the arts center are open Monday, Wednesday, and Friday 9:00 A.M. to 4:00 P.M. at 1200 Main Street. Admission charged. (901) 784–1842.

The spirit in the small community of Green Frog is to capture the feel of rural West Tennessee of days gone by. Today there are seven buildings making up this privately owned community, located on Highway 412, 14 miles west of Jackson in Bells. The buildings are all original to this area of the state and were saved, dismantled, brought here, and restored. Each houses a shop or a store now, including an ice cream parlor and a candy store. The antiques shop is housed in an old mule barn with vendors set up in the original mule stalls.

The star of the community is the Grist Mill Restaurant, housed in the old ... well, you figure that one out. There's a luncheon Blue Plate Special each day for $4.95, and on Sunday, there's an old-fashioned Sunday dinner, featuring one meat, three veggies, bread, and dessert for $6.95. There are several salads and sandwiches on the menu, and of course, they serve frog legs.

Open Wednesday through Saturday 11:00 A.M. to 9:00 P.M. and Sunday 11:00 A.M. to 3:00 P.M. Closed Monday and Tuesday. (901) 663–FROG.

Crockett County was established in 1871 and named in honor of the famed Tennessee frontiersman, Davy Crockett. The county seat of the 14,000 residents of the county is Alamo, where the Crockett Times newspaper has been published for more than 120 years. (901) 696–4558.

Crockett had already been killed when the county was formed, so when it came to finding a name for the new county, locals thought naming an entire county after the man would be an appropriate tribute. Cageville was renamed Alamo and became the county's center.

Crockett never lived in the county and there is no record that he ever visited here, but the people are proud of their living monument to one of the state's best-known sons.

Remember the Elvis Presley hit of 1956, "Blue Suede Shoes"? It was written by the late Tennessean Carl Perkins, who spent his teen years in Jackson. Today the walls of **Suede's,** Perkins's restaurant in Jackson, are lined with his personal collection of memorabilia from the early rock years. You'll find a telegram from the Beatles, gold records, photographs, and a showcase with several of Perkins's stage costumes.

Among the items you'll find on the menu in this family eatery are "Rockabilly Sandwiches" featuring fish, hamburgers, and country ham; "Bopping the Blues" west Tennessee barbecue; and "A Whole Lota Steaking Going On," a choice of grilled steaks. There's also a great children's menu featuring pizza, hamburgers, and chicken. The restaurant is run by Perkins's son-in-law, Bart Swift, who takes great pride in pointing out the more outstanding pieces of memorabilia to guests.

Suede's is located 1 block off I–40 exit 82A at 2263 North Highland

Tennessee's Only Archeofest

A unique two-day festival takes place each fall deep in the heart of Pinson Mounds State Archaeological Park. Archeofest is a celebration of Native American culture and archaeology and features Native American dancers, haywagon tours, story- telling, Native American foods and crafts, wildlife programs, flint knapping, and artifact identification. And it's all FREE. Pinson Mounds is a 1,086-acre prehistoric Indian ceremo- nial center containing the second highest mound in the United States. The fest takes place the last week- end of September. Located off Highway 45, south of I–40, southeast of Jackson. (901) 988–5614.

Avenue. Open Monday through Saturday 11:00 A.M. to 9:00 P.M. and Sunday 11:00 A.M. to 2:00 P.M.; (901) 664–1956.

Take a right on Highland Avenue as you leave Suede's, and about 5 miles later, you'll be at the Jackson Courthouse Square, where you'll find several antiques stores. Right off the square, the West Tennessee Farmers Market features fresh- from-the-garden produce and flowers during the growing season. Located at New Market Street and North College, the covered market is open daily, except Sunday, and features various activi- ties and festivals during the year.

Jackson's original Greyhound Bus Terminal is still in operation and is as beautiful as ever in its 1920s art-deco glory! Several movies have been filmed here, and it's a popular spot for still pho- tographers from all over the mid-South. Located across from city hall at North Cumberland and East Main Streets.

A few blocks from downtown Jackson, on South Royal Street just after you cross the railroad tracks on your left, is the site of the city's first modern waterworks. During its construction in the mid-1880s, one of the area's most prolific underground mineral rivers was discovered. By the early 1900s thousands were visiting and drinking water from this artesian well, searching for a cure for their stomach, liver, and kidney ailments. Today the powerful *Electro Chalybeate Well* still bubbles forth inside a gazebo built adjacent to the city's restored art-deco water plant. A small park separates the well from the railroad tracks. Cham- ber of Commerce; (901) 425–8333.

On the other side of the tracks is a local railroad museum, created inside the restored turn-of-the-century railroad depot. The city pur- chased the depot from the railroad, who had not used it for twenty years and had plans to tear it down. Restoration was completed in 1994, and it was opened as a museum in late 1995. Inside are exhibits, photos, a model railroad, and other memorabilia that tell the story of the five different railroads that serviced Jackson through the years. Known locally as the N.C. & St. L Railroad Depot, the museum is open Monday through Saturday 10:00 A.M. to 3:00 P.M. (901) 425–8223.

You can bet on one thing if you decide to stay at the **Highland Place Bed & Breakfast** in Jackson: You'll find a well-designed inn. In 1995 the circa-1911 mansion was the designer showcase home for the Jackson area. Over a three-month period, twenty-five interior decorators and three landscape designers did their best to create the best.

Innkeepers Janice and Glenn Wall are mighty proud of their facility and are quite the congenial Southern hosts. Rooms start at $75 per night. While you're here, pick up a copy of the cookbook Janice wrote, it's called *Magic Potions—Favorite Recipes from the Good Times of Our Lives.* Located at 519 Highland Avenue. (901) 427–1472; www.bbon-line.com/tn/highlandplace/

"Come all you rounders if you want to hear a story about a brave engineer." That's the beginning of the tale of Casey Jones, an engineer who became a legend after being killed in a much-publicized train crash. The **Casey Jones Home and Railroad Museum** tells the story of that fateful night. Casey was at the throttle of "Old 382" when it approached a stalled train on the same track near Vaughn, Mississippi, on April 30, 1900. The fireman jumped, and yelled to Casey to do the same, but instead he stayed on and valiantly tried to stop the train. He didn't succeed, but he slowed it down enough so that he was the only casualty of the wreck. The engineer immediately became a folk hero, and his story has been recounted for more than a half-century in story and song.

Casey was living in Jackson at the time of his death. His home has since been moved and now serves as the centerpiece of the museum, located in Jackson's Casey Jones Village on the Highway 45 Bypass, just off I–40. In addition to the museum, the village contains specialty shops and the **Brooks Shaw and Son Old Country Store,** a country restaurant complete with an 1880s-style soda fountain and large gift shop. Shops are free; admission is charged to the museum, which is open daily, year-round. Call the country store and restaurant at (800) 784–9588 and the museum at (901) 668–1222.

Along historic Front Street in Henderson, Hugh Harville's two businesses are bringing worldwide attention to this small community. Known throughout the world for the soft plastic fishing lures he creates, the **Harville Manufacturing Co.** creates and ships out nearly five million lures a year.

Three doors down from the factory, at 125 Front Street, his retail outlet, **Hugh's Tackle Box,** sells "several million" more lures, according to the entrepreneur. He invented the machines the lures are made on, and he not

Casy Jones Home and Railroad Museum, Jackson

only sells his own brand but he also makes custom lures for other companies, who package them under their own brand names, and makes and ships out soft plastic lure parts for those who want to assemble their own lures.

Located in historic, pre–Civil War buildings, Harville has been in the business since the late 1960s. Due to insurance and security reasons, Hugh can't offer tours of his manufacturing plant, but if you stop by his retail store and he's around, he'll be happy to chat about fishing and, more specifically, about lures with you. Open Monday through Friday 8:00 A.M. to 4:30 P.M.; (901) 989–5846.

Covering 43,000 acres, the **Natchez Trace State Resort Park** is Tennessee's largest state-run facility. It is also the home of the **"World's Third Largest Pecan Tree."** The tree is 106 feet tall, has a spread of 136 feet, and was planted in 1815. Legend says that one of General Andrew Jackson's men returning home from the Battle of New Orleans gave a pecan to a man called Sukey Morris, who then planted it because he didn't want to eat it.

The size of the tree is quite impressive, but what is more amazing is that the tree has been chronicled, by photos, almost since its "birth." Those photos are on display at the park's visitors center. The tree still gives a few pecans, but as one ranger said as she looked up at the tree, "It's hardly worth the effort to try and eat one. They aren't that good."

The massive park, with its lakes, trails, and heavily forested areas, is a success story for one of President Roosevelt's New Deal programs. When the U.S. Department of Agriculture acquired the land in the early 1930s, the area was some of the most heavily abused and eroded land in the state. The area's occupants were relocated, and a "Land-Use Area" project was set up to demonstrate how wasteland could again be made productive through proper conservation practices.

Picturesque **Pin Oak Lodge and Restaurant,** situated in a heavily wooded area of the park next to a lake, offers some of the best food and lodging in this part of the state. Cabins, a swimming beach, family camping, off-road vehicle trails, fishing, boating, and miles of hiking are other attractions at the park. Open year-round; (901) 968–3742.

Each April coon hunters gather at the Decatur County fairgrounds just south of Parsons on Route 69 to take part in an event that is billed as the *"World's Largest Coon Hunt."* Depending on the year and the weather, about 600 hunters from thirty-five states come here to hunt for the state's "official" animal, the raccoon.

This is basically a competition for dogs, so no guns are allowed and no coons are hurt. The hunter with the dog who does the best "tracking and treeing" goes away as the winner. Since coons are nocturnal, most of the action on this weekend takes place at night. A country band plays until 3:00 A.M., and the local Jaycees keep their concession stands open around the clock for the entire weekend.

The event is considered to be the biggest independent fund raiser for *St. Jude's Children's Research Hospital* in Memphis. More than $100,000 are raised and donated each year.

If you're in the area on a Monday, make sure you drop by the *County Courthouse* in Decaturville. That's when the judges come to town for court. The circuit and juvenile courts are held each Monday, and there's usually a crowd gathered to watch the action. "It's a real big and busy day around here, especially if there's a murder trial going on," said one local observer.

As you drive the highways of life, some roadside eateries jump out and seem to pull you off the road by some unseen force. It almost feels as if you have no choice but to stop and check things out. *Broadway Farms* is one of these. The inviting, rustic-looking restaurant is located along Old Perryville Road, Highway 100, 3 miles east of Decaturville.

Open Friday through Sunday, the folks here specialize in country cooking. On the front of the menu, they state their guarantee that you'll like their food: "We aim to please . . . if'n we don't, just holler at us and we'll shore try!" There's a seafood buffet every Friday and Saturday night, a special Sunday buffet, fried catfish (fillet or whole fry), country ham dinners, barbecue pork dinners, clams, fried shrimp, hamburgers, and a great kids' menu. All meals, except for steak, are served with hush puppies!

What a fun and funky place to give in to your hunger pangs. Open Friday and Saturday at 5:00 P.M. and on Sunday at noon; (901) 852–4559.

Down the road apiece, where Highway 100 meets Highway 412, is the little riverside community of Perryville. In town, up on the very top of

Pentecostal Hill, the **Tennessee River Flea Market** does business year-round every Friday through Sunday. Carl and Evelyn Moore have taken over an old church camp and now feature more than fifty dealers within their 12,000-square-foot building. What a collector's heaven this is! You'll find some great stuff, and the best part, it's off the beaten path. Follow Pentecostal Campground Road to the top; (901) 847–9383.

Southern Plains

The *Shiloh National Military Park and Cemetery,* 12 miles south of Savannah on Route 22, is a grim reminder of how bloody the Civil War really was.

On April 6 and 7, 1862, the North and South fought the first major battle in the western theater of the war here, just a few miles north of the Mississippi state line. More than 23,000 soldiers, about one-fourth of the total forces that fought, were casualties. The casualties in this one battle exceeded the total American casualties from the nation's three preceding wars, the Revolutionary War, the War of 1812, and the Mexican War.

Known as Bloody Shiloh, the battle went down in the history books as one of the most gruesome in all American warfare. The park was established in 1894 and includes the battlefield and environs. A 9-mile self-guided auto tour highlights the battle and explains the various monuments that have been erected. The visitors center has a library and a museum complete with relics and maps and a movie explaining the battle. Open daily, year-round; admission is charged; (901) 689–5275.

For a month prior to the Shiloh battle, the Union forces, under the leadership of General Ulysses S. Grant, used the grounds of **Cherry Mansion,** 101 Main Street in nearby Savannah, as Union headquarters. Tents were set up in the yard, and Grant slept in the house and dined with the Cherry family. He was eating breakfast on April 6 when he got word of the battle of Shiloh.

Built in 1830 the house is the oldest structure in Savannah and is currently a private residence. The owner doesn't mind your taking pictures and looking at the exterior of the house, but please be considerate.

South of Shiloh, in the small community of Counce, the Packaging Corporation of America has developed an **arboretum** on its corporate property. Pull into the parking lot off Highway 57 and follow the signs directing you to the paved nature trails that will lead you into the woods. There you'll find seventy native tree species from Tennessee, Mississippi, and Alabama. The trees are well marked and the walk is an easy one and is handicapped accessible. Brochures are available at the gate. Open daily during daylight hours; free; (901) 689–1274.

The Tennessee River Museum in Savannah is a tribute to the Tennessee River—from Paducah, Kentucky, to Muscle Shoals, Alabama—and the influences it has had on the people who lived and worked along it. Several exhibit areas include displays on the early steamboats that plied the river, paleontology, archaeology, the Civil War, and a great collection of locally made musical instruments. Several gunboats are on display. Officials say their ceremonial "Shiloh Effigy Pipe" is world famous. Located in the old post office building at 507 Main Street, the museum is open daily, year round. (800) 552–3866.

About 11 miles north of Savannah on Highway 128, take a left turn at the Saltillo Ferry sign and go down to the river. The *Saltillo Ferry* is owned by Hardin County and runs Monday through Saturday 6:00 A.M. to 4:00 P.M. For $1.00 you can take your car for a ride across the Tennessee River to Saltillo. Blow your horn if the ferry is on the other side.

Both Saltillo and Cerro Gordo were named after Mexican communities by soldiers returning to their Tennessee farmlands following the Mexican War. A brochure listing seventeen points of interest in Saltillo is available from city hall.

The signs along Highway 64 outside *Adamsville* proclaim the community to be the "Biggest Little Town in Tennessee." A lot of that obvious pride may come from the fact that the town was home to one of America's most celebrated lawmen, Buford Pusser.

Pusser, who died in an auto accident in 1974, is immortalized today in the *Buford Pusser Home and Museum,* located at 342 Pusser Street. He was sheriff of McNairy County from 1964 to 1970 and had the reputation of a no-nonsense, hard-nosed lawman. The exploits of this 6-foot, 6-inch tall, 250-pound "legend" were the basis of the three *Walking Tall* movies.

Today in the quiet residential area that he called home, his brick ranch house is overflowing with artifacts of his life. Following his death, his mother allowed nothing to be removed. Opened officially in 1988 as a museum, the facility is owned and operated by the city. Everything from his credit cards to his toothbrush to the roll of $100 bills he had in his pocket when he was killed are on display. An advertisement from a mattress company rests on his bed. "Big Buford Bedding, designed to honor a man who walked tall in Tennessee."

The years he spent as sheriff were hard ones on this "soft-spoken country gentleman." He was shot eight times, knifed seven times, and gunned down in an ambush that killed his wife. Many residents believe the flaming auto crash that took his life was no accident.

According to the museum's hostess, Pusser was constantly on guard and often remarked that he was "on borrowed time." His home is a reflection of that attitude. He had a special entrance built on the lower level, where his underground bedroom and living quarters were. He slept with his head against the earthen wall to help protect himself against the continuous threats.

In addition to his personal belongings, numerous scrapbooks of newspaper clippings, a videotape of television interviews, and a copy of his 1956 high school yearbook are on display. Admission is charged. (901) 632–4080.

Up Highway 224 near Leapwood, the **Coon Creek Science Center** reveals that this whole area was under a sea about 70 million years ago. The center, opened in late 1989, is owned and operated by the Memphis Museum System, although it is more than 100 miles from that city.

When emptied, the warm, shallow ocean left behind an abundance of unusual and significant geological treasures. The marine shells found here in the bottomlands are not actually fossils but the real things, since they have not undergone the process of mineralization and have not turned to stone. The clay of the area has preserved the shells in their original form.

Known as the Coon Creek fossil formation, the entire area attracts geologists from all over the world. The center has been established to preserve the area and to provide an educational facility for the study of the earth sciences.

Various educational exhibits and programs have been established and are available for groups of fifteen or more. If you're not in a specific group and want to see the place, the center sponsors several "family days" during the year when individuals can sign up for a program. (901) 632–4850.

The hog is king at **Pappy Johns** whole hog barbecue, located on Highway 45 South, a few miles outside Selmer. Here you gotta be hungry for pork, because that's the only meat served. Open daily except Sunday, pork ribs are cooked up three nights a week, Wednesday, Friday, and Saturday, while the rest of the hog is available all the other times. A good deal of the business here is take-out, but if you enjoy eating near the hickory pits where the cooking is done, there are tables inside. (901) 645–4353.

THE WESTERN PLAINS

Along Highway 57 just east of Ramer city limits, you'll find a nice piece of folk art in the Deming family's front yard. A tall bicycle sculpture made out of old wagon wheels and various other pieces of "junk," the item is a true piece of roadside Americana.

Hardeman County's first courthouse, now known as the **Little Courthouse,** was built in 1824, making it one of the oldest original courthouses in western Tennessee. Located at 116 East Market Street in **Bolivar,** the restored structure now houses the county museum.

The original part of the existing building was a two-story log structure that served as the courthouse. In 1827 the building was purchased and moved to its current site, where additions were made to the log structure. It was converted into a family residence in 1849 and more additions were made, turning it into a large Federal-style home.

The building itself is worth the stop, but some of the items inside highlighting this county are fascinating in themselves. Open by appointment or by chance; admission charged; (901) 658–6554.

Another historic structure in Bolivar is **The Pillars,** former home of John Houston Bills, one of the original settlers of West Tennessee. Built prior to 1826 the building saw the likes of James K. Polk, Davy Crockett, General Ulysses S. Grant, and Sam Houston. Open by appointment or chance; admission charged; (901) 658–6554.

The **Magnolia Manor** is this area's premier bed and breakfast. The 1849 structure has been completely restored to its early splendor with wooden floors throughout. Owners James and Elaine Cox currently run the three-guest-room inn. Rates to stay at the antebellum inn range from $75 to $85, including a choice of meals. In the hallway you'll find portraits of four famous generals who stayed here many years before you found out about the place. Commissioned by the Cox family, the portraits feature Ulysses S. Grant, William T. Sherman, John A. Logan, and James B. McPherson. Located at 418 North Main Street; (901) 658–6700.

The small community of **Grand Junction,** located near the point where Highway 57 is joined by Highway 368, is known throughout the world as the home of the **National Field Trial Championships.** Held nearby at the 18,600-acre Ames Plantation since 1896, the annual February event is often called the "Super Bowl of Bird Dogs."

Competition lasts eight to ten days, with the winning dog earning the title of World Champion Bird Dog. Hunting mostly for quail, the dogs and handlers are followed by a large gallery of spectators on horseback. As quail raiser Joe Jordan says about the mounted spectators: "There must be 4,000 or 5,000 of them out there at a time. They never see a dog, but they sure have a good time."

Ames Plantation, located 4.3 miles off Highway 18 just north of Highway 57, is not only synonymous with the quest for canine excellence, it also plays an integral part in the University of Tennessee's livestock and agriculture program. The facility is one of the eleven branch experiment stations in the university's system. Built in 1847 the magnificent **Ames Manor House** is open for tours on the fourth Thursday afternoon of each month, March through October, with a $2.00 admission charged. Adjacent to the manor house is a small collection of original log cabins that have been moved here to create a small farmstead, which is open daily. There is no fee to walk about the cabins, but it's wise to check in with the office in the manor house first. (901) 878–1067.

Although Ames Plantation is the official headquarters, **Dunn's Supply Company** in downtown Grand Junction is the gathering place for local as well as international bird-dog aficionados. The store carries just about anything one would need for bird hunting and other outdoor activities. (901) 764–6901.

Across the street from Dunn's is the **Field Trial Hall of Fame and National Wildlife Heritage Center.** Created by the Bird Dog Foundation, the dedication plaque reads: "Dedicated to preserving the past, protecting the future for sporting dog fanciers the world over."

Films, paintings of some of the most famous bird dogs of the past hundred years, artifacts, literature, photography, and other memorabilia are featured here and help tell the story of the talents of well-trained bird dogs. If you're not familiar with any of this, don't worry; the folks working here are more than eager to share their love of the sport and of the dogs with you. Admission is free. (901) 764–2058.

Over at 133 Madison Avenue on the town square in Grand Junction, you'll find a real gem. The **Tennessee Pewter Showroom** is the only commercial producer of a full line of pewter products in the South. Pewtersmith Byron Black uses both the spin and the cast method of production to make all kinds of things ranging from beer steins to sugar bowls to pitchers to dinner plates. In all, he and the other craftsmen make about 435 different items.

The showroom is open Monday through Friday 9:00 A.M. to 4:00 P.M., but if you want to see Black in action, you'll have to show up between 7:30 A.M. and 4:00 P.M. on Tuesday or Wednesday. Those are the days he's most apt to be casting the molten pewter. (901) 764–2064.

Heading toward Memphis on Highway 57, you'll find *LaGrange,* a quaint little village that has been able to avoid the commercialization that the others have fallen to along this busy highway corridor. In addition to a couple of antiques shops, the streets are lined with a plethora of well-kept little white cottages with green shutters and trim. Settled in 1819 on the site of an Indian trading post, it was named for General Lafayette's ancestral home in France. Translated to mean "beautiful village," it was occupied by Union forces from 1862 to 1865. It was an antebellum center of wealth, education, and culture, having had two colleges, four academies, two newspapers, and 3,000 residents in 1862.

Lucy Cogbill runs *Cogbill's Store and Museum,* a business her great, great, great grandfather started in 1868. The original building was destroyed by a tornado in 1900, and the current structure was built in 1901. Inside the classy old general store, Lucy peddles a wide range of antiques, collectibles, local crafts items, and has a small area devoted to a display of old tools. Located at the intersection of LaGrange Road and Highway 57, she's open Thursday through Sunday except for January and February when it gets a bit cold in this area. "I just can't seem to get this old 1901 building very warm, so I don't open when it gets that cold," she told me. When she does differ from her posted hours, she'll leave a message on her answering machine, so it's wise to call before venturing forth during the winter. (901) 878–1235.

The Delta Region

With a population of about 700,000, *Memphis* rests along the Mississippi River and is one of the river's largest inland ports. Among many other things, the city is famous for its impact on the development of popular American music as well as the blues.

The history of music in the Memphis area revolves around the "King of Rock and Roll," Elvis Presley. Although he died in 1977, Elvis is more popular today than when he was alive; and his estate is worth much more now ($75 million) than it was when he died ($4.9 million) because of his home (Graceland Mansion), souvenir and tourist shops, and museums. Estate revenues were topping $15 million by the late 1980s, more than the singer made in any one year of his career.

Little-Known Facts About Tennessee

Thanks to Tennessee, women are allowed to vote. It was the state's ratification on August 21, 1920, that put the 19th Amendment into the Constitution of the United States, giving franchise power to the country's 17 million women.

Graceland Mansion, at 3765 Elvis Presley Boulevard, is one of the many unique places in the state where the beaten path catches up with the unbeaten path. There's nothing like this anywhere in the world, and it shouldn't be missed. Elvis and his family are buried here in the Meditation Garden, and tours of the mansion are run daily, year-round, except for Christmas, Thanksgiving, and New Year's Day. Closed Tuesday in November and December.

You'll get a chance to walk the grounds, see his private recording studio, and tour his bus and his private jet, the Lisa Marie, named after his daughter. You'll also have the opportunity to add to his estate at a variety of merchandise shops across the street from the mansion. It would be a good idea to make reservations, because the lines can get very long, especially during the summer months. Admission charged; (901) 332–3322.

Each year in mid-August Memphis hosts the *Elvis International Tribute Week,* an action-packed week of events that include trivia contests, candlelight vigils, special tours, tournaments, and parties. Humes Junior High School, where Elvis graduated from in 1953, is also open for tours and features a special exhibit room and a chance to walk across the stage where Elvis performed in a talent show.

Sun Studio, where Elvis recorded a song for his mother for $4.00, is open to the public. Founded by disc jockey Sam Phillips, Sun was the first studio to record such musicians as Presley, Jerry Lee Lewis, Carl Perkins, and Johnny Cash. The studio is located at 706 Union Avenue, just a few blocks from Baptist Hospital, where Elvis was pronounced dead on August 16, 1977. Open seven days a week, with tours scheduled every hour on the half-hour from 9:30 A.M. to 5:30 P.M. Longer hours during the summer. Admission charged; (901) 521–0664.

Beale Street, in downtown Memphis, is considered the spiritual home of the other type of music the city is famous for, the blues. During its heyday in the twenties and thirties, there wasn't a tougher, more swinging street in America. The zoot suit originated here, and Machine Gun Kelly peddled bootleg on the streets. Always a mecca for musicians, the street's nightclubs were frequented by the country's best blues artists, including the man known as the Father of the Blues, the legendary William Christopher (W. C.) Handy.

Today the street is once again a hot nightspot with numerous clubs, restaurants, and shops. And the best part is that the sound of the blues has not been forgotten. Three clubs now offer traditional blues and jazz music: *Mr. Handy's Blues Hall* at 174 Beale; the *Rum Boogie Cafe* at 182 Beale; and *B. B. King's Blues Club,* at 147 Beale. *The Center for Southern Folklore,* which also serves as a folk art gallery and outlet, features an informal and funky view of southern culture. 209 Beale Street; (901) 525–3655. Call the Beale Street visitors center for more information. (901) 543–5333.

The first entertainment venue to ever bear Elvis's name is located at 126 Beale Street. *Elvis Presley's Memphis* is a fun nightclub and restaurant that features contemporary southern cuisine, live entertainment, and a Sunday gospel music brunch. Open daily at 11:00 A.M. (901) 527–6900.

Virtually unchanged through the years is *Schwab's* dry goods store, where a sign still hangs in the window proclaiming "If you can't find it here, you're better off without it." The clerks still offer old-time service with a written receipt for each item purchased.

Downstairs, the Schwab family has created a museum. Having been on Beale Street since 1876, they have been able to collect quite a few memories of the "good ole days" to display. Upstairs, the store sells all sorts of items, from dream books to straw sailors to crystal balls to size 74 men's pants. Forty-four kinds of suspenders are kept in stock. (901) 523–9782.

The *Memphis Police Museum* is located at 159 Beale Street. It's located in an active police substation and is open every day, all day, all night. This precinct currently houses the walking and bicycle details for the Beale Street and downtown areas of the city.

Among items the museum has on display is a tape of the first car-to-car radio broadcast that took place in the city in 1940. Elvis also is saluted here. He was a reserve police captain, and the picture of him and his chief along with special orders taking him off the roll call following his death are on display, as are other Elvis/police-related memorabilia. Admission free.

A new taste treat awaits you a few doors down from the police museum. *Dyers Burgers* features deep-fried hamburgers, and the grease they are cooked in has not been changed since 1912! It has been strained, but the same basic grease has been used all these years, and officials say it has never been allowed to cool and has never been solidified. When the restaurant was moved here from another part of town, the truck with the hot grease was given a police escort to make sure they could make it before the grease got cold. Open daily; located at 205 Beale Street. (901) 527–3937.

If it's history you came to Memphis for, take the short trip out to *Mud Island,* out in the Mississippi River across from downtown. The city has developed this area to display its rich river heritage. The *River Walk* is a 5-block-long scale model of the entire Lower Mississippi's 1,000 miles from Cairo, Illinois, to the Gulf of Mexico. Every twist, turn, and split the river makes is shown on the model. Each step equals 1 mile along the miniriver, where each bridge and town is also depicted. Markers along the way point out interesting facts and figures. Water flows down the model into a one-acre Gulf of Mexico.

The eighteen-gallery *Mississippi River Museum* is also located on the island and is a showcase for the people and the history of the river, with exhibits ranging from Indian arrowheads to a replica of the pilothouse of a modern diesel towboat.

One of the galleries traces the wreck of the steamboat *Sultana,* which burned and sank nearby killing 1,547 people. It is considered the worst maritime disaster in United States history. (901) 576–7241.

A visit to the *Peabody Hotel,* at 149 Union Street in downtown, is a must. Built in 1925 the grand hotel has been restored and carries on a tradition started back in the mid-thirties. Each morning at eleven o'clock, five ducks are transported by elevator from their penthouse facilities to the lobby of the hotel.

As the doors slowly open, a red carpet is unrolled from the big fountain to the elevator as the "King Cotton March" is played over the sound system. With Toby Carter, the official Duck Master in control, the ducks waddle to the fountain where they will spend the day. At 5:00 P.M. the action is reversed, and the ducks go back to their duck palace on the roof. During the day, if you visit the roof home of the ducks, you'll find a sign on their door proclaiming: GONE TO WORK IN THE LOBBY. BE BACK AT 5:00 P.M.

The palace is open to visitors, but that's not all you'll find up there. You'll also find a very impressive view of the river and downtown Memphis. (901) 529–4000.

Metalsmithing, everything from delicate gold jewelry to massive wrought-iron fencing, is the subject of one of the area's most unusual museums. Located in downtown Memphis on a bluff overlooking the Mississippi River, the *National Ornamental Metal Museum* was opened to the public in 1979 as a memorial to metalsmithing.

Changing exhibits are the basis of the museum, but its permanent collection contains a variety of items from jewelry to handmade nails to large outdoor sculptures to ancient iron locks. In the museum's smithy (anyplace where metal is worked) work is done daily by resident artists and members of museum classes. On the third weekend of October each year, "Repair Days" is held. People from all over the South bring in their broken metal items to be fixed. On an average, sixty craftspeople are available during that time to repair "broken, bent or otherwise mutilated metalwork."

Make sure you pay attention to the front gates as you enter. Known as the Anni-

The Peabody Ducks

versary Gates, the tall metal gates contain nearly 200 specially designed rosettes, each made by a different metal craftsman. Each was submitted as part of the museum's tenth anniversary project and placed in an S scroll on the gate. Designs range from the traditional to contemporary, abstract, and whimsical. This is a great piece of unique art, and in no way should you visit Memphis without seeing it.

The grounds immediately surrounding the museum are also unique. Talk about artistic yard art! Wonderful metal sculptures and doo-dads are placed throughout. In the gazebo, you can see the Mississippi River from high above.

The museum grounds, at 374 Metal Museum Drive (formerly known as West California), are a part of what was once known as the Marine Hospital, with the oldest of the three large brick buildings dating from 1870. That building was used in the extensive Memphis research that led to a cure for the yellow fever epidemics that once swept the area. The museum's main exhibit building was built as a Works Progress Administration project in 1932 and once served as a nurse's dormitory for the hospital complex. Admission charged; (901) 774–6380.

Remember when you had to drive out West to get Coors beer? Well those days came to an end when the company started shipping their brew east of the Mississippi in 1981. First they opened a brewery in Shenandoah, Virginia; then, in September 1991, the *Memphis Brewery* opened in the old Joseph Schlitz Brewery.

This facility now brews, bottles or cans, and ships Coors Cutters, a non-alcoholic beer, and Zima Clearmalt. Coors and Coors Light are brewed in Golden, Colorado, and shipped to Memphis in refrigerated tanker cars. Upon arrival here those products are canned or bottled and shipped.

There are three can lines in operation, each filling up to 1,600 cans per minute. Four bottle lines are also in use. Free tours are given Monday through Saturday from noon to 4:00 P.M. During the thirty-minute trek you'll be briefed on the history of the brewery and you'll get to see all facets of the operation. The tour ends in the Belle Hospitality Center, where you'll get to sample the great Coors products. The brewery is at 5151 East Raines Road; (901) 375–2100 or (901) 368–BEER, for up-to-the-minute tour times.

At *Huey's restaurant and bar* you are encouraged to use your straw to shoot toothpicks into the ceiling! Name another eatery that permits that. The menu consists mostly of burgers, salads, pitas, and other sandwiches. Make sure you bring your Sharpie—you're allowed to write on the walls. Open daily at 11:00 A.M. or noon, closes well after midnight. Located at 77 South Second Street, across from the Peabody Hotel. (901) 276–6934.

A few doors down from Huey's is the *Memphis Music Hall of Fame, Museum and Archive.* It's a public display of one man's huge collection of Memphis-related musical artifacts, recordings, and memorabilia. The private museum belongs to John Montague, a prominent local barrister, and presents more than 100 years of Memphis music, from the "Father of the Blues" to the "King of Rock and Roll." On display is the largest collection of W. C. Handy memorabilia and the largest collection of Elvis Presley memorabilia outside Graceland. Others represented are the Box Tops, Jerry Lee Lewis, Booker T. and the MGs, and Otis Redding.

There's great audio interpretation, and the displays are packed solid. There's absolutely nothing sophisticated about this museum, but it certainly ranks up there with the top music museums in the world. The Rock and Roll Hall of Fame and Museum in Cleveland has nothing on this place. This place does what a museum should do—it tells the story. Open daily at 10:00 A.M. or noon, closes at 6:00 or 9:00 P.M. 97 South Second Street, (901) 525–4007. Admission charged.

The *National Civil Rights Museum* is the nation's first museum dedicated to documenting the complete history of the American civil rights movement. Constructed around the Lorraine Motel, where Dr. Martin Luther King Jr. was assassinated on April 4, 1968, the center features an interpretive education center, audiovisual displays, interactive exhibits, and civil rights memorabilia. Large exhibits portray several memorable moments in the movement, including the arrest of Rosa Parks for not moving to the back of the bus when requested, the sanitation workers' strike in Memphis, and the assassination of Dr. King.

King used to stay in Room 307 at the motel when he came to Memphis, and it was outside that room on the balcony that he was shot. Visitors can now walk into that room and be immersed in the assassination story. It's quite moving, and if you see nothing else, this is the one exhibit you shouldn't miss. Located at 450 Mulberry Street, the museum is open daily year-round. Admission charged. (901) 521–9699.

Jacqueline Smith lived in the Lorraine Motel until she was evicted on March 2, 1988, so the work to build the museum could begin. Since the time of her eviction she has lived across the street on a couch on the sidewalk and has protested the presence of the museum. She says the museum is "a disgrace to the life and works of Dr. King, a scam and a landgrab that is inflating real estate values and displacing people who have lived in the area for years." She has been on the couch every day for more than ten years and says she won't leave until her work is done, which she predicts will be another ten to fifteen years.

Danny Thomas, entertainer, humanitarian, and founder of St. Jude Children's Hospital, is buried in a memorial garden in front of the hospital, next to a beautiful pavilion that features his life, his career, his hospital, and his love for his fellow man. There are videos of his *Make Room for Daddy* television series and a wall full of photos of Thomas posed with other legendary stars. In addition, there are hundreds of personal items and most of the trophies and awards he won during his illustrious career. Located in downtown Memphis at 332 North Lauderdale, the pavilion and gardens are open Monday through Saturday, 10:00 A.M. to 4:30 P.M. (901) 495–3508.

There's nothing off the beaten path about the ***Sleep Inn at Court Square,*** in downtown. In fact, it's on the path as well as on the trolley line. It's the best place for your dollars if you want to stay downtown and within a 5-block walk of most of the downtown attractions listed in this chapter, including Beale Street and Mud Island. On one side of the hotel is the riverfront Confederate Park; the other side is the trolley line and the historic Court Square. It's new and a great continental breakfast is included. 40 North Front Street; (901) 522–9700.

The **Map Room** is an eclectic coffee shop, reading room, concert venue, and gathering spot for downtown residents located in downtown at the corner of Madison and South Main, just 2 blocks south of the Sleep Inn. It's owned by Virginia Ivy, who with her friends transformed the 120-plus-year-old storefront into a funky oasis. The ornamental plaster ceiling was redone and is now a sky-blue color. There are a few light sandwiches, soups and salads on the menu, but the coffees and the teas are the stars here. Make sure you try one of the twenty-five flavors of the La Teas. Virginia describes them "like a cap-

A Sampling of African-American Sites and Attractions

Meharry Medical College
1005 D. B. Todd Boulevard, Nashville
First medical education program in
United States for African-Americans
(615) 327–6111

Fisk University Historic District
1000 17th Avenue North, Nashville
Founded in 1887 as "free school"
for blacks
Area consists of vintage
buildings, theaters, galleries
(615) 329–8720

Bethlehem Cemetery
Highway 51 North, Henning
Alex Haley's family burial plot,
where Chicken George is buried
(901) 738–2240

National Civil Rights Museum
450 Mulberry Street, Memphis
Housed in Lorraine Motel, where
Martin Luther King Jr. was assassinated
(901) 521–9699

W. C. Handy Home & Gallery
352 Beale Street, Memphis
Where W. C. Handy penned his
many famous songs; memorabilia,
and artifacts (901) 522–1556

WDIA Radio Station
47 Union Avenue, Memphis
Founded in 1948 as first African
American formatted radio station
in the United States
(901) 529–4300

Beck Cultural Exchange Center
1927 Dandridge Avenue, Knoxville
Archives, research, and museum for
the city's African-American citizens
(423) 524–8461

Highlander Research Foundation
1959 Highlander Way, New Market
An important training center for the
modern civil rights movement
Graduates include Dr. Martin Luther
King Jr. and Rosa Parks
(423) 933–3443

**Afro-American Museum &
Research Center**
200 East Martin Luther King
Boulevard, Chattanooga
Portrays history and culture of the
city's African-Americans and their
contributions to society
(423) 266–8658

puccino with tea flavor." The blackberry sage and cinnamon plum are quite good. (901) 579–9924.

The Map Room serves as the meeting place for several downtown tours, including the hip Pink 1955 Cadillac Tour of Memphis. Put on your sunglasses and settle into the back seat while an experienced downtown guide offers you the choice of several routes. One of the most popular is The Greatest Hits Tour. It's a two-and-a-half-hour trek through the city's musical heritage and mansion-lined streets.

Another tour out of the Map Room is the Manhole Cover Tour. Jimmy Ogle, whose day job is as general manager of the Memphis Queen Line (which also offers some great river tours), is the city's unofficial riverfront expert and manhole cover guru. He has identified 191 different types of manholes in the downtown area. He'll point out the covers while he talks about downtown in general. He's quite the entertainer as well as a great guide.

The *Crystal Shrine Grotto,* inside the Memorial Park Cemetery is a must stop if you're looking for the unusual located in unusual locations. A unique cave was constructed by cemetery founder Clovis Hinds and Mexican artist Dionicio Rodriquez during the period of 1935–1938. The cave and exterior environs were built of concrete in imitation of rocks, boulders, and trees. The entranceway appears to be through a tree trunk.

Natural rock and quartz crystal collected from the Ozarks form the background for nine different scenes from the life of Christ. Because of those scenes, the local kids often call the cavern the Jesus Cave. It's beautiful and quite an unusual work of naturalistic art. The Shrine is open daily 8:00 A.M. to 4:00 P.M. Located at 5668 Poplar Avenue, just off I–240 east of downtown. (901) 767–8930.

Of all the sites listed in this guide, the one that seems most out of place in Tennessee is the magnificent *Pyramid,* located in Memphis along the banks of the Mississippi River at One Auction Avenue. The 32-story stainless steel structure, built in the shape of a pyramid, opened to the public in late 1991. It is currently the home of a 20,000-seat arena where concerts, sporting events, and ice shows take place.

From the floor of the arena you can look straight up 321 feet to the top floor, which will become a glass-enclosed observation deck in the future. A glass-enclosed incline elevator will take guests up the outside of the building to the deck. In addition there is 180,000 square feet of space in the four corners of the building that will be developed into museums, restaurants, and other attractions.

From April through Labor Day, tours start on the plaza level and are conducted Monday through Saturday 10:00 A.M. to 4:00 P.M. and on Sunday noon to 4:00 P.M. After Labor Day, tours are conducted daily at noon, 1:00, and 2:00 P.M. Admission is charged. (901) 521–9675.

In **Mason,** just across the Tipton County line at 342 Highway 70, is **Bozo's Restaurant.** Look for one of those tiled cafe buildings that dotted America's landscape in the 1950s and you'll find Bozo's.

Founded in 1923 by Bozo Williams, the restaurant has stayed in the family and is now owned by the founder's great-grandson, Jeff Thompson. Famous for its pork shoulder barbecue sandwiches and plates, Bozo's has a full menu that has not changed since shortly after World War II.

When he took over ownership in 1988, Thompson was told by "just about everybody" not to change a thing. One thing he did do, however, was to bottle and sell the establishment's popular sauces. Food comes with no sauce, allowing the diner to choose between the hot and mild concoctions located on each table.

Having never advertised, the restaurant's one-hundred seats are filled by longtime customers and newcomers who have heard about the place from a friend. On weekends about 50 percent of the business comes from Memphis, 35 miles away. Bozo's is open Tuesday through Saturday from 10:30 A.M. to 9:00 P.M. and offers the same menu items all day. (901) 294–3400.

For a totally different culinary experience, stop by **Gus's Fried Chicken** restaurant, across the street and down about a block from Bozo's. Here you'll discover the hottest, spiciest fried chicken in this part of the state. It's the family's secret recipe, developed in 1953 by Napoleon Vanderbilt, that makes this chicken so tasty. Vanderbilt's son, Gus, and Gus's son, Terry, run the business now, and they keep it open every day of the week. "We're closed Thanksgiving and Christmas days, but you know, we'd be packed even on those days if we were open," laughed Terry, who noted that his grandfather, Napoleon, brought the first hot-and-spicy chicken to Tennessee.

As at Bozo's, Gus's Fried Chicken has a longtime, loyal following, and a good portion of the business comes from nearby Memphis. (901) 294–2028.

Don't go through the tiny town of Munford, northeast of Memphis, without stopping to meet J. B. Curtis. His **J. B. Curtis Trading Post,** at the corner of Highway 51 and Munford Street, isn't easy to miss. Junk and antiques literally overflow from several buildings, including an old ice plant. "People have come in and told me I must be a genius to display the stuff out there the way I do because it attracts so much attention," J. B. said. "It's only piled out there because I ran out of room in here."

You name it, he has it. The eighty-one-year-old retiree started this business as a little place to repair jewelry and guns. "It grew little by little and got out of hand," he claims. When you walk in, you may have to wait for him to take your money. He's probably over in the corner entertaining some other customers. His heroes are country singers Jerry Lee Lewis and Mickey Gilley, and he sounds just like either of them, depending on your request. He has a speaker system and piano, and he takes plenty of time to play for everyone. He's a neat guy, with a lot of talent, and he can tell you story after story about a whole bunch of things. Open nearly every day. (901) 837–8181.

Further north on Highway 51 in Tipton County is Covington, where you'll find an eclectic architectural area known as the *South Main Historic District.* In all, there are seventy-five different structures reflecting "architectural styles that were sought by the emerging, affluent members of society in the late 19th and early 20th century," reads the historic marker. Among the styles represented: American Four-Square, Prairie Bungalow, Colonial Revival, and Queen Anne. (901) 476–9727.

The restored Ruffin Theater on East Pleasant is part of the historic district. Built in the art-deco style in 1937, it now serves as a performing arts center for the community. (901) 476–9727.

Over in Brownsville, West Tennessee's most unusual outdoor sculpture is located 3 blocks from the courthouse on West Main Street. Reaching heights of seventy-five feet, *Mindfield* is a work in progress by local artist and welder Billy Tripp. He lives in his welding shop behind the sculpture. The huge, eclectic, steel structure symbolizes life and the process of growing up, and it's up to everyone who sees it to interpret it for themselves. He adds to it constantly and says he will do so for as long as he physically can. While many residents don't get it, many do, including the county's tourism director, Belinda Sellari. "It's a great technical achievement," the art lover said.

Nestled among the old structures in the city's College Hill historic district is the College Hill Community Center. Situated at the top of the hill at 129 North Grand Avenue is the College Hill Center, which houses the Morton Felsenthal Lincoln Collection. Now property of the city, the large collection of books and memorabilia concerning the sixteenth U.S. president is an all-encompassing exhibit. Open Sunday through Friday. (901) 772–4883.

The **Haywood County Museum** is located at 127 North Grand Avenue and features a good view into this part of the Mississippi Delta region. Open Saturday afternoons. A walking tour of the historic homes in this historic area is available; brochures can be obtained at the chamber of commerce at 121 West Main Street.

The blues music heritage is alive and well and in good hands around here. The annual Brownsville Blues Fall Fest is held the last Saturday of every September and features live blues music all day, a BBQ contest, a scarecrow contest, and various children's activities.

The house where **Sleepy John Estes** last strummed his guitar is now open to the public next to the Elma Ross Library at 1011 East Main Street. This is where the blues legend was living when he died in 1977. There are photos and memorabilia, and blues music fills the house. Open daily except Monday. Call the chamber of commerce for more information. (901) 772–2193.

Up Highway 19 from Brownsville, in the small community of Nutbush, Anna Mae Bullock was born on November 26, 1939, to sharecropper parents. She was a young girl surrounded by cotton fields and plenty of dreams. With a few lucky breaks and an immense amount of talent, this young lady moved away, got married, and became Tina Turner, Queen of Rock and Roll.

She immortalized her hometown in her 1973 hit, "Nutbush City Limits," and she was inducted into the Rock and Roll Hall of Fame in 1991. The sharecropper's shack in which she was born has long since disappeared, but the farm where that shack stood still stands, as does the elementary school where she was educated. A sign now marks the farm, located on Highway 19 adjacent to the cotton gin. The high school she attended in Brownsville and the elementary school she attended in Ripley are both still in service.

Sharon Norris, another Nutbush native, has created a little business centered around Tina Turner, Nutbush, and the blues heritage of the area. She and her group own and run the **Nutbush Tina Turner Resource Center and Exhibit,** where a Turner and blues archive, including videos, photos, and memorabilia, is on display. There must be something in the water out there, because many other notable blues musicians have come from the Nutbush and Brownsville area as well, including Sleepy John Estes, Alex Harvey, and the Reverend Clay Evans.

Admission to **Wild Onion Ridge,** Norris's twenty-two-acre blues heritage resource center and music park is by appointment only, and special personalized auto tours of the area are available from Norris. In mid-June the annual Nutbush Wild Onion Ridge Blues Heritage Celebration takes place at Wild Onion Ridge and features blues entertainers, food, and other activities.

The center is way out in the cotton fields. Head toward Ripley on Highway 19 and turn onto Nunn Road. Continue past the historic cemetery and turn left onto Sam Williams Road, then take a right onto Willette Beard Road. At the end of the road is Wild Onion Ridge, located in an old farm homestead. (901) 772–4265 or (901) 772–8157; www.nutbush.com

Henning, the boyhood home of the late author Alex Haley, is a picturesque town of Victorian homes and turn-of-the-century storefronts. The town probably would have progressed quietly like many small towns had it not been for native son Haley.

His 1976 Pulitzer-prize-winning novel, **Roots,** and the subsequent TV miniseries, based on the family stories his grandmother and aunt told him, brought international fame to Henning, where Haley's family home is now the ***Alex Haley House Museum.***

Those stories inspired Haley to research his family members, who were brought to America as slaves, and the book came as a result. He recalls sitting on the front porch of his boyhood home and listening for hours to the stories.

Haley's museum by description is a "tribute to Kunta Kinte's worldwide family." Built in 1918 by a Kunta Kinte descendant, the house has been restored and not only serves as a tribute to Haley but also as a good example of rural small-town life in west Tennessee. It is also the first African-American state historic site and the only writer's home open to the public in Tennessee.

Following his death on February 10, 1992, Haley was buried in the front yard of the house, and his grave site is available for viewing at any time. Located at 200 South Church Street at Haley Avenue, the museum is open Tuesday through Sunday. Admission charged; (901) 738–2240.

In a bright red caboose in downtown Henning, the area's historical society has its records and artifacts on display in its heritage museum. Located on Main Street, adjacent to the city hall. If you'd like to visit, go into city hall and someone will come out and unlock the doors for you.

Here's one for the engineers who are looking for off-the-beaten-path mechanical wonders. Outside Dyersburg is the world's only surviving "swing span, pony Pratt through truss bridge." Known for the town from which it came, the **Lenox Bridge,** as it is now known, was built in 1917 and moved and restored in 1985. The bridge was positioned for land travel, and when a ship would need to go through it would blow its whistle to alert the bridge tender who would come down, walk out to the center pier, and hand crank the bridge open. The bridge would turn away from both riverbanks and line up out of the way of the ship in the middle of the river, parallel with the shores, supported only in the middle.

The bridge is 150 feet in length, 14 feet wide, and the pier is 18 feet in diameter. Jere Kirk, whose grandfather helped with the construction of the original bridge, bought and refurbished the bridge. It is now on display over a body of water in the Lakewood subdivsion. Take Highway 78 north out of Dyersburg. From Highway 155, go 2.7 miles and turn left on Highway 182 South. Go 1 mile and turn left into Lakewood. Stay right and the bridge is on your right, just past the lake.

Delta Flyway

The **Obion County Museum** in Union City is the only regional history museum in this part of the state. All the other museums are specialized, so this is the place to go to get a good overview of what northwest Tennessee is all about.

County historian Rebel C. Forrester is the perfect guide as he walks you through the displays and explains little tidbits of history that only a county historian would know. An amazing collection of "documentary" photos from 1919 to 1924 gives a good visual feeling to the other exhibits. Among the items on permanent display are a Model-T Ford, Indian artifacts, and a horse-drawn hearse.

Adjacent to the museum is a two-room log cabin with exhibits. The museum is open Saturday and Sunday afternoons and is located at 1004 Edwards Street, directly behind the high school. Admission free; (901) 885–6774.

About a block from the museum at the end of Edwards Street is the first monument erected in honor of the unknown Confederate soldier. It was dedicated on October 21, 1869. Some of the twenty-nine buried died in training at Camp Brown, here in Union City.

Gun collectors worldwide probably already know about this city's **Dixie Gun Works,** while noncollectors across town may never have heard of it. Founded by the late Turner Kirkland in the early 1950s, the business is now considered the world's largest supplier of antique guns and parts. The firm sells about 80,000 guns a year, including antique reproductions.

At any given time a walk through the Dixie Gun Works' showroom is like walking through an antique firearms museum, except that you can buy most of the guns you see here. Usually, more than 1,500 guns are on display. Kirkland's other passion, antique automobiles, is also in evidence. Adjacent to the gun showroom is an auto museum with more than thirty cars, including a 1908 Maxwell.

A small log cabin gunshop is a part of this attraction. Originally built in this area around 1850, the shop contains two rifling machines and more than 1,000 gun-making tools. The complex is located on the Highway 51S Union City By-Pass. Admission is charged for the museum. (901) 885–0561.

Adjacent to the county courthouse in the center of Union City is the *Flame of Freedom,* an eternal flame dedicated to "all veterans of Obion County in all wars and conflicts, past, present, and future." It was dedicated in 1971. Along the railroad tracks on South Depot Street next to the municipal building, Kiwanis Park offers a nice place to rest for a spell. Make note of the Confederate monument in the park. It's one of the few in the South that looks north. There's a bandshell, fountains, playground equipment, and plenty of huge shade trees.

If it's architecture you like, don't overlook the First Christian Church at West Lee and South Second streets. The circa-1912 domed church is the third to be built on the site. The bell that is on display on the church lawn was the first bell of the brick church built on this site after the 1862 destruction of the 1857 frame church by Union forces. Check out the beautiful stained glass windows of the church.

The Masquerade Theatre Company, a community theater group in Union City, raised the money to buy and are now about finished restoring the beautiful, circa-1927 *Capitol Theater,* at 118 South First Street. Through the years, it was used as a film house, a stage for traveling legitimate theater, and as a vaudeville stage. The theater group will produce several shows a year in the 364-seat venue and will host a bevy of local entertainment events such as recitals. Make sure you check out the ticket box out front. Inside is a life-size cutout likeness of Louise Harper, who sold most of the tickets used at the Capitol from 1930 to 1962.

Kaye Logan owns the *Ivy Cottage gift shop* next to the Capitol Theater, and will be offering gourmet coffee and homemade fudge the nights of shows at the Capitol. The shop now offers the fudge as well as a large selection of coffee beans, and they have a coffeepot going all the time. They only brew one kind each day, their choice. The shop offers an eclectic selection of gifts and crafts.

When questioned about where to get a hamburger in town, Johnna Rogers, executive director of the county chamber of commerce did not hesitate. "*P.V.'s Hut* has the best cheeseburger in the world. Period," she said. With an endorsement like that, you definitely need to stop by and enjoy a burger personally made by Jim Isbell, the owner and cook. Located at East Florida and South Perkins Streets, the eatery is open Monday through Saturday, 11:00 A.M. to 7:00 P.M. (901) 885–5737.

Following World War II, housing was in demand throughout the United States, and as a result many all-steel prefabricated homes were built. They were quick to put up and reasonably inexpensive for the returning servicemen. Only one remains in Obion County. It's at 1020 Church Street, and has been maintained quite nicely through the years.

A couple streets over in the oldest residential neighborhood in town, the home of Lexie Parks still stands at 822 East Main. The house contains the first elevator in town, and it contains the ghost and spirits of the wealthy Mr. Parks. He was killed in the house by his butler who was never convicted of the crime. Residents who have lived here since have documented Parks and his congenial hauntings as he walks through the house. It seems he is upset that the butler got away with the crime.

The Jack Flippen family, all three generations of them, are actively involved in the family's *Flippens Hillbilly Barn* business just outside Hornbeak about 16 miles from Union City. Originally established as an orchard, various parts of their business have grown from circumstances.

The Hillbilly Barn still sells apples and peaches but is into much more. Several years ago the Flippens started selling apple cider and individual fried fruit pies at the encouragement of a local festival promoter. They have been frying pies and making cider ever since.

Mrs. Flippen started frying hamburgers when an orchard worker forgot to bring his lunch one day and asked her to fix him something to eat. That good deed on Mrs. Flippen's part has turned into a full-service "country-cooking" restaurant. The homemade jams and jellies are quite popular, but through it all, the apple and peach fried pies remain the major reason for much of the return business. More than twenty-two varieties of apples and twenty-eight varieties of peaches are available. They use their "over-ripe" peaches to make a wonderful peach ice cream that is up to 75 percent peaches. Yum, talk about a fuzzy taste! Menu items include fried catfish, country ham, and grilled quail.

To find the establishment, head west out of Union City on Highway 22. Go 8 miles and turn off the highway onto Shawtown Road, and go 8 miles to the barn. Open daily for breakfast and lunch. Dinner is also served on Friday and Saturday; (901) 538–2933.

About ten minutes west of the Hillbilly Barn is **Reelfoot Lake,** the result of a true quirk of nature. The **worst earthquake ever measured** in American history took place in this area in 1812. On February 7 the quake hit, and the lands of northwest Tennessee near the Mississippi River dropped as much as 20 feet.

For fifteen minutes the river's water flowed backward to fill this major void, which had been a swampy forestland. Now the area is a 13,000-acre shallow lake, an average of 5.2 feet deep, with the remains of the forest

The "Real Legend" of Reelfoot

*O*nce upon a time in the early 1800s, there ruled a mighty Chickasaw chieftain whose only son had a deformed foot. The son ran with a rolling motion, so the tribe nicknamed him Kaolin, meaning Reelfoot. When the son became chief and was to be married, he found he had no feelings for any maidens in his tribe.

He went searching for a wondrous beauty and found her among the Choctaws. She was the daughter of the chief. Reelfoot immediately fell under the spell of the princess and asked her father to allow a marriage.

The old chief replied: "It is true that my daughter is enchanting, and she will only be given in wedlock to a Choctaw chieftain. I will not ever permit her to join a tribe which is so unfortunate as to have a clubfooted chieftain." Reelfoot was more determined than ever, but the Great Spirit had a few words for him. "An Indian must not take his wife

from a neighboring tribe, and if you disobey and take the princess, I will cause the earth to rock and the waters to swallow up your village and bury your people in a watery grave."

Reelfoot chose not to believe the Great Spirit, and within months he had captured the princess and brought her back to west Tennessee. As the marriage rites took place, the earth began to roll, and Reelfoot cried out for mercy on his people. The Great Spirit answered, "I will show you and your people mercy, but you will have to pay for your disobedience. I will form a lake where I stamp my foot, and you and your people will forever watch over the lake, for I will rest your souls in the cypress."

The 1811 earthquake continued, the lands dropped, and the Mississippi River filled the new basin. Cypress trees became abundant. Reelfoot Lake was formed.

just under the surface, which makes boating quite an adventure. The water is a dark green color, with visibility never more than a few inches. The area surrounding the lake is now a state park, and a journey through here is truly a trek into unspoiled nature. The combination of shaggy cypress trees, some of them centuries old, and water lilies is most unusual for this state.

Reelfoot Lake is the winter home to more than 100 American bald eagles. The birds, with wingspans of 6 to 8 feet, come here from their northern summer homes to spend the winter in a warmer, ice-free environment. The park provides numerous eagle programs, including bus tours of the area during winter.

The park's museum offers the chance to experience an earthquake firsthand. The 1812 quake has been reproduced, to a lesser degree, and allows guests to feel and hear what took place during those fifteen minutes. You can also sit in a stump jumper, learn about its creators, the Calhoun family, see Indian artifacts, and read firsthand accounts of the creation of the lake. The museum is also the loading site for the lake's sight-seeing cruises.

Each morning at 9:00, a three-hour pontoon boat cruise leaves for a trek around the southernmost part of the lake. The guide is usually David Pike, a naturalist with the park. He grew up in these parts and really knows the lake, the animals, and the history of the area.

The park has camping sites, a camp store, and hiking trails. Guided "swamp tromps" are offered during the year. A resort inn and restaurant, both owned by the state, are built out over the lake among the cypress trees. The entrance to the park is located off Highway 21.

An annual calendar lists the best times, month by month, to see the various wildlife around the lake. A copy can be obtained by calling the ranger's office; (901) 253–7756. A three-day arts and crafts festival is held each October at the park.

A fantastic place to stay while you're in this area is the ***Bluebank Resort,*** on Highway 21 a few miles east of Tiptonville. Located on the water's edge, the rooms are rustic in style but are new, clean, and offer great views of the lake. The water practically comes up to your door! Rates range from $60 to $90 a room per night. Special hunting and fishing packages, which include lodging, boat, motor, bait, and ice, are available and can save you quite a bit of money.

The *Bluebank Fish House & Grill* is located closer to Tiptonville, at the Bluebank Motel, and is owned by the same people. The restaurant is open early each morning with a hearty breakfast, and has steaks, quail, frog legs, crappie, country ham, ribs, and chicken for dinner. The house special is a twenty-ounce porterhouse steak, for $16.95! (901) 253-6878; www.bluebankresort.com

PLACES TO STAY IN THE WESTERN PLAINS

BOLIVAR
Magnolia Manor
418 North Main Street
Antebellum bed
and breakfast
(901) 658-6700

CORDOVA
Bridgewater House B&B
7015 Raleigh-
La Grange Road
Quiet, quaint, in century-
old schoolhouse
(901) 384-0080

COUNCE
Little Andy's
Sportsman's Lodge
Highway 57
1950-era motel with
knotty-pine rooms
(901) 689-3750

DYERSBURG
Hampton Inn
2750 Mall Loop Road
Close to all northwest
Tennessee attractions
(901) 285-4778

JACKSON
Highland Place
Bed & Breakfast
519 Highland Avenue
Circa-1911 mansion
(901) 427-1472

MEMPHIS
Memphis Graceland KOA
3691 Elvis Presley
Boulevard
Laundry, showers,
pool, store
(901) 396-7125

Ridgeway Inn
5679 Poplar Avenue
(at I-240)
Known for service
and elegance
Member of Peabody
Hotel Group
(901) 766-4000

Sleep Inn at Court Square
40 North Front Street
Close to downtown
attractions
(901) 522-9700

PARIS
Sunset View Inn B&B
1330 Shady Grove Road
Great views, screened
porch, antiques
(901) 642-4778

PICKWICK DAM
Pickwick Landing State
Park Inn
Highway 57
Pool, tennis, restaurant
(901) 689-3135

TIPTONVILLE
Backyard Birds Lodge B&B
Air Park Road
On shore of Reelfoot Lake
in old fishing lodge
(901) 253-9064

Bluebank Resort
Highway 21
Rustic rooms
with lake views
(901) 253-6878

WILDERSVILLE
Pin Oak Lodge
and Restaurant
In Natchez Trace State
Resort Park
Cabins, swimming, hiking,
fishing, camping
Open year-round
(901) 968-3742

PLACES TO EAT IN THE WESTERN PLAINS

CLIFTON
Riverside Restaurant
Highway 128
Featuring Tennessee
River catfish
Overlooking Tennessee
River
Open at 6:00 A.M.
Closed Monday
(931) 676-3944

DECATURVILLE
Broadway Farms
Old Perryville Road
Country cooking in
rustic setting
Open Friday and Saturday
5:00 P.M., Sunday at noon
(901) 852-4559

GREEN FROG
Grist Mill Restaurant
Highway 412
Frog legs and more
traditional food
Wednesday through
Saturday 11:00 A.M.
to 9:00 P.M., Sunday
11:00 A.M. to 3:00 P.M.
(901) 663–FROG

HORNBREAK
Flippens Hillbilly Barn
Shawton Road
Country cooking, apple
and peach fried pies,
peach ice cream
Breakfast and lunch daily;
dinner on Friday
and Saturday
(901) 538–2933

P.V.'s Hut
At East Florida
and South Perkins Streets
Best cheeseburgers
in the world
Monday through Saturday,
11:00 A.M. to 7:00 P.M.
(901) 885–5737

JACKSON
Royal Street Smokehouse
1673 North Royal
BBQ, ribs, chicken,
Sunday buffet
Open daily, 11:00 A.M. to
7:00 P.M.
(901) 424–9410

Suede's
2263 North
Highland Avenue
Rock memorabilia; fish,
barbecue, pizza
Monday through Saturday
11:00 A.M. to 9:00 P.M.,
Sunday 11:00 A.M.
to 2:00 P.M.
(901) 664–1956

MASON
Bozo's Restaurant
342 Highway 70
Pork shoulder barbecue
sandwiches
Tuesday through Saturday
10:30 A.M. to 9:00 P.M.
(901) 294–3400

Gus's Fried Chicken
Highway 70
Hot-and-spicy chicken
Open daily 10:30 A.M. to
6:45 P.M.
(901) 294–2028

MEMPHIS
Arcade Restaurant
540 South Main Street
Breakfast all day;
plate lunch specials
Since 1919; neon signs,
vinyl booths
Tuesday through Sunday,
7:00 A.M. to 3:00 P.M.
Closed Monday
(901) 526–5757

Automatic Slims
Tonga Club
83 South Second
Southwestern and
Caribbean cuisine
and decor
Coconut Mango Shrimp,
Caribbean Voodoo Stew
Lunch Monday through
Friday, 11:00 A.M.
to 2:30 P.M.
Dinner Monday through
Saturday, 5:00 to 11:00 P.M.
(901) 525–7948

Dyers Burgers
205 Beale Street
Hamburgers cooked in
grease not changed
since 1912
Open daily at 11:00 A.M.
Closes when everyone
leaves.
(901) 527–3937

Elvis Presley's Memphis
126 Beale Street
Contemporary southern
cuisine and
live entertainment
Open daily at 11:00 A.M.
(901) 527–6900

Huey's restaurant and bar
77 South Second Street
Allowed to write on walls
and shoot toothpicks
into ceiling
Open daily at 11:00 A.M. or
noon until after midnight
(901) 276–6934

Memphis Queen Dinner
Cruises
On Mississippi River,
downtown
BBQ, chicken, prime rib
Two-hour sunset cruise;
great views
May through October
(901) 527–5694

Rendezvous
52 South Second
World famous
barbecued ribs
Since 1948; a Memphis
tradition
Tuesday through Thursday,
4:30 to 11:30 P.M.
Friday and Saturday,
noon to midnight
(901) 523–2746

SAVANNAH
Christie's Restaurant
2304 Wayne Road
Breakfasts, prime rib,
seafood, catfish
Open daily, 5:00 A.M.
to 9:00 P.M.
(901) 925–5566

Sa'von's Restaurant
Highway 64, 9 miles from
Somerville
Great fried green tomatoes,
tomato bread
Open daily 6:00 A.M.
to 10:00 P.M.
(901) 465–7678

SELMER
Pappy Johns
On Highway 45 South
Whole-hog barbecue
Open daily except Sunday
(901) 645–4353

SPRINGVILLE
The Crows Nest
435 Graceland
Prime rib, jumbo shrimp
Waterfront dining,
with boat docks
Wednesday through
Saturday, 5:00 to 10:00 P.M.
(901) 593–0340

TIPTONVILLE
Bluebank Fish House
& Grill
Highway 21
Steak, quail, frog legs,
crappie, country ham
Open for breakfast
and dinner
(901) 253–6878

Boyette's Dining Room
Highway 21
Famous for
family-style meals
Since 1921 adjacent
to Reelfoot Lake
Open daily 11:00 A.M.
to 9:00 P.M.
(901) 253–7307

Indexes

Entries for Museums, Restaurants, Fairs and Festivals, and Lodgings appear in the special indexes on pages 205–8.

INDEX

INDEX

INDEX

INDEX

Special Indexes

Museums

INDEX

INDEX

About the Author

Tim O'Brien is a veteran news reporter and editor who now travels the world's highways for a living as Southeast editor for *Amusement Business Newsweekly*. His specialty area of reportage is amusement parks and other types of tourist attractions.

When he's not traveling, he's at his home base in Nashville, Tennessee, where he lives with his wife, Kathleen, and his two daughters, Carrie and Molly.

A graduate of Ohio State University with a Masters degree in Journalism/Film Production, Tim is also an accomplished photographer and a roller-coaster fanatic, having ridden many of the world's greatest coasters.

He has written three other Globe Pequot books: *The Amusement Park Guide, Where the Animals Are,* and *Family Adventure Guide: Tennessee.*

Indulge in some southern comfort

  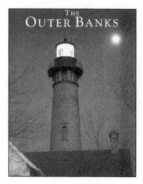

Fun with the Family™ in Tennessee
Hiking South Carolina Trails
North Carolina is My Home
North Carolina Curiosities
Fun with the Family™ in North Carolina
Short Bike Rides™ in North Carolina
Outerbanks
Romantic Days & Nights™ Savannah
Romantic Days & Nights™ Atlanta
Quick Escapes™ Atlanta
Georgia: Off the Beaten Path™
Romantic Days & Nights™ New Orleans
Quick Escapes™ in Florida
Choose Florida for Retirement: Retirement Discoveries for Every Budget
Guide to Sea Kayaking Southern Florida
Great Family Vacations: South
Recommended Country Inns®: South
Southeastern Lighthouses
Gulf Coast Lighthouses
Choose the South for Retirement: Retirement Discoveries for Every Budget
The Best Bike Rides™ in the South
Dixie: A Traveler's Guide

And an *Off the Beaten Path™* guide for every state in the South!